DATE DUE

| | | | |
|---|---|---|---|
| NOV 11 '93 | | | |
| JUN 24 | | | |
| MAY 25 '94 | | | |
| OCT 11 '95 | | | |
| MAR 27 '96 | | | |
| DEC 10 '97 | | | |
| | | | |
| | | | |
| | | | |
| | | | |

JAN 27 '92

# THE CHOICE:

*The Issue of Black Survival in America*

# THE CHOICE:

## THE ISSUE OF BLACK SURVIVAL IN AMERICA

### by *Samuel F. Yette*

Cottage Books
P.O. Box 2071
Silver Spring, Md. 20902

ISBN 0-911253-00-9 (Hard cover)
ISBN 0-911253-01-7 (Soft cover)

Library of Congress Catalog Card Number: 82-083686

PRINTED IN THE UNITED STATES OF AMERICA

## PERMISSIONS

For a permission to quote from copyrighted or otherwise special works, the author is grateful to the following:

Charles R. Allen, Jr., for permission to quote from "Concentration Camps, U.S.A.," a study commissioned by the Citizens Committee for Constitutional Liberties and published in 1966.

*The American Mercury* and its managing editor, LaVonne D. Furr, for permission to quote from U.S. Representative John R. Rarick's article, "Americans Do Not Support the Genocide Treaty," which appeared in the Summer, 1970, issue.

Joan Daves for permission to quote from "I Have a Dream," a speech by Dr. Martin Luther King, Jr., at the Lincoln Memorial, August 28, 1963.

*The Chicago Daily Defender* and its publisher, John Sengstacke, for permission to quote from Charles V. Hamilton's article, "Is Genocide Possible in America?," which appeared in the August 3, 1968, edition.

The Johnson Publishing Company and publisher's assistant June A. Rhinehart for permission to quote from John Britton's article, "Black Militants Face Showdown in Struggle to Avoid Prison," which appeared in *Jet*, January 16, 1969, and from Carl T. Rowan's article, "How Racists Use 'Science' to Degrade Black People," which appeared in *Ebony*, May, 1970.

Floyd B. McKissick for permission to quote from "Genocide U.S.A.," a speech delivered at the Newark Black Power Conference, July 21, 1967, and circulated by the National Congress of Racial Equality.

*The National Observer* and its assistant editor, John F. Bridge, for permission to quote from Jerrold K. Footlick's article, "A New Look at the Northern Ghettos," which appeared in the July 11, 1966, edition.

*The New York Times* for permission to quote from articles on the use of computer data processing in surveillance of civilians, the articles appearing in the July 9, 1969, and June 28, 1970, editions. © 1969/1970 by The New York Times Company. Reprinted by permission.

J. F. terHorst, author of "The Business Role in the Great Society," which appeared in *The Reporter,* October 21, 1965.

*The Washington Monthly* and its editor, Charles A. Peters, for permission to quote from Christopher Pyle's article, "CONUS Intelligence: The Army Watches Civilian Politics," which appeared in the January, 1970, issue.

iv

To the hope and determination that the conclusions implicit in this book will not come about, but rather that my country—the United States of America—will reverse her present course toward repression and national suicide and will achieve, instead, a true birth of freedom, mercy, and justice for *all*

# ACKNOWLEDGEMENTS

As stated in the original publication of this book in 1971, "For the most part, the author alone must stand with any merits and shortcomings of the work." In this republication, however, I am pleased to acknowledge the art work of my son, Michael, who designed the Cottage Books logo, and to a most esteemed colleague, John Oliver Killens, whose perceptive foreword gives this book a contemporary context, especially for those reading the book for the first time.

Also, in the years since 1971, I have become indebted to the many individuals and groups who have invited me to discuss the book and related matters, and who have shared their points of view and encouragement.

I remain indebted to my beloved family, who bring meaning and joy to this and every challenge.

# Contents

Now is the time to make justice
a reality for all of God's children.
It would be fatal for the Nation to
overlook the urgency of the moment. . . .
I have a dream that one day this Nation
will rise up, live out the true meaning
of its creed: "We hold these truths to
be self-evident, that all men are created
equal."

I have a dream that one day on the red
hills of Georgia sons of former slaves and the
sons of former slaveowners will be able to sit
down together at the table of brotherhood. I
have a dream that one day even the State of
Mississippi, a State sweltering with the heat of
injustice, sweltering with the heat of
oppression, will be transformed into an oasis
of freedom and justice.

I have a dream that my four little children
will one day live in a Nation where they will
not be judged by the color of their skin but by
the content of their character. . . . With this
faith we will be able to transform the jangling
discords of our Nation into a beautiful
symphony of brotherhood.

  —MARTIN LUTHER KING, JR. (1963) *

* Excerpt from "I Have a Dream," August 28, 1963, reprinted by permission of Joan Daves.

OR

The time must come when American
slavery shall cease, and when that
day shall arrive (unless early and
effectual means are devised to obviate
it) two races will exist in the same
region, whose feelings will be
embittered by inextinguishable hatred,
and who carry on their faces the respective
stamps of their factions. The struggle
that will follow will necessarily
be a war of extermination. The evil day may
be delayed, but can scarcely be averted.
—JAMES FENIMORE COOPER (1838) *

* *The American Democrat: or Hints on the Social and Civic Relations of the United States of America* (Cooperstown, H. & E. Phinney, 1838) p. 167.

# FOREWORD

by John Oliver Killens

In 1971, a book was published entitled, THE CHOICE by Samuel Yette. The book had a cataclysmic impact on the American Republic. The author made a strong case for the fact that the American ruling class had made a hard decision, a *choice*, and THE CHOICE was that Americans of African descent would either accept their miserable lot or *die!* Like a meticulous attorney, he gathered the evidence, collected the witnesses and made an eloquent and dramatic presentation to a jury of his peers, the great American reading public. Simply stated, THE CHOICE was clear. *Accommodation* or *Extinction. Deny your humanity or perish!*

The author was a prophet warning a generation of exuberant Black folk, flushed with the taste of apparent victory and progress, a taste that was already swiftly turning to bile.

Repeat: The American Corporate Structure had made a *choice*. Now it was up to Black America. Sam Yette warned of concentration camps, genocide through lynchings, starvation, birth control devices, etc., but few could hear him, due to the great euphoria of the times. "Three little words," Brother Martin had proclaimed. "We want it *all!* We want it *here!* We want it *now!*" Even as the glorious revolutionary decade of the Sixties was winding down, the evidence was collecting and becoming conclusive that the prophecy was accurate. Medgar, Malcolm and Martin were gone, the martyred victims of hired guns.

A hard choice for Black men and women. I believe it was then when the venerable Saturday Evening Post issued what might be termed as a

7

"White Paper," in which it warned Black America that they had better understand and accept the fact that absolute freedom and equality were not part of the game plan for them, and that the consequence of nonacceptance would be wholesale genocide. Apparently speaking for white Americans, North and South, the bottom line was, as quiet as it was kept, that,—*At heart, we are, all of us, Mississippians!*

The problem for Black people was how to reconcile this fact with Frederick Douglass's admonition to us—"Power concedes nothing without a demand. It never did and it never will. Find out just what any people will quietly submit to and you have found out the exact measure of injustice and wrong which will be imposed upon them, and these will continue till they are resisted with either words or blows, or with both."

The news that THE CHOICE is being republished is both dire and an occasion for celebration. It is dire because it is a sharp reminder that the dreadful prediction is unfolding. It is a cause for celebration, because the book is sorely needed, more than ever, in these terrible times. I am suggesting, that, in order for a generation of oppressed people to fulfill its historic mission, it must first, shed of all illusions, know the nature of its opposition. For George Santayana was absolutely right in saying: "Those who cannot remember the past are condemned to repeat it." A people's movement must have continuity.

This book is doubly important, especially for the current generation, who never sat in a jim crow coach of a train, never saw a "White Only" sign, never knew the wrath of *Southern Hospitality*, the fire hose or the cattle prods, nor the deprivation of the Northern cities. This book is triply important for the current Black generation, if it makes the choice that any freedom-loving people are compelled to make, i.e., to refuse to make accommodation with their own degradation, which is itself a fatal kind of genocide, self-destruction. This book is important, moreover, because, once the only possible choice is made, the people must then map out for themselves a strategy for survival. And yes, to go beyond survival toward the goal of liberation. For the dialectics of the situation are such, that a people who concentrate their struggle solely on survival are setting themselves up for ultimate extinction. It is an axiom of almost any athletic contest that "the best defense is a good offense."

For example, we must pursue, vigorously, the demand for reparations raised by SNCC leader James Forman. Not only because the wealth and power of this mighty nation was constructed on the backs and with the sweat and blood of our ancestors, but because our people have suffered the most horrendous holocaust known to human history, the American Slave Trade, in which the lives of over 100 million Africans were sacrificed. Also we must, without delay, forge an indestructible unity with our natural allies, i.e., with African people wherever they may find themselves (especially in Africa) and in the Caribbean, English, French and Spanish-speaking (what does it matter the language spoken by our colonizers and enslavers?), in South America and Canada, and with the First World people of Asia and throughout the earth, including the Native Americans who certainly know the reality of genocide and concentration camps.

And finally, even as we struggle for survival and for our own self-fulfillment, we must struggle for a coalition with and for a time of clarity for the white masses in this country, a struggle with them for their ultimate understanding that what is good for Black people is good for the entire masses of this nation; that when the bottom rises everything above is simultaneously elevated. Surely if they learn nothing more from Reaganomics, it is that when humanistic services are withdrawn from Black people, more whites suffer than Blacks. When the Blacks and the masses are denied food stamps, educational assistance, when Social Security and Medicaid and Medicare are threatened, when unemployment steadily increases, the majority of this entire nation suffers. This was the meaning of Brother Martin's "Poor People's March." None of this will be easy. Certainly, Samuel Yette never promised us a rose garden. We are discussing a strategy for survival and advancement, which means an all-out struggle for permanent alliances and temporary coalitions. This is to carry Brother Malcolm's slogan "by any means necessary" to its logical conclusion, i.e., "by every means necessary."

For THE CHOICE is reality and truth, a truth the author gives us to set the people free. It is a book that *must* be read by every Black (and white) who cares about the people and the nation. For the nation is not Reagan, or Rockefeller, or Morgan, or H.L. Hunt, or Getty, or Standard Oil, or General Motors. The nation is the people.

We should remember Winston Churchill's rallying call to the British
people when they faced the Nazi blitzkreig. Significantly, Churchill
quoted the Black Jamaican Claude McKay, who had addressed his
poetry to African-Americans at a time similar to these times—when we
were faced with wholesale liquidation:

> *If we must die, let it not be like hogs*
> *Hunted and penned in an inglorious spot,*
> *While around us bark the mad and hungry dogs,*
> *Making their mock at our accursed lot.*
> *If we must die, O let us nobly die,*
> *So that our precious blood may not be shed*
> *In vain; then even the monsters we defy*
> *Shall be constrained to honor us though dead!*
> *O kinsmen! we must meet the common foe!*
> *Though far outnumbered let us show us brave,*
> *And for their thousand blows deal one death blow!*
> *What though before us lies the open grave?*
> *Like men we'll face the murderous, cowardly pack,*
> *Pressed to the wall, dying, but fighting back!*

John Oliver Killens
September 1982

# PREFACE

There are no changes in the original text of this book, first published in 1971. This republication responds to a popular and welcome demand.

Republication under my own label—Cottage Books—responds, however, to two even greater exigencies:

(1) The nation's major publishers now rigidly resist publication of meaningful and instructive literature by and about Black people; and

(2) There is an obvious and urgent need for Black self-reliance in publishing, as elsewhere.

Before THE CHOICE went out of print in 1978, there were 8 hardcover printings (by Putnam's) and 11 soft-cover printings (by Berkley). And, although the demand for the book has remained strong, the demand increased sharply following the 1980 elections that brought Republican Ronald Reagan to the White House and Reagan majorities to both houses of Congress—Republicans in the Senate, and conservative Democrats in the House.

Clearly, Senator Lowell P. Weicker, Jr. (R-Conn.) was right when he termed the "Watergate" schemes of the early 1970s schemes designed by some "to steal America." However, the discovery, publicity, and partial adjudication of Watergate crimes merely interrupted—and did not end—schemes to steal the nation, and destroy its freedoms and oppressed peoples in the process.

In Chapter 6 ("The Laws: The Legal Police State"), THE CHOICE had already reported such schemes as Watergate, and emphasized that the ultimate danger to Black Americans was enforced by the erosion of constitutional due process. That is, the stealing of America—the successful carrying out of Watergate schemes—was a necessary antecedent to conditions and a climate in which genocidal schemes could also succeed. Indeed, genocidal schemes are subsumed in Watergates, by whatever name.

Since THE CHOICE was first published, the legal police state has expanded significantly, and a Watergate climate has re-emerged, but this time, with potential victims even more defenseless.

Expansions of the police state include re-instatement of the death penalty; legalization of such police crimes as those evident in Abscam and various other unlawful activities by so-called officers of the law; and the federal use of concentration camps to hold Haitian refugees captive—without charge—while searching the high seas for anyone with white skin who might be dragged ashore and anointed with the status of honored citizen.

But, perhaps the most consequential police-state expansion—state involvement in the destruction of unborn human life—comes, incredibly, with the urging of many Black and poor peoples themselves. Chapter 4 ("Starvation and Birth Control: The Ultimate Weapons") warns against state-sponsored (potentially enforced) birth control.

In its 1973 Roe v. Wade ruling, the U.S. Supreme Court sanctioned destruction of the unborn, which dangerously cheapens the value of human life. (See Chapter 5: "The Threat and Tactics.")

Pretexts created for destroying life on the pre-birth side of the womb include a suspected abnormality, or the mere inconvenience of the unborn. Thus created are pretexts for destroying life on the after-birth side of the womb also. These pretexts—abnormality and/or inconvenience—are society's frequent descriptions of oppressed peoples: the unemployed, the wrong color, the slow learner, etc.

Potential victims of Watergate-type schemes are seriously less protected now than in the 1970s. Today's legal climate is even colder.

In 1982, for example, the Congress—with merely half a dozen Senate votes against it—passed the Intelligence Identities Protection Act. That law makes it a crime (punishable by heavy fines and imprisonment) for any person (journalist, government worker, former agent, etc.) to reveal the identity of a spy, even if the spy is the most obvious and dangerous agent of the so-called "intelligence community."

Consequently, the Watergates of the 1980s may proceed without fear of the revelations that forced Richard Nixon to resign his presidency and sent some of his above-the-law hoodlums to jail.

So, in terms of survival, where were the Black and poor when Frank Wills, the Black night watchman, discovered a taped lock on a Watergate door that June night in 1972?

Chapter 2 ("The Great Society's Pacification Programs") discusses the three levels at which an oppressor may deal with those oppressed: liberation, pacification, or liquidation.

The 1960s were a decade in which the nation, consciously or otherwise, decided to deny Black people liberation. Richard Nixon was busy shutting down the Great Society Pacification programs when he was interrupted by the revelations of Watergate in 1974. That shutting down has been resumed by President Reagan in the 1980s. In place of pacification, Reagan, his budget director, David Stockman, and others instituted Reaganomics—the politics of "supply-side economics."

Reduced to fact, "supply-side" means that those who have some can get more; those who have much or most are in the running to get it all; and those who have little or nothing stand to lose even what they have been promised—such as public schools, Social Security, and other entitlements. Ultimately threatened is the right of the socio-economically dispossessed to exist.

This radical transfer of wealth and resources from the low and middle-income groups to the rich and super-rich has required economic chaos, hardship, and contradictions: "stagflation" (record-high inflation and interest rates, even in a stagnant economy), rapidly-increased automation and the permanent displacement of workers by the thousands, and the highest unemployment rates since the Great Depression of the 1930s.

So, where are we now?

Reaganomics has replaced Watergate. "Supply-side" is the new scheme "to steal America." This time, however, much of the danger that once was secret and illegal is now either publicly acceptable and legal, or legally hidden from the public—and, therefore, not sufficiently challenged, legally or otherwise.

Now, with even pacification a closing option, the survival of Black Americans is still at issue, but with oppressive control having been strengthened by the recent pacification era. This is true, despite significant political and isolated socio-economic gains of the last decade. For the group, socio-economic obsolescence deepens at robotic speed.

The decent mind still rebels against the reality of mass harm. Meanwhile, however, society's oppressed masses, increasingly obsolete, languish on pacification's bottom rung without evident strategies to meet the choices open to police state operations no longer as legally subject to public scrutiny.

—Samuel F. Yette
October 4, 1982

# INTRODUCTION:
# A Question of Survival

When the decade of the 1970's began, the United States government was officially—but unconstitutionally—in the midst of two wars: (1) a war of "attrition" (genocide) against the colonized colored people of Indochina, and (2) an expeditionary "law and order" campaign (repression—selective genocide) against the colonized colored people of the United States.

Although nonaligned, both colonized groups had much in common. As discussed in Part Two, they were, in fact, victims of the *same* war, though in different theaters.

In the United States, as in Indochina, victims of these undeclared wars painfully achieved high visibility during the 1960's. The colonized Blacks inside the United States were the subject of numerous and extensive studies, special programs, White House conferences, and plain gawking curiosity. Occasionally, a collection of what American society regarded as social antiques would present themselves for inspection in the nation's Capital. Such a group arrived in the spring of 1966. A motley collection of Blackpoor, they were a spectacle, even for Lafayette Park, where they spent the night. Rest-broken, poorly clothed, and shivering, the two dozen Mississippi outcasts* could not have

* "A young university economics instructor just made a trip to Mississippi and returned convinced that some 100,000 Negro sharecroppers may shortly be thrown off Delta plantations and forced by whites to move north," Marianne Means reported in the New York *World Journal Tribune,* January 31, 1967. "The practical economics of the wage increase (to 84¢ per hour) hardly warrant the sudden eviction of huge numbers of impoverished Negro families . . . but

been less in tune with the opulence around them. Some still crowded inside and others huddled outside the several tents they had pitched in the park across Pennsylvania Avenue—squarely in front of the White House.

These uninvited campers had braved a bone-chilling mist that shrouded the park. Two years earlier, some of them had dared vote in the Presidential election—for the first time in their many adult years. Others were accused of participating in the "Meredith March Against Fear," a walk quickly interrupted by the blasts of a white man's shotgun that nearly took the life of James Meredith. Some of them might even have joined in that chorus along the Meredith March that gave the first audible shouts of "Black Power!"

Now they were homeless.

They kept explaining that they were *not* the Negroes who had "lived in" at the deactivated Greenville (Mississippi) Air Force Base and were finally dragged out by the military. Instead, they insisted, they had relied on "the people in Washington" to help them work out their needs in an orderly way. All of them had outlived their rights as tenants in the Mississippi feudal system, but they had not outlived their faith in the government. They had been evicted from the land they had worked as sharecroppers, but they still allowed that the failing might be theirs, that it must have been they who had not made clear that their need was great and their cause just.

They hoped that federal antipoverty funds could be arranged for them to build houses and stay in the Delta, for that was home. Paper appeals failing, they brought their bodies to Washington to support their cause and demonstrate their need.

The bureaucratic charades had reduced them to this tent-setting spectacle, a desperate effort to get the attention of President Lyndon B. Johnson, and possibly embarrass him into action on their behalf. The Washington *Post* that morning

---

the political realities are something else again. The [instructor's] memorandum points out: 'the incentive [to evict] is rendered particularly strong by the fact that Negroes now constitute a majority of registered voters in a number of Delta counties and all major state and county offices will be up for election this fall.' "

carried a story of the telegram they sent to the President. It was signed "Your Neighbors." Their humor was lost on the President. There was no neighborly response. There was no response at all.

In time, they were driven by harsh weather and dysentery back, hungry and homeless, to the rigors of survival in the Mississippi Delta.

The spectacle of Lafayette Park kept alive the symbolic depravity of an inhumane history. Those anguished inhabitants of the park were truly a dying people. So were their legions of millions left in the valleys of the Black Belt and in the teeming ghettos of Chicago, New York, Los Angeles, Cleveland, and all the other welfare-swelled urban centers of the East, North, and West.

They were obsolete people, described by the then Labor Secretary W. Willard Wirtz as a "human scrap heap":

We are piling up a human scrap heap of between 250,000 and 500,000 people a year, many of whom never appear in the unemployment statistics.

They are often not counted among the unemployed because they have given up looking for work and thus count themselves out of the labor market. The rate of nonparticipation in the labor force by men in their prime years increased from 4.7 percent in 1953 to 5.2 percent in 1962. The increase has been the sharpest among non-whites, increasing from 5.3 percent to 8.2 percent in that period.

The human scrap heap is composed of persons who, as a consequence of technological development, of their own educational failures, of environments of poverty and other causes that disqualify them for employment in a skilled economy, cannot and will not find work without special help.

The 115,000 boys who failed the Selective Service educational tests in 1963 are candidates for the human scrap heap.

If we are to turn the human scrap heap into the materials for richer progress and more rewarding lives, then private industry and our private institutions must help us to do the job that government actions have only suggested need doing.*

* Reported in a Department of Labor press release, June 15, 1964, from a lecture by Wirtz to a seminar on automation and technological change in Los Angeles.

A people whom the society had always denied social value—personality—had also lost economic value. Theirs was the problem of *all* black America: survival.

Examination of the problem must begin with a single, overpowering socioeconomic condition in the society: black Americans *are* obsolete people.

While this certainly is not accurate in a moral scense, nor, at the moment, biologically, it is true where, in the 1970's, it becomes the issue: it is true in the minds and schemes of those who, with inordinate power and authority, control the nation. While it may not be so true among the general population, mass sentiments against oppression and possible genocide are not sufficiently strong to cause these schemes to fail. Black Americans have outlived their usefulness. Their *raison d'être* to this society has ceased to be a compelling issue. Once an economic asset, they are now considered an economic drag. The wood is all hewn, the water all drawn, the cotton all picked, and the rails reach from coast to coast. The ditches are all dug, the dishes are put away, and only a few shoes remain to be shined.

Thanks to old black backs and newfangled machines, the sweat chores of the nation are done. Now the some 25 million Blacks face a society that is brutally pragmatic, technologically accomplished, deeply racist, increasingly overcrowded, and surly. In such a society, the absence of social and economic value is a crucial factor in anyone's fight for a future.

Blacks in America have had 250 years of nationally sanctioned slavery and another hundred years of deceitful enslavement outside the national law. Now they are irreconcilably committed to personal dignity and justice as a people. Their patience, like the oxcart, is gone. But the hope remains that they, *un*like the oxen, can cease to be driven and can be permitted to stay—on human and civil terms.

They want to survive, but only as men and women—no longer as pawns or chattel. Can they?

This is the most frightful and pressing question facing America in the 1970's. Those who say the most urgent question is the "environment" should recognize that it is Blackness that is unsightly in America. Those who say it is war should face the fact that racism—an arrogance of superiority that seeks economic and military exploitation—is as much the nation's role in Birmingham as it is in Vietnam. And those who say that the most pressing issue is "law and order" should recognize the term for what it is: a euphemism for the total repression and possible extermination of those in the society who cry for justice where little justice can be found.

Whether Blacks have a place in U.S. society is a choice that belongs to the nation. That choice was audaciously called to the attention of white America early in 1960, when four black college students sat down at a North Carolina lunch counter reserved for whites. For the ten raw years of the 1960's, the nation noisily grappled with its choice: freedom or death for Afro-Americans.

By the end of the decade, Blacks were forced to face the evidence heaped painfully upon them. The evidence showed that a choice had been made, and freedom was denied.

True, the decade of the 1960's provided some contrary indications. There were, for example, outpourings of new laws and pronouncements that ostensibly guaranteed not only freedom and security but also socioeconomic progress. Blacks were visibly appointed to a handful of high federal positions. This was a kind of progress, but it was also confusing: it helped obscure from many Blacks and whites alike the true dangers being designed by repressive elements. In significant instances, what appeared to be progress was, in fact, the vehicle of the danger itself. For example, black appointees to high office generally included men of some standing and/or credibility in the black communities. Without that fact, of course, the value of their appointment was greatly, if not totally, diminished. Appointees included such men as Robert C. Weaver as Secretary of Housing and Urban Development, the first nonwhite member of any President's Cabinet; Andrew Brimmer, the first black governor of the Federal Reserve Board; Lisle C. Carter, Jr., as Assistant Secretary of Health, Education, and Welfare; Theodore M. Berry, as community action director of the Office of Economic

Opportunity; and Thurgood Marshall as Solicitor General, then Associate Justice of the Supreme Court, both unprecedented.

While the black appointees were highly visible, they were, for the most part, powerless. And their powerless visibility in and around the bureaucratic councils added an aura of legitimacy to illegitimate acts, providing a smokescreen for dirty dealing.

This is neither to criticize nor exonerate the appointees. The fault was not theirs. The fault was in the system—by design. Those who attribute the major fault to the appointees do so mainly out of their failure to grasp the cleverness and ruthlessness in the bureaucratic design to which these men were attached.

This is not to say that those who hoped should not have hoped, and that those who tried should have done otherwise. When the 1960 decade began, there was every reason both to hope and to try.

This cycle of hope, lost hope, promise, aborted promise, then rank oppression began with the election, in 1960, of Senator John F. Kennedy to the Presidency. What with the Freedom Rides in full swing, and with black people singing a bold, new song, what real choice had black people between candidate Richard M. Nixon, who had authored concentration camp legislation (see Part Three), and a superbly glamorous young man who promised to "get America moving again"?

When President Kennedy brought into the White House Andrew Hatcher, the first black White House assistant press secretary, that appointment served to indicate that he was willing to hear the black man's story. Subsequently, he received at the White House the leaders of a massive 1963 march on Washington for "Jobs and Freedom." He promised those leaders—Dr. Martin Luther King, Jr., A. Philip Randolph, Whitney Young, Jr., Roy Wilkins, and John Lewis—a new strategy to attack poverty and injustice.

Less than four months later, President Kennedy was dead, and the decade's first brief hope and promise had died with him.

New hope and bigger promises, nonetheless, sprang up in their places.

Kennedy's successor, Lyndon B. Johnson, offered his sequel to President Kennedy's "Let us begin." Said President Johnson: "Let us continue."

The Johnson promise: "The Great Society."

― Within a few months after President Kennedy was shot down in Dallas, November 22, 1963, President Johnson announced a new "unconditional war on poverty" and succeeded in getting an aggrieved Congress to pass the Civil Rights Act of 1964 (signed on July 2), and to create, on August 20, the Office of Economic Opportunity (OEO).

Beyond that, President Johnson made highly publicized speeches pledging to open doors for poor Blacks and to help them "walk through those doors" into a "Great Society." Those were the promises of the Great Society. The floods of government promise and black hope both crested at that point in the mid-1960's.

But . . . slowly, almost imperceptibly, the glint began to wear from Uncle Sam's shiny new armor. It tarnished, even while Uncle Sam stood like a colossus in the middle of the poverty and civil rights battlefield, swearing to take on all comers on behalf of Negroes and the poor. Still early in that new day of hope, wary Negroes, straining to see some sign of battle, could not perceive the paralysis that stayed the federal giant.

But as the day wore on, the go-slow motions of the federal giant did not match the fast, rhythmic rhetoric. In time, Negroes began to know that what they heard was aimed *at* them— not for them.

The cruelest hoax since the vain promise of "20 acres and a mule" following the Civil War had been set in motion against Africans transplanted in America. The raised hand of Uncle Sam was swatting poor Negroes while rewarding rich whites with the spoils of black misery. As this truth became known, hope turned to hatred, dedication became disgust, hands raised for help became clenched fists, and eyes searching for acceptance turned inward.

Negroes turned Black.

Blacks could see clearer what Negroes could not: If help would come, they, themselves, would bring it. Beauty was where they found it: Finding beauty meant *being* beautiful. They could win only if the system lost, and vice versa. And what truly was at stake was their natural lives.

And so it went—a decade of freedom rides, promises, public con games, black rebellions, and armed invasions of campus "sanctuaries." Even so, through it all, Blacks did manage more togetherness—whether it was in Vietnam or campsites on this side; the college campus or at wakes for the martyrs; in jail cells or on OEO community action boards.

The black togetherness of the 1960's—the newfound Blackness—produced a new visibility and a grip on the issues affecting black lives. Consequently, through a residue of confidence in the political system, hundreds of Blacks were elected to public office. But even some of them foresaw, as the new decade began, concentration camps and oppression.*

Thus, even the Blacks who hoped most and were most rewarded in the tradition of the system saw in the nation's choice a clear and present danger.

The schemes of the 1970's promised new martyrs, bigger jails, more wars (at home and abroad), data banks, wiretaps, and a genuinely regimented society, including the sharp curtailment of black college students, a white establishment take-over of

* Reported *Ebony* in its February, 1970, issue (p. 77): "Optimism, guarded, qualified and very cautious, was the general tone of the responses of a score of the nation's black mayors to a ten-question *Ebony* poll dealing with the status, present and future, of black people in America. . . . As many as 14 of them generally agreed on a single question (that black people will be better off 20 years from now in the United States), but on another issue they were sharply divided (the possibility of black Americans being 'preventively detained' as Japanese-Americans were during World War II) . . . . Mayor Carl Stokes of Cleveland predicted a much improved situation for blacks over the next two decades. Mayor Richard Hatcher of Gary foresaw black fortunes plummeting to 'a desperately low level,' unless some unlikely changes are made. The two men agreed that police state-type detention is a very real possibility for blacks and other groups of Americans."

black colleges, and psychological barbed wire around all learning institutions.

In short, the 1970's promised a reversal of those processes that, in the 1960's, tended to bring black people a modicum of socioeconomic advancement.

In the 1970's, for black Americans, it is clearly a question of survival.

# PART I:

# THE DECISIVE DECADE:
# THE 1960'S

# Chapter 1

# A Plan to "Destroy" the Obsolete People

The murder of Dr. King tells Negroes that if one of the greatest among them is not safe from the assassin's bullet, then what can the least of them hope for? In this context, those young black militants who have resorted to violence feel vindicated. "Look what happened to Dr. King," they say. "He was non-violent, he didn't hurt anybody. And look what they did to him. If we have to go down, let's go down shooting. Let's take whitey with us."

—BAYARD RUSTIN, in *The American Federationist*, May, 1968, p. 3.

Martin Luther King, Jr., had been dead for exactly a week, and fresh fires still sprang up almost hourly, even during daylight and within blocks of the White House in the nation's Capital.

In the charred ruins of Northwest Washington, a young black gangster* told how it was—what it was like to lose a leader he would not have followed, and yet why the murder had to be avenged, even at the risk of his own death.

"It killed a lot of hopes," said Spanky, raising his shades to look at the reporter with his natural eyes. "Don't get me wrong," he went on, readjusting his shades, "I don't necessarily say that I would have been in one of those nonviolent marches with him, but everybody knows that he was out there trying to work this thing out the right way. But after he was killed, I said,

* In an interview with me. See *Newsweek*, April 22, 1968, p. 33.

'What's the use?' There ain't nothing left, man. A lot of people feel that way. All hope is gone now. Nobody's going to get out there like he did."

Though still under twenty-five, Spanky (not his real name) was a little older than most of his gang. A little more mature, too. Some would say that he had less "reason" to loot, but loot he did—and would again. And yet his manner was so quiet and orderly that it was hard to picture him looting and burning, except when he described it.

"The other guys where I work felt that the people down at the White House and the Capitol knew that this assassination was going to be done. You know? Same way with President Kennedy. Same shit. Nobody feels that the real killer will be caught."

Spanky was at work (making more than $2 an hour) when he heard of the assassination of Dr. King on the evening of April 4, 1968. He and his working partner left the job and headed for Washington's northwest corridor. They crashed a pawnshop window and loaded the trunk of their car with cameras and electric shavers. Then they set fire to the shop. They drove up and down the main drag hitting their favorite targets, looting until the establishment was either empty or being approached by police; then they set fire and moved on.

"I can't quite explain it, you understand, but, yea: I felt good doing it. I felt that me participating in this was for his cause—I don't mean that he would *appreciate* this violence, you understand, but it was because they had killed him. I had to do something. I can't let Whitey get away with that. I think everybody felt that way. A lot of people just didn't care whether police shot or anything else."

Spanky said Washington had to be hit hard "so Whitey would get the message. A lot of people thought this kind of thing wouldn't happen in Washington—the nation's Capital and all."

"No, it ain't over yet," Spanky said, "and finding the assassin won't prevent further fire and looting. It wouldn't help much; it wouldn't bring him [Dr. King] back. And besides, the man who did it couldn't be punished enough to satisfy me. And again, even if they did get some cat I ain't so sure that Whitey would get the right man."

Spanky's distrust of "Whitey" was total, but even that was not his reason for looting and burning. The reason: "This whole bag [establishment or system] owes me something. It owes me something," he repeated. Again.

A few years earlier, as Spanky described it, he was an above average student in a slum high school. His family had hoped to move from the slum, but his father died, leaving his mother with three other children. They were stuck.

"I really liked school," he said, without pretense. "I was always anxious to get to arithmetic classes. But, you remember, about that time the gangs were bad, jim, and they didn't like me making all those good grades. So they roughed me up, and I had to join them for protection. Next thing I knew I was on the corner more than I was in school. Then it got kinda good to me, you know—laying up with chicks and jiving around. I needed some change, so I got me a job.

"So this was where the bad thing happened. Of course, I think if my old man had been living, I wouldn't have been in that neighborhood and I'd been in school. But, anyway, I was coming home from work one night and saw a couple of cats hitting on this chick—for money. It was a woman that I didn't know, but I knew the cats from on the corner, and I was going to rescue the chick. So while I was telling the cats not to do it, the cops came up. They ran. I didn't run nowhere because I knew that the woman would tell the cops that I was trying to help her. But the cops took me on down anyway and said they'd turn me loose if they found that it was like I said.

"They took the chick in one room and me in another. They beat my head with blackjacks, jim, and told me that they would make me tell who the other cats were. But I was mad as hell then, and I wouldn't tell them if it killed me. . . .

"This lawyer they gave me didn't believe me neither, and he kept telling me to cop out [confess] and get a lighter sentence. But I got out on bond while my mother was trying to find me another lawyer. I went to church and asked the Man upstairs for some help, you know. But I got a hung jury, and the judge put some prejudice in it. He told the jury that my trial was costing a lot of money, and they went back and said I was guilty. They owe me something. They owe me something."

The boss of Spanky's gang entered the room and told him to "scatter." He did.

Like Spanky, Roy (not his real name) was an exceptional student, and a dropout. But unlike Spanky, Roy almost never enjoyed going to school.

His native intelligence was unquestionably of a very high order. He was categorical, direct in his speech, quick and thorough in his assessments, and exuded personal charm at the moment he deemed it appropriate. Still a teen-ager, he was younger than most of his associates but, nonetheless, their leader.

Did he loot and burn?

"Yes, of course," he said impatiently.

His anger almost leaped from his finely chiseled face. Sensitive and intelligent, he was well versed on the good life afforded some in America and had decided that he would rather die young than be left out.

"Dr. King was a Negro trying to do something for us. They made a great mistake in killing him. I was hurt. Bad. But they made us realize what Whitey's trying to do. I had believed Stokely and Rap for a long time. But now I know that what they say is true—we built Whitey's country; now he wants to kill us."

Would "Whitey" really do such a thing? Would he systematically kill off Negroes or place them in concentration camps?

Roy sat up straight and adjusted the cuffs of his shirt sleeves—which had the same effect for him as mounting a stage.

"I believe the white man would do this," he said carefully. "I believe this is worth dying for. To stop him, I would burn this country down. This is my country. If I can't have it, then nobody can. Whitey brought us over here, and we built this country. It's as much mine as his, and I'll burn it down if I can't have it."

Roy's fierce pride helped force him out of school while he was still in junior high school.

"My mother died and left the bunch of us with my father. He's just a laborer. He couldn't take care of us. I'd go to school with torn pants. People could see my ass. I didn't even have no shoes at all sometimes. People wanted to give us things, but I don't want nobody giving me a damned thing. So I didn't like school. I had to start some kind of hustle."

Like other teen-agers, Roy was pained by the draft. He was angry at the likelihood that he would be called soon.

"I'm not going to any war!" he said in a near shout. "It's not my war any more than that World War II was my daddy's war. What the hell did he get for it?—bad health and a hole to dig. Stokely's right. Hell no, I ain't going to Vietnam."

Roy admitted that he was not a pacifist. Nor even nonviolent. But would he have marched with Dr. King?

"Yes, I would have marched with him. And I would have been nonviolent, for a while—until some white man did something I didn't appreciate. I admired the man. I didn't dig his ways, because I don't want to wait 400 years for my rights. I really feel hurt behind the fact that they killed the man. When I heard they killed Dr. King I wanted to go out and kill me a couple of white men. I think death is too good for the man who did it.

"I believe there're a whole lot of people in it [the assassination]," reasoned Roy. "Because for $100,000 [reward money] any white man would tell on his mama. If he's crazy enough to do it, he's crazy enough to want to tell somebody about it. He's doing it for recognition or money. The most honest man in the world would talk for $100,000. So the guys who did it don't need the money. That means they're doing well in politics or somewhere else. He's got to be a big man. Just like the man that got Kennedy."

The "good life" Roy envisioned includes love and family. A home. But it takes money to live the good life.

"When this man [Uncle Sam] asks me to go to the army he

insults me. He thinks I'm a fool. We got a war here. He talks about Communism. What does he think *this* is?

"This is hell. It's a bitch. A fellow wants to get married to a broad and he's tired of stealing, you understand. But he's got no education and no money, you dig? So if I got married, she'd be making more money than me."

Roy writhed painfully in his chair.

"We *are* inferior to our women because the white man likes our women and he gives her a break. Look at me," he said, pointing to his thick, tan arms, "I wouldn't be this damned color if the white man hadn't been fucking around with our women. So she gets the break. She goes to school. She's smarter than you. She should be the man, and you the woman—lying home and having the babies.

"No," Roy said, almost in tears. "This disturbance ain't over. This white man has made a savage out of me. The only way I can survive is to kill, hustle, and step on people. I don't want to do that, but I have to survive."

What Roy called black "survival" Congressional members of the House Un-American Activities Committee (HUAC) called "guerrilla warfare." Whom Roy regarded as avengers of a martyr's death, HUAC, a standing committee of the U.S. House of Representatives, regarded as "black guerrilla fighters." And three weeks later, under the chairmanship of Representative Edwin E. Willis, a Louisiana Democrat, the committee recommended to President Johnson a plan by which such black citizens could be "isolated and destroyed in a short period of time."

Recommended the committee:

Guerrilla warfare, as envisioned by its proponents at this stage, would have to have its base in the ghetto. This being the case, the ghetto would have to be sealed off from the rest of the city. Police, State troopers, and the National Guard could adequately handle this chore and, if they needed help, the Regular Army would be brought into service.

Once the ghetto is sealed off, and depending upon the violence being perpetrated by the guerrillas, the following actions could be taken by the authorities:

(1) A curfew would be imposed in the enclosed isolated area. No one would be allowed out of or into the area after sundown.

(2) During the night the authorities would not only patrol the boundary lines, but would also attempt to control the streets and, if necessary, send out foot patrols through the entire area. If the guerrillas attempted to either break out of the area or to engage the authorities in open combat they would be readily suppressed.

(3) During a guerrilla uprising most civil liberties would have to be suspended, search and seizure operations would be instituted during the daylight hours, and anyone found armed or without proper identification would immediately be arrested. Most of the people of the ghetto would not be involved in the guerrilla operation and, under conditions of police and military control, some would help in ferreting out the guerrillas. Their help would be invaluable.

(4) If the guerrillas were able to hold out for a period of time then the population of the ghetto would be classified through an office for the "control and organization of the inhabitants." This office would distribute "census cards" which would bear a photograph of the individual, the letter of the district in which he lives, his house and street number, and a letter designating his home city. This classification would aid the authorities in knowing the exact location of any suspect and who is in control of any given district. Under such a system, movement would be proscribed and the ability of the guerrilla to move freely from place to place seriously curtailed.

(5) The population within the ghetto would be exhorted to work with the authorities and to report both on guerrillas and any suspicious activity they might note. The police agencies would be in a position to make immediate arrests, without warrants, under suspension of guarantees usually provided by the Constitution.

(6) Acts of overt violence by the guerrillas would mean that they had declared a "state of war" within the country and, therefore, would forfeit their rights as in wartime. The McCarran Act provides for various detention centers to be operated throughout the country and these might well be utilized for the temporary imprisonment of warring guerrillas.

(7) The very nature of the guerrilla operation as presently

envisioned by certain Communists and black nationalists would be impossible to sustain. According to the most knowledgeable guerrilla war experts in this country the revolutionaries could be isolated and destroyed in a short period of time.*

Like any other U.S. President since passage of the Internal Security Act of 1950, President Johnson could have taken the action recommended by HUAC without any consultation with Congress, and upon lesser provocation than the uprisings following Dr. King's death. President Johnson, however, chose not to take the recommended action. But that was a choice delayed—not necessarily canceled. Such action might await riper circumstances, a new cast of possible executioners, and societal conditions which would facilitate it. In short, such a choice would require such conditioning as is possible only under a more complete police state. A fuller rationale—a scapegoat syndrome—would also be required. Both of these would have to precede the execution of a liquidation plan on the order and scale proposed by HUAC. *However,* a *de facto* police state and a rationale *were* achieved by mid-1970. By that time, legalization of the police state and selective liquidations (particularly of the Black Panther Party members†) had already begun.

The obsolescence of Blacks in America and their will to survive nobly—demand and fight for their rights—provide some with an adequate rationale for black extinction. Legal sanctions for the systematic invasions of black sanctuaries—homes, schools, and establishments—were signed into law before Congress adjourned for the fall, 1970, elections. But, in America, as in Asia, these essentially military measures bespoke the failure of insincere or basically unsound efforts to help black people.

* *Guerrilla Warfare Advocates in the United States,* a report by the Committee on Un-American Activities, House of Representatives, Ninetieth Congress, May 6, 1968, pp. 59–60.

† "Gordon Parks on the Panthers," *Life,* February 6, 1970, pp. 18–27.

# Chapter 2

# The Great Society Pacification Programs

True to his promise to the leaders of the August 28, 1963, march "For Jobs and Freedom," President Kennedy ordered federal agencies to begin studies into the problems of civil rights and poverty. The fate he met only a few months later might have been a first stern warning that the controlling forces in America would pay any price to deny the choice President Kennedy symbolized.

On an unforgettable Friday afternoon in November, the President died, cruelly and almost too suddenly for comprehension.

In Alabama, some white schoolchildren cheered the murder.

As regards the destiny of the Blackpoor, the swift and symbolic destruction of the Kennedy administration had served notice on two points: (1) an equitable solution to socioeconomic oppression would have to be found, or violence and death would have to put an end to the aspirations for change; and (2) the initial choice had been violence and death.

On the day before his fatal trip, President Kennedy told his new ambassador to Finland, Carl Rowan:

Carl, a lot has happened in the six months you've been out of Washington. Hatred is spreading across this country like a cancer. The bigots, the Birchites, are like a plague. They get bolder every day. I suppose you read about the disgraceful things that they did to Adlai Stevenson down in Texas. This trend is dangerous for the country. It endangers you, me and human rights and all that this administration stands for. I have made up my mind that a President is obligated to use the prestige of his office to try to halt this damned madness. I have concluded that I am partly to blame because I haven't got out among the people enough. I'm going to Texas tomorrow partly because I believe it is something I am obligated to do.*

The legacy of the assassination is the staggering fact that a President had been slain in broad daylight, in the view of thousands, and neither was anyone ever placed on trial for the deed nor did any of those directly accused at the time live to tell any coherent details of their involvement or information.

The central message was hard to miss: high-level vigilante action had begun to replace due process in America. Such action began with "justice" to a President and had only one way to go from there—downward to the rest of the people.

But President Johnson moved quickly to map out the regions to which his predecessor had merely pointed. "My good friends and my fellow Americans," he stated in his State of the Union message, January 8, 1964, "in these last seven sorrowful weeks, we have learned anew that nothing is so enduring as faith, and nothing is so degrading as hate. John Kennedy was a victim of hate, but he was also a great builder of faith—faith in our fellow Americans, whatever their creed or color or their station in life; faith in the future of man, whatever his divisions and differences."

Earlier in that message to Congress, President Johnson had announced what were to become not the progressive actions he called for but the two major holding actions of the decade—the Civil Rights Act of 1964 and the so-called war on poverty:

"Let this session of Congress be known as the session which did more for civil rights than the last hundred sessions combined—as the session which declared all-out war on human poverty and unemployment in these United States. . . . We have in 1964 a unique opportunity and obligation—to prove the

* *Ebony,* April, 1967, p. 28.

success of our system; to disprove those cynics and critics at home and abroad who question our purpose and our competence."

But President Johnson also touched on the historical flaw of efforts toward sustained socioeconomic progress in America—the fact of color and racism:

"Unfortunately, many Americans live on the outskirts of hope—some because of their poverty, and some because of their color, and all too many because of both. Our task is to help to replace their despair. Let me make the principle of this Administration abundantly clear. All of these increased opportunities—in employment, in education, in housing and in every field—must be open to Americans of every color. As far as the writ of Federal law will run, we must abolish not some, but all racial discrimination."

Despite the rhetoric, President Johnson's "unconditional war on poverty" never became a general war. Except in the rhetorical sense, it was never intended to be. At best, it was a kind of bureaucratic and political civil war. The rhetoric and occasional good intentions aside, the effect of it all was mainly to further the establishment war against those in the society already defeated. OEO, in fact, would become a new vehicle for black oppression—at white profit. President Kennedy had taken official notice of black discontent; President Johnson would move to pacify it.

There are two choices other than pacification. One is liberation. The other is liquidation. Of the three, only liberation is honest. Pacification delays liquidation, but stops far short of liberation.

The 1960's was a decade of decision. Conflicts built into free enterprise and the U.S. political fabric prohibited the liberation of colonized Blacks in America and, yet, in their private consciences, many white Americans regarded liquidation as too extreme and immoral, if not "un-American." Thus, the 1960's, a period of black liberation struggles, wavered between liberation and liquidation and became a decade of pacification, giving rise to two major pacification programs—the OEO and a collection of civil rights measures spearheaded by the Civil Rights Act of 1964.

In the ghettos, as in Southeast Asia, the need for pacification rises out of a history of colonization—the economic and cultural exploitation of a subject group. An honest determination to relinquish such exploitation would obviate any need to pacify. Schemes short of this determination, however, merely attempt to calm and contain the exploited groups while the schemes provide a cover for extending the exploitation, tightening control, and generally furthering the unworthy aims of the colonialists.

Under such a scheme the U.S. State Department's chief pacification agency, the Agency for International Development (AID), operates in such "neutral" countries as Laos. In a radio interview with Metromedia reporter Dan Blackburn on June 5, 1970, AID administrator, Dr. John A. Hannah, was forced to admit that AID was a cover operation for the Central Intelligence Agency (CIA) in Laos under the guise of assisting Laotians with development of agriculture, hospitals, and other benefits.* AID's pacification programs in Vietnam and Cambodia were similarly implicated in the interview.

Domestic pacification programs are basically identical to those in Laos and elsewhere. Distinguishing features include the facts that pacification is a game which cleverly continues an oppressor's options but is limited by the resourcefulness and alertness of the oppressed and their determination to be truly free. Thus, unsuccessful pacifications in Indochina were followed by military intervention and wars of attrition. And thus, the HUAC plan to destroy black citizens came in 1968 after two major pacification programs ceased to beguile the Blackpoor and failed to contain their liberation struggle.

* Blackburn: "Doctor, how do you respond to complaints that the AID program is being used as a cover for CIA operations in Laos?"

Dr. Hannah: "Well, I just have to admit that that is true. This was a decision that was made back in 1962 and by administrations from now until then, and it is the only place in the world that we are. I don't like the way that CIA cover, but we have had people that have been associated with the CIA and doing things in Laos that were believed to be in the national interest, but not routine AID operations."

The Great Society pacification programs, then, must be judged as failures, both in the honesty of their designs and in their truer aims of placating people justly aroused. In view of their maximum goals, the funds and personnel provided, and the authority to do the job, the OEO and civil rights program did not relinquish the original aims of white establishment exploitation. They left ultimate control and financial benefits with the colonialists—not with the colonized; nor even were control and profits shared equitably between them.

It would be difficult to overestimate the importance of these pacification failures; they represent a kind of last ditch effort to delay an ultimate choice regarding the disposition of black citizens, their aspirations, and their history of incipient genocide. The cause and manner of these catalytic failures in pacification become an essential part of understanding what lies ahead.

Like pacifications elsewhere, pacifications in the black U.S. colonies tended, in reality, to strengthen the options of the colonizer, tighten control, and earn him profits. By mid-1970, the status of major pacifications begun in 1964 clearly indicated that the colonizer had achieved these advantages.

—The Job Corps, that billion-dollar program that promised to rescue poor teen-agers with training and jobs, instead of being an economic boon to the poor, became an alternative base for the military-industrial complex; not a vehicle for getting boys into the labor unions, but a major source of boypower for Vietnam; not a reasonably priced, soundly based training course for existing jobs, but the basis for a new educational-industrial complex, a place for the conglomerates to dump their worthless gadgets at inflated prices; and, instead of providing campsites for wholesome surroundings and conservation programming, the Job Corps camps, when 59 of them were closed during 1969, became ready-made concentration camps, places for the "human scrap heaps" of the unskilled, the unconnected, and those Blacks unwilling to stop procreating and demonstrating in a society that neither cared about their problem nor wanted any more of their kind.

—The Community Action Program (CAP), a billion-dollar

con game about "involvement," pledged "maximum feasible participation" of the Black and poor in local decision-making but actually became a name-taking web that helped identify and isolate the natural leaders of every black community in America, each leader's name ultimately fixed to a massive pickup list at the Pentagon, awaiting the moment when the order is given.

—Volunteers in Service to America (VISTA), the so-called "domestic Peace Corps," sprinkled throughout the poor black neighborhoods enough spies among the sincere workers to keep tabs not only on the numbers players in Harlem, for example, but also in-depth information on any and all new thought, plan, or development—any strategies Blacks might devise to aid in their own defense. It was understandable, then, that in 1967, when police began accurate raids on lottery operations in Harlem, residents complained that VISTA worker Laurance Rockefeller had his nerve sending cops on them while his uncle, New York Governor Nelson Rockefeller, was urging public support of the state's multi-million-dollar lottery to finance education.

—Head Start, a program to give deprived preschoolers a better chance to compete with rich kids by first grade, was perverted into a white Southern strategy for prolonging school segregation. Throughout America, it became the forerunner of a new scheme for "documenting," in various studies, the inferior learning capability of deprived black children.

Beyond the OEO programs, Title VII of the Civil Rights Act of 1964 requires equal opportunity in hiring; but the government admittedly handed out multi-million-dollar defense contracts to Southern textilers in violation of the existing civil rights laws and the Nixon administration chose to demonstrate its interest in fair hiring by pitting black and civil rights groups against their only consistent, well-financed ally—the labor unions.* In a year-end editorial, the December 30, 1969, edition of the Washington *Afro-American* observed:

* Civil rights strategist Bayard Rustin, a black man, told an AFL–CIO convention in 1969: "The fight against Judge Haynsworth is important because he makes us remember . . . that whatever differences we may have among ourselves, we have a lot more in common. For one thing, we have enemies in common."

President Nixon took a firm stand in favor of the "Philadelphia Plan" drawn up by Assistant Secretary of Labor Art Fletcher. The plan aims at forcing federal contractors in the construction business to hire more black workers, in fact, to require this.

Pressure by the White House convinced Congress to accept the Philadelphia Plan.

Two questions, though, are obvious.

One is, whether or not this was another ploy of the Nixon Administration to set civil rights leaders and labor leaders at odds, since labor did not want the Philly plan.

The second is, why should black citizens expect President Nixon to enforce this contract requirement when he has done such a lousy job on federal contracts handed out to Dixie firms, and others, that violate discriminatory hiring and promotion standards? In one instance, Bethlehem Steel in Baltimore, Mr. Nixon has not backed Mr. Fletcher in getting the necessary conformity but the federal funds keep flowing.

Few motives are more enduring than the profit motive in pacification. Always present in the purchase, contract, and grant phases of OEO, financial interests also dominated the major titles of the Civil Rights Act of 1964. Title IV offers federal money for local (white) school districts to learn how to desegregate; Title VI would cut off funds to schools which did not desegregate, that is to say, they would receive federal money if they obeyed the law; and Title VII would gradually require employers—particularly those receiving federal contracts—to cease discriminatory hiring, and upon compliance or an "effort" at legal compliance, they could sit at the federal trough.

The OEO became headquarters for the war on poverty. Sargent Shriver, former Peace Corps director and brother-in-law of President Kennedy, was named by President Johnson as the first OEO director. Shriver's first statement following the funding of the OEO on October 8, 1964, could have been a warning of just how revolutionary this war would be. It was not widely interpreted so at that time, but in retrospect Shriver's initial statement was an eloquent statement of profit-motivated, insincere pacification:

This program not only starts a war against poverty, but a campaign for opportunity—opportunity for the poor people of America. This is not a relief program. There isn't going to be any cash mailed out. There isn't going to be a dole: there is no hand-out here. The only thing we're giving is a new chance, a new opportunity for self-help. We're offering a chance for one million poor people who are young men and women out of school and out of work. We're offering a new chance for the aged, for mothers on relief, for fathers who can't get a job. . . .

Seventy-eight percent of these poor are white. The majority live in depressing urban slums. They prefer *work* over charity. They prefer a new *chance* most of all. *We're not taking cash from the rich to give to the poor.* We're going to be sharing what most of us have—the chance to do our best—we're going to be sharing that with *all* Americans. [Emphasis original.]

Indeed, OEO would not take "cash from the rich to give to the poor." The opposite would more likely be true.

There was a seldom-voiced but strong feeling among many whites at OEO that the anti-poverty effort was something they were doing *for* poor Blacks. Permitting a black person to participate, they felt, was permitting an usurpation of the rights of rich, well-motivated whites. Because OEO had the responsibility—though not the authority—to coordinate the efforts of all other federal agencies toward the elimination of poverty, the OEO Task Force was studded with interagency representatives —all white. They included Labor Assistant Secretary Daniel P. Moynihan, Deputy Under Secretary of Agriculture James Sundquist, Peace Corps Latin America regional director Frank Mankiewicz, and, second in command to Shriver, Adam Yarmolinsky, Special Assistant to Defense Secretary Robert McNamara.

Nonbureaucrats on the Task Force included private industry's C. Virgil Martin of Carson, Pirie, Scott, and Co., department store; Donald Petrie of Avis Rent A Car, and Litton Industries' Charles B. (Tex) Thornton. It also included authors Michael Harrington (*The Other America*), Edgar May (*The Wasted Americans*), and professional liberal Hyman Bookbinder. From the beginning of OEO, military and industrial interests were prominently represented—but not Blacks or the poor.

While it competed with the strong *noblesse oblige* undertone that preferred no Blacks at all, the selection of black appointees to OEO administrative and policy jobs was, as always, an art unto itself. For what the appointment managers sought were classic anomalies: black men who were really white; bright men who were stupid; honest men whose honor was flexible; strong men who, at the appropriate moment, were weak. Fortunately, this generally was not what the personnel czars found. Nevertheless, the system did succeed often enough to reveal three of its essential goals in the selection and appointment of black talent: (1) to provide color credibility wherever such credibility was crucial to selling an otherwise invalid product; (2) to neutralize such talent by taking it from potentially radical stations (the hiring off of militants) and placing it officially on the side of the establishment (a technique not unlike the President's nationalizing of a National Guard unit to prevent its misuse, disuse, or proper use by a governor) ; and (3) to have a black person in position to take responsibility for antiblack policies and decisions, usually made exclusively by whites— without the black appointee's knowledge, consent, or ability.

For Blacks, who never had such jobs before and who were anxious to do a job, this hiring deception was most difficult to perceive.

More than anyone else, Yarmolinsky, the man Shriver wanted as his deputy, was the chief architect of the Job Corps. Another prominent voice on the OEO Task Force was John Rubel, a former Pentagon aide, but then a fast-rising star in Thornton's gigantic conglomerate, Litton Industries, a major defense contractor.

Asked in those early days why he surrounded himself with so many industrialists, Shriver replied: "They have good judgment."* It would not be fair to say that Shriver involved only industrialists in OEO planning, but it is obvious that the counsel of these magnates with "good judgment" went a long

* Eve Edstrom, Washington *Post*, February 23, 1964.

way. Indeed, it was they who eventually walked away with the lion's share of the money the Blackpoor was told was coming to them. It went to these industrialists in the form of multi-million-dollar contracts to deliver—not jobs—but "employability" training to Job Corps enrollees.

A favorable report on the big business gambit was presented in the pro-business trade journal *Business Management*. The January, 1966, issue of the publication reported the *fait accompli* nearly two years after the fact: "Probably the most visible evidence of industry's attack on public problems lies in the Job Corps program. Last year the Office of Economic Opportunity began letting contracts to operate the first of 75 Job Corps retraining centers for disadvantaged young men and women. The contracts were quickly snapped up by such companies as Burroughs Corps., ITT, Philco, Packard-Bell Electronics, Xerox, IBM, Westinghouse Air Brake, Litton Industries and U.S. Industries. In fact, with as many as 12 more training center contracts to be let by next July, there's even a waiting list of companies."*

Not surprisingly, Thomas Watson of IBM, Thornton of Litton, Sol Linowitz of Xerox, and others among the major contractors were members of the OEO's Business Leadership Advisory Council. While they might well have been in the poverty business to perform a public service, they came to that endeavor with guaranteed, fixed profits of four to six percent, plus a broad vested interest in the success of pacification. The financial payoff was not so much in the profit guarantees (modest compared to defense contracts), but in the hardware and software capabilities and markets developed while using Job Corps trainees as guinea pigs. Neither the poor nor any other group not locked into the socio-military-industrial complex ever had the slightest chance of siphoning capital gains from the Job Corps and related big-money programs.

Although OEO press releases boasted that Job Corps trainees were able to send home part of their modest allotment to their

---

* *Business Management*, January, 1966, p. 39.

needy parents and guardians* these sums were small pinches from Job Corps budgets which poured millions into the big business coffers. In 1966, Job Corps contributed $6 million directly and an equal amount indirectly to the families of needy enrollees. That $12 million was undoubtedly helpful to the poor families, but the Job Corps' direct contribution ($6 million) was less than single contracts awarded to each of several blue-chip military industrialists.

For example, in fiscal 1968, the industrialists hauled off contracts in these amounts: Litton Industries, for Camp Parks in California, $15.9 million; Federal Electric, a subsidiary of International Telephone and Telegraph, for Camp Kilmer in New Jersey, $10 million; Graflex Inc., a subsidiary of General Precision Equipment, Inc., for Camp Breckinridge in Kentucky, $9.7 million; Burroughs Corporation, for the Omaha Job Corps center in Nebraska, $8 million; the Thiokol Chemical Corporation, for the Clearfield Center in Utah, $6.8 million; Philco, for the Tongue Point center in Oregon, $6.3 million; and Westinghouse, for Camp Atterbury in Indiana, $6.3 million.

Although the numbers fluctuated slightly from 1964 to 1969, about 25 of the 110 Job Corps centers were run by the private sector, an indication of substantial profit incentives from the outset. The others are run by such public agencies as the Forest Service of the Department of Agriculture, a few state agencies, and several bureaus within the Department of the Interior: Bureau of Reclamation, Bureau of Sport Fisheries and Wild-

* Reported a January 22, 1967, OEO news release:
Job Corpsmen and women are sending allotments home to needy dependents at the rate of more than $1 million each month, Acting Director William P. Kelly of Job Corps announced today.

In December 1966, he said, 72 percent of the young men and women in the program made allotments to needy dependents. The allotments by these 20,737 young men and women totalled $1,022,870 that month.

Kelly said that 96.5 percent of those making allotments send the maximum of $25 a month, with Job Corps matching the amount of the allotment.

The share of the allotment by the Corpsman or woman is taken from the $50 a month readjustment allowance, which is paid the youth on leaving the program.

life, Bureau of Indian Affairs, Bureau of Land Management, and the National Park Service.

A few of the private sector contractors are nonprofit: the Alpha Kappa Alpha Sorority, the only basically black group—nonprofit or otherwise—among contractors running Job Corps centers; the Texas Educational Foundation, Inc.; the National Board of the YWCA; and, to the extent that they can be considered nonprofit, several universities.

Although the public agencies operated more centers, their centers were small and handled comparatively few enrollees. Consequently, two-thirds of all enrollees passed through the bigger centers run by the giant profit-making corporations.

One of the first Job Corps profit-makers to sign up was Thornton's multifaceted Litton Industries, which, on April 26, 1965, hauled in a two-year, $13.4-million contract to operate Camp Parks in Pleasanton, California. Parks, with its 2,300 enrollees, is larger than all except the state-sponsored 3,000-enrollee Gary Center in San Marcos, Texas.

The big-industry centers literally spanned the country. For example, AVCO Economics Systems Corporation, a big defense contractor, operates Job Corps centers both in Maine, on the East Coast, and in the western-most state of Washington. Westinghouse Learning Corporation's Camp Atterbury in Edinburg, Indiana, had 1,600 enrollees; Graflex, Inc., won the 1,900-enrollee Camp Breckinridge in Morganfield, Kentucky, from Southern Illinois University; the Thiokol Chemical Corporation broadly diversified by taking on the 1,300-enrollee Clearfield Center in Utah; and Federal Electric won the 1,700-capacity Camp Kilmer, New Jersey, in the first round of contracts, February 11, 1965.

At the height of the "socio-commercial enterprise," other centers were run by Science Research Associates (a subsidiary of Thomas Watson's IBM), RCA, U.S. Industries, and Northern Natural Gas. For reasons to be discussed later, these centers were ordered closed, vociferous lobbying notwithstanding.

The Job Corps was virtually the ideal vehicle for this ultra-capitalist venture of superbusiness to the "rescue" of the imperiled poor. Had there already been a Job Corps in some equitable form, the industrialists would surely have used it; but having a chance to influence its inception was immeasurably more advantageous.

While Yarmolinsky is credited with designing the Job Corps, perhaps no single individual had more influence on both the Job Corps concept and its tie-in with industry than Rubel of Litton. Like Yarmolinsky, Rubel was present at the first meetings of the OEO Task Force and, also like Yarmolinsky, Rubel was a Pentagon veteran. Both Yarmolinsky and Rubel had a chance to share the intellectual stimulation of economist-sociologist Moynihan while the three served on the Task Force. For good measure, Pentagon boss McNamara had once been an aide to Litton's Thornton while both Thornton and McNamara were at the Ford Motor Company.

These varied influences meshed reasonably well on a memorandum Rubel sent to Shriver in the Job Corps' formulative days as big business made its move:

I think of the Job Corps as a complex transforming machine with many internal parts. The input—the raw material—that is fed into this machine is people. The output is people. It is the function of this machine to transform these people. . . .

Here we have a new government echelon aimed at altering the behavior of a class of people that isn't being duplicated elsewhere. The programs of OEO offer the country a chance of creating a new environment for these people and thus modifying their own past inadequate social behavior. It won't happen all at once, sure, but the knowledge gained in the behavioral sciences may bring pocketbook benefits to everybody, including business. . . .*

Thus, two years later, in the fall of 1967, the profits of Thiokol Chemical Corporation were typical of those realized by the big Job Corps military contractors. Thiokol's $11.2-million contract was set at 4.8 percent profit. Under the headline "Thiokol Sales Soar," the August 4, 1967, Trenton *Evening News* reported:

* Jerald Terhorst, "The Business Role in the Great Society," *The Reporter,* October 21, 1965, pp. 27–28.

Thiokol Chemical Corporation reports earnings of 68 cents per share for the first six months of the year, sales totaling $122,522,385. This compares with earnings of 65 cents per share and sales of $89,217,453 for the like period of 1966. The major portion of the increase in the sales and earnings resulted from production of flares and related devices at the company's Longhorn Division, Marshall, Texas, and from the operation of the Job Corps Training Center at Clearfield, Utah.

Thiokol decided to get into the poverty business after losing its defense contract for development of big solid-fuel booster rockets. Like other contractors, Thiokol found the poverty-education route an attractive avenue for insuring profits, but, also like others who turned to this fallback position, Thiokol found need both to explain its altruism and why it cost so much to exercise it. Thiokol's vice-president for economic development, Robert L. Marquardt, put it this way:

People say the Job Corps is too expensive. Public schools educate youngsters for $500 to $800 a year per pupil, while Job Corps costs run around $6000 each. Sure, conventional education works for the average middle-class youngster, but for the other 20%—the deprived 20%—it just plain doesn't. The regular school system is not adequate for kids without the right functional and intelligence quotients. Industry and OEO can take a boy any day of the week and put that boy through a progress program and succeed—if he's willing to stick it out. We are doing it. So is Litton, AVCO, and RCA.*

While most of the contractors were knowing enough to hire at least enough Blacks to satisfy the "cosmetic" requirements for credibility among black Corpsmen, it is nonetheless true that not one contractor was subjected to a civil rights compliance review as legally required. Shriver and the OEO management-legal apparatus simply would not permit it, and Shriver generally succeeded in delaying a confrontation on the issue. But the profit splash of big business into social programming was

* *Chemical & Engineering*, August 28, 1967, pp. 42–43.

not without its critical observers. In his comprehensive look at "The Business Role in the Great Society," for example, journalist Jerald terHorst reported:

Other criticism of the business approach to social programs is being heard around the country. ITT, it is charged, picked up its $11.5 million Job Corps contract at Camp Kilmer merely as part of a diversification policy that led it to acquire Avis, Inc., several months later. And despite their professed commitments to social change, Litton, Philco, and other companies have been accused in some quarters of sermonizing all the way to the bank. Shriver's office, and indeed the White House itself, is being criticized for promising an attack on the causes of poverty while merely attacking its effects—the educational and behavioral inadequacies of the unemployed. Eli Ginzburg, a Columbia University manpower specialist, has taken the position that the object of the Job Corps should be to train people for specific jobs, not to improve their "employability."*

Perhaps lucrative contracts to run Job Corps centers should, alone, have answered Rubel's vision of corporate-size profits, but the growth factors—experimentation and production gimmicks—only began there. Profitable though they were, running the centers was merely a foot in the door; for once inside, OEO officially invited Job Corps contractors to "develop new instructional techniques and materials to help the enrollees become more employable." This was an invitation to develop the software and hardware which would produce the profit windfalls more characteristic of military industrialists. They were further invited to establish consortiums between business and universities and, later on, with the education establishment at all levels, to further experimentation and development of "materials."

All such experimentation and development would be with guaranteed profits, of course.

The entry of these industrial giants into the nontraditional

---

* Jerald terHorst, "The Business Role in the Great Society," *The Reporter*, October 21, 1965, p. 29.

field of social improvement occurred ostensibly to fulfill needs
Moynihan had "documented." What these giants of industry set
out to do, then, was to make black youths, in particular, and
other deprived youngsters more employable, OEO said.
In essence, the theme was education and training—not jobs.
Nothing done by OEO reversed or even moderated black exclusion by trade unions. In reality, the twofold design was rather to
(1) establish an economic base in the education system, and
(2) accommodate poor youths to the military machine while
getting them off the streets, away from picket lines and other
points of possible confrontation.

But "education" was the password. As terHorst further
observed:

> A new partnership between government and business is evolving
> that may bring about profound social changes in American life: the
> vast technical and managerial resources of the big defense and aero-
> space firms are being put to use in an attack on social problems that
> range from poverty and crime to water pollution and transporta-
> tion. Elected politicians and government administrators are leading
> the way, and business is going along willingly, and for profit.
> The collaboration is already a reality in the Job Corps program
> of the Office of Economic Opportunity—and while technocratic
> dangers exist and may well increase in such a partnership, there is
> every indication that private corporations will increasingly carry
> out programs now assumed to be the sole prerogative of the bureau-
> cratic agencies of the government.
> Although the overriding reason for this shift in corporate activity
> is the reduction in defense and space spending, there are other
> explanations. One is that the service industries, in contrast with
> manufacturing, are generally viewed by economists as the growth
> industries of the future. . . . And among the service industries,
> education is the fastest-growing of all.*

The government-industry-education-establishment cycle of
billion-dollar funding was a hand-in-glove situation. Such OEO
involvement was by no means limited to Job Corps; neither,

---

* *Ibid.,* p. 26.

moreover, was the government's generosity to business and their joint subversion of the school establishment even primarily managed by OEO.

True, by fiscal 1967—only two years after the first Job Corps contract was let—18 firms were running 23 Job Corps centers to the tune of $105,552,711. Meanwhile, in fiscal '67, Health, Education, and Welfare's (HEW) Office of Education spent $442 million (of its total budget of $3,852 billion) for such education ventures as private industry was able to sell state and local school boards. Yet, by comparison, both were far behind the Defense Department, whose $4-billion education budget doubled the entire budget of the Office of Education.

The educational-industrial complex developed as a fallback support for the producers of military hardware who saw the end of the Vietnam War an eventuality, and who, therefore, felt the need to diversify. The fallback was rationalized as a need to accommodate the government by becoming involved in what George Champion, chairman of the board of directors of the Chase Manhattan Bank, antiseptically described as the "socio-commercial enterprise."*

The sociocommercial enterprise, or educational-industrial complex, was rooted deeply in the earliest strategies of the Job Corps and the so-called war on poverty.

Quite literally, in fact, some military industrialists and various breeds of systems cultists were taking over management of schools and school systems—much as they had run Job Corps camps, thereby gaining experience and running test models. Litton Industries, for example, put together a community college in Oakland, Michigan, performing every chore—right down to devising the curriculum and teaching the teachers how to implement it.

Obviously, there is a bonanza for the producers of both the hardware and software being introduced into these new schools, as well as into old schools where grandiose claims are made on behalf of newfangled hardware to teach the "unteachable."

* George Champion, "Creative Competition," *Harvard Business Review*, May–June, 1967, p. 67.

Obvious also is the fact that the willingness of the government to pick up the tabs for experimental equipment (albeit with money earmarked for the poor) is the break industry had in mind from the outset. A routine travesty committed by OEO in 1966 shows clearly how the agency substituted the interests of the rich for those of the poor.

On the first day of the new fiscal year—July 1, 1966—OEO announced a $1.17-million contract for an array of computerized gadgetry.

About 44 percent of the money—$443,750—went to the Board of Education of the City of New York, with the remainder—$666,000—used to purchase 20 "talking typewriters," formally called the Edison Responsive Environment (ERE).

The point of the deal, according to the OEO release, was "to help New York's culturally deprived children and adults learn to read quickly. . . . The revolutionary talking computers will also be used to teach reading skills to school dropouts and functionally illiterate adults during afternoon and evening classes."

OEO had earlier completed a similar deal, providing the same machines for the Chicago Welfare Department. The cost: $600,000.

Beginning in about 1964, the military-industrial educationalists were obviously on a binge of producing gadgets at high cost, experimenting with the unwitting poor while raking off the money ostensibly aimed at the poor.

As OEO had the Economic Opportunity Act of 1964, the Office of Education had its Elementary and Secondary Education Act (ESEA) of 1965—a measure specifically passed to help educate the poor. But, like OEO, the Office of Education was a sitting duck for the educational gadgeteers (producers mainly of audio-visual aids—small computers which virtually no teachers knew how to use, even if they'd had the time—and an undigestible assortment of so-called "institutional" materials).

Thanks to the ESEA, millions passed through the slightly numb hands of state and local school administrators and into the coffers of the gadgeteers. How fast the businessmen moved is evident in the Office of Education budget outlays for their wares.

In fiscal '65, the year *before* the ESEA was effective, the total Office of Education budget was $954,717,000, with $115,150,-000 of it spent with the industrialists. However, fiscal '66 was a bumper year for the industrialists, who raked off profits from the poor in both Job Corps and the Office of Education.

In fiscal '66, the Office of Education doubled its total budget to $1,972,000,000; but its spending with the industrialists quadrupled—from $115,100,000 to $522,130,000. A crucial point, however, is the fact that although the Office of Education's total budget doubled again in fiscal '67 (from $1.9 billion to $3.8 billion), its spending with industrialists actually dropped (from $522.1 million to $442.0 million).

Eventually, a reckoning of some kind was inevitable—but forced more by an industrial dilemma than by any enlightened recognition of the poor's need by the government and the industrialists. The school warehouses were simply filled to the gills, finally alerting state and local school administrators that their common judgment would have to prevail if, indeed, the federal bureaucrats and the corporate gadgeteers were to be halted.

Despite the fact that the industrialists managed a slight new spurt in spending in the Office of Education's fiscal '68 budget ($465 million from a swollen total budget of $3.9 billion), the budget events of fiscal '69 removed all doubt that the downturn was solid. The $6-billion Johnson administration cut demanded by the Congress had a sobering effect, of course, but considering the increase given the Office of Education's total fiscal '69 budget of $4.1 billion, the industrialists' share of only $350 million was clearly bad news.

The change had been evident at least a year earlier in the education programs industry had run for OEO.

Under pressure from such tireless critics as Congresswoman Edith Green (Democrat of Oregon) of the House Education and Labor Committee, Job Corps began cutting back on costs by closing Job Corps centers in the last quarter of fiscal '68.

Despite hurried objections from the business community and protests from even such liberal lawmakers as Senator Wayne Morse (Democrat of Oregon) (whose victorious opponent, Republican Robert W. Packwood, twitted him during the 1968 campaign for not being able to keep business pouring into the state) , OEO had to close four centers, knocking three firms out of the circle: Rodman Center in New Bedford, Massachusetts, was closed, ending a lucrative skein of IBM; termination of the Lincoln Center in Lincoln, Nebraska, knocked out Northern Natural Gas; the closing of the Custer Center in Battle Creek, Michigan, eliminated U.S. Industries, Inc.; and although RCA lost the McCoy Center in Sparta, Wisconsin, it stayed in the Job Corps business with the Keystone Center in Pennsylvania.

Although the Job Corps cutback order was not effective until March, 1968, the order was handed down in January—early enough to reduce the Job Corps' educational expenditures more than a million dollars, from $105,552,711 in fiscal '67 to $104,440,751 in fiscal '68. Even deeper cuts were effected in fiscal '69, reassuring the industrialists that they were right to be concerned at the first evidence of fairness and sanity two years earlier.

It was this concern that brought education commissioner Harold Howe II before the annual convention of the National Audio-Visual Association at Washington's Sheraton-Park Hotel on July 13, 1968. It was a watermark in the public relationships between the education establishment and the corporate gadgeteers. Howe was immersed in pressures both from superintendents in need of warehouse space and from businessmen who reminded him that President Johnson's chief emissaries had urged the private sector to enter the Great Society (ahead of the poor) a few years earlier.

Howe told the association: "Some of our social critics have become increasingly concerned over what seems to them the ominous emergence of a new 'social-industrial complex'—rivalling in its iniquity and influence the 'military-industrial complex' against which President Eisenhower warned us nearly a decade ago. About the only similarity I see between education and defense industries is that both have developed well-oiled routes to the Congress—a development to be expected by any except the politically naive. . . . I would urge you not to confine your concerns simply to the making and selling of educational hard goods—or even of educational systems. I do not assume that your interests and those of education are exactly identical. But neither do I assume that they are inherently incompatible. I see no reason why the new educational technology cannot prove immensely profitable both for the students of America and for the stockholders of our educational industry. There are those . . . who fear that the education industry will exert an undue influence upon American education and usurp the decision-making functions that ought to be reserved to educators and to the society and citizenry as a whole. I do not discount this danger. But I do not think it is the only problem or the most immediate."

Any modicum of candor required Howe to face up to the industrial dilemma brought on by the profits-from-the-poor schemes. He did: "It must be said that the reluctance of some educators to talk to business is not necessarily the result of any excessively puritanical attitude toward profits. For industry has not always served American education well. I could cite, for example, the hardware-selling spree of a few years ago."

The "spree" was the result of a new relationship between business and education, and it necessitated "some readjustment," Dr. George Redfern, associate secretary of the 18,000-member American Association of School Administration, stated later in an interview.

"As industry and business have moved into the development of hardware and software to incorporate the new technology into education," Dr. Redfern explained, "there has been a new kind of relationship between business and education. Corporations such as General Learning have been formed. Business and industry now say, 'We're going into education not only to perform a service, but to sell a service.' This seems to be a more activist kind of relationship, whereas before it was a kind of advisory relationship."

Educator Redfern spoke charitably of the pressure-selling tactics that victimized school administrators, loading them with useless hardware:

"Some of these ventures business has undertaken have not worked out and some administrators have been disappointed. We thought they [the industrialists] could provide more than time has proved that they can. Certain experiments looked very promising, but they are still in the experimental stage. Such devices as the 'talking typewriter' have not become the miracle that can solve all education problems. But we should not condemn industry; there was an unrealistic expectation on the part of some of us school people."

Dr. Redfern was quite specific, however, in pointing to the emergency produced by education's industrial dilemma:

"In the beginning of the federal programs, we bought more machinery than we needed and got overstocked on that, and they were not wisely used. I think that is a great danger. If you can get federal money, you are tempted to overbuy. But when 30,000 school administrators come to our conventions, as they did in Atlantic City, and look at this new equipment brought there by seven or eight firms, they have become more hesitant to buy. And this is good for business and industry, as well as for administrators. So, we are having some readjusting in the market."

A knowledgeable official in the Office of Education stated flatly that this "readjusting" means that "some of the smaller guys [retailers] are overstocked and they're having to go into the warehousing business, because the fluctuation might put them out of business."

"You see," the Office of Education official continued, "when this money first became available, a lot of little guys figured that this was a good deal, and that they'd better get in on it in a hurry. They did, but then, a year later, the holes were all filled up. It's all evened out now. Naturally this fluctuation will hit the little guy harder than the big guys."

But the outlook is for the big producers—those well enough diversified—to weather the low-key revolt of the school administrators. If and as the need increases for the industrialists to substitute domestic gadgets for those no longer shipped to Southeast Asia, the hardware spree of antipoverty's vintage years will be on again. The pressures will mount once more on the school hierarchy, and the administrators will fight back, realizing that their own hallowed policy and decision-making roles are challenged by an array of "talking machines."

One of the best informed and strategically located men in this arena thinks the industrialists and their machines have already won that battle—thanks to federal antipoverty financing. This key man is Dr. Robert C. Snider, assistant director of the National Education Association's Division of Educational Technology and, more importantly, a special consultant to the Commission on Instructional Technology (CIT). The CIT was created pursuant to provisions of Title III of the Public Broadcasting Act of 1967. Its job: to look broadly into what former education commissioner Howe termed the "instructional technology, including television, radio, the computer, films, and recordings both in their relation to each other and to instruction."

Dr. Snider, whose views are given urgent consideration by the commission, thinks that it is too late to worry *whether* industry is going to influence educational policy but that it is time, rather, to consider the *content* of the influence.

"The classroom teacher becomes more and more dependent on an array of materials—movies, slides, and the like produced by private industry," Dr. Snider said, without a hint of unhappiness. "The more schools buy, the more the things bought will influence instruction and eventually school policy. The handwriting is on the wall. There is a danger here that the American schools will be taught by General Motors and General Foods. But, we must admit that the classroom teacher standing before the classroom talking is a very primitive form of communication. The new knowledge is going to force reorganization of the schools."

Several years after President Johnson declared his "unconditional" war on poverty, the Wall Street corporations were

counting higher profits and discounting the changes that offer
shares to the poor. The poor, meanwhile, were no less institutionalized in their poverty.

The meaning of the episode was put correctly, and in cruel
innocence, by Shriver's successor, acting director Bertrand
Harding, speaking on OEO's fourth anniversary:

Perhaps the most powerful institution OEO has effected [sic] is
that of the business world. When the war on poverty began, among
our loudest critics were the U.S. Chamber of Commerce, the
National Association of Manufacturers and countless private corporations. They saw it as another tax-consuming welfare-style program
—one that the Democrats brag about and the Republicans pay for.
Worse, they saw it as an attack on free enterprise and self-reliance.

But then something happened. Last year, when it looked doubt-
ful that the Economic Opportunity Act would get through Congress, some of our strongest defenders turned out to be the Chamber
of Commerce, the NAM, people like Tex Thornton of Litton,
Thomas Watson of IBM and Henry Ford.

The reason for this turnabout was clear: the business world took
a closer look at the war on poverty. They saw it was basically
conservative in outlook. It was relatively inexpensive, it was run
locally and programs were based on self-reliance—a virtue long
espoused by this segment of American society.

Most of all, the business world saw that it was to its own economic interest to end poverty in America.*

The economic phase of the Blackpoor pacification program
was clearly a victory for the military industrialists. Just as
clearly, it was an economic setback for the Blackpoor, who still
had hopes of social gains to offset the relative economic losses.

The "opportunities" outlined in the new Great Society pacification rhetoric were inviting, if not compelling. But alongside
that rhetoric were seeds for the full-blown, cleverly woven
police web that was also encircling the Blackpoor. Some confusion was inevitable. On the one hand was the warning of a

* Speech delivered at the New School for Social Research, New York, N.Y.,
October 8, 1968.

veteran radical, Bayard Rustin, and on the other were glowing promises from such proven liberals as Hubert H. Humphrey, the nation's number two citizen.

Paradoxically, both the warning and the promise had been made possible by the paper milestones of 1964, along with the elections that fall. But laws, being only tools, were to be used by the bureaucratic mechanics—the system—along patterns set by ultimate political pressures. The bureaucrats and politicians could build either fortresses of hope and justice or camps to contain those mangled and aggrieved by injustice and hopelessness.

"Bayard Rustin, the backstage organizer of last summer's march on Washington, is calling upon Negroes to enlist the support of poor whites in a 'social revolution,' " reported syndicated columnist Jack Anderson (in the Washington *Post*, November 15, 1964).

". . . As part of his pitch, Rustin has set up a cry against President Johnson's anti-poverty czar, Sargent Shriver.

" 'Shriver is immoral when he claims he can give our youths vocational training in his work camps. All he wants to do is get our boys off the streets. We must not allow our sons to be picked up and hauled off to remote concentration camps.' "

That, of course, was a pointed warning of how civil rights and antipoverty laws could, at the mercy of bad bureaucrats and power-sick politicians, be used in totally negative ways. Thus, personnel and the whims of the bureaucracy itself became crucial.

While Shriver obviously had his personal credibility problems with some Negroes, President Johnson was saying things most Negroes wanted to hear, and two simultaneous—essentially bureaucratic—moves made his most cynical Negro critics take notice. Without question, President Johnson, that veteran of every level and shade of the bureaucracy, understood the bureaucracy. He knew the game could be won or lost there. Two moves early in 1965 were designed to win.

First, shortly after the election, Johnson announced that the new Vice President, longtime civil rights advocate Hubert H.

Humphrey, would have an overall role to play in the war on poverty—a move welcomed by the sprinkling of liberal bureaucrats in the federal system. They felt that Shriver's title of "Director" scarcely equipped him to "coordinate" the antipoverty progress of recalcitrant department heads who carried cabinet-level rank and status. The move also improved OEO's credibility among some Negroes who had not learned to trust Shriver.

As a junior Senator from Minnesota in 1948, Humphrey sparked a Dixiecrat walkout of the Democratic national convention because of his insistence on a strong civil rights plank. Just as gallantly, he went about his new job as federal civil rights overseer assigned him by President Johnson. Humphrey began calling on each agency and department head in the federal establishment and explaining that he fully intended to carry out the President's assignment in getting the Civil Rights Act of 1964 implemented. When it was Shriver's turn to go over to see the Vice President, Humphrey said with astonishing directness, "Now, Sarge, there's no use in our fiddling around on this matter. Let's get right down to it."

The Vice President went on to tell Shriver that OEO had a "special mission" in the civil rights struggle, for the antipoverty program could "put flesh on the bones of the Civil Rights Act of 1964."

In that meeting, the Vice President represented personally what OEO symbolized in theory. But, down the bureaucratic line, the wheels were already turning—in the opposite direction. Veteran bureaucrats who knew the potential of the law and a tough backer like Humphrey were already busy moving the wrong men into the right places, and the right men into the wrong places—proven bureaucratic techniques.

Specifically, the OEO official in charge of personnel and management drafted an appointment order for Shriver, which, when Shriver signed it, made OEO's chief civil rights officer a low-grade management employee who would handle civil rights along with his other chores and in his spare time. The announcement was spotted by Lisle Carter, the only Negro on the senior staff at the time. Carter, who had been the civil rights enforcement officer at HEW prior to coming to OEO as inter-agency relations director, sent a stiff memorandum to Shriver complaining that the job at OEO was much too important to be handled in the manner Shriver intended.

A few days later, Shriver asked me to take the job. It wasn't long before I realized that some careful wording in the announcement of my appointment was neither incidental nor to be taken lightly. It had made me the chief civil rights officer, but carefully provided that enforcement of nondiscrimination in contracts awarded by OEO would be a responsibility of OEO's deputy director, Jack Conway. Conway, a high union official with the United Auto Workers, warmly assured me that he would permit me to assist him in the contract work whenever my help was needed. But—he would call me. He never did. Not once.

In time, though, it was clear that his interest was very much a union interest. Nondiscrimination was fine—so long as it did not interfere with unionism; that is, sacrosanct seniority rules that automatically exclude nonwhites, legislative policies that tended neither to lower union wages nor to put poor job trainees in competition with unionists, and various other union hall concerns—all of which meant that I would never review an OEO contract and that no contract would ever be stopped for civil rights reasons.

Among the most difficult aspects of enforcement of civil rights laws were the obstinate bureaucrats, such as OEO general counsel Donald Baker, who were able to stand in the way of enforcement. Beyond them, however, was a fact of paramount importance in enforcement strategy. The lines of authority, responsibility, and budget were so studiously chaotic and diffuse that any coordinated attack on any tangible phase of racism under government was difficult, at best. This deliberate bureaucratic hokus-pokus involved a diffusion of civil rights responsibility and confusion of authority that extended across agency lines and, indeed, across the three branches as well as the three levels of government.

But President Johnson, an accomplished student of the bureaucracy, understood all this when he put a superbureaucrat, the Vice President, at the top of the system to streamline authority.

His second move, however, was by far the most significant civil rights move of the pacification era: it offered the only hope of bringing federal programs to bear on problems of the Black-poor by counteracting scheming Congressional cliques and their carefully placed civil servants. Essentially the game they play involves keeping the bureaucratic machinery slightly tilted so that in efforts to "solve" certain problems, all the necessary ingredients are never present at any one time or place. Or, to put it another way, it is much like the shell game of con men. The bean is theoretically under one of three shells; you guess which one as the con artist works his sleight of hand.

The basic move is keeping the three required ingredients to any solution—authority, responsibility, funds and/or personnel—in a delicate suspension. One agency, for example, is given responsibility for a particular job, while another has the authority (but not the responsibility), while still another has either the funds or the staff—and never the three shall meet. This was precisely the game being played on the homeless black Mississippians who, in early 1966, came to Washington for help, and after days of circling the bureaucratic bases, resorted to sleeping on the ground among the mums of the wet and cold of Lafayette Park while many bureaucrats looked on in amusement.

Perhaps more than any other single act, President Johnson's establishment of a Council on Equal Opportunity indicated a sincere attempt at genuine change—not mere vested interest pacification.

That Johnson move in February, 1965, aligned federal agencies in a way that assured coordination by a single individual directly responsible to him—Vice President Humphrey. President Johnson was, as it were, removing two of the con man's three shells. There would be only one shell to watch, and the bean should be there.

This bold antibureaucratic move began to take shape when

Vice President Humphrey wrote the President on January 4, 1965:

". . . I, and members of my staff, have also met with, or solicited views from, the representatives of State and local governments and of many private organizations. These included Governors, Mayors, city managers, police chiefs, civil rights leaders, the Leadership Conference on Civil Rights, official human relations bodies, labor organizations, businesses, educational institutions and the major religious bodies.

"On the basis of information developed from these consultations and other studies, and from the extensive written material which has been submitted, I have concluded *that there is need for establishment by Executive Order of a President's Council on Equal Opportunity,* [Emphasis added.] composed of the highest level representatives of those departments and agencies most directly involved in the civil rights field, and charted by the Vice President. . . ."

Vice President Humphrey's report underscored the new federal intent to use its massive spending power via contracts to eliminate job discrimination.

This new antibureaucratic approach by the President would either begin to improve conditions of the Blackpoor or it would soon have to be a target of the strongest reactionary forces.

It became a target.

During the spring Congressional recess in 1965, rumors seeped back to Washington about powerful Southern Congressmen meeting secretly in their home states and designing ways to sabotage what was beginning to look like a nonviolent revolution in America.

The President's Council on Equal Opportunity (PCEO) was headed for a daring but very brief existence.

The first meeting, on March 3, got right down to business. Heads of all contracting agencies, civil rights agencies, and Attorney General Nicholas Katzenbach were all brought together in one room, the Indian Treaty Room, under the aegis of the Vice President, who had enough administrative clout to pinpoint problems and other solutions by the men who were directly in control of them. Task forces were assigned in the major social areas—education, labor, and community relations, for example.

By the time of the second meeting, on May 19, the council, under daily orders from the Vice President, had begun to mobilize to hit where it hurt—in the financial statements of private industry and those of state and local governments. Computers were being organized to ferret out civil rights violators (much as they ferret out tax-dodgers) and to indicate where withholding federal money would be possible and effective.

For example, that second meeting heard a report on Alabama by William L. Taylor, staff director of the U.S. Commission on Civil Rights.*

The report was a typically dismal survey of the plight of black people in the South. But there was singular significance to the report coming as it did before the council: the focus of the council was on concerted action by twelve federal agencies represented, the result being that the state of Alabama would be forced to change many racist policies—or lose $1 billion in federal revenue.

The council was no paper tiger: thus it had to go. But while this fact was axiomatic from the outset, two specific events sealed its doom. The council's involvement in two cases drew together two of the most encrusted, resourceful, and determined exploiters of the Blackpoor—big city bosses and Southern governors.

The two events were (1) the council's endorsement of federal intervention on behalf of Dr. King's Selma-to-Montgomery march on March 20, and (2) an aborted cutoff of funds to the *de facto* segregated schools of Mayor Richard J. Daley's Chicago on September 29, 1965.

* "Enforcement of Federal Civil Rights Policies in Alabama"
Every year the State of Alabama receives about $1 billion from the federal government, and most of this assistance involves programs now covered by one or more federal policies of nondiscrimination. Reports from twelve agencies reflect three basic problem areas in carrying out these policies in Alabama and elsewhere. . . .

Actually, arch segregationists themselves could not have chosen better tactical strategy to draw together Mayor Richard Daley and Alabama Governor George Wallace.

The first catalytic involvement of the council emerged suddenly and within two weeks after the council's first meeting.

In the organization meeting, Vice President Humphrey had stated that the President, from time to time, would ask the advice of the council on major policy decisions involving civil rights.

In January, Dr. King had announced a new voter registration drive in Selma, Alabama—a city with a history of violent suppression of the Negro's right to vote. Incident followed incident until, on a Sunday afternoon, March 7, some 500 black protest marchers were attacked by 200 Alabama state troopers and sheriff's deputies (many of them on horseback), who spewed tear gas, then mercilessly clubbed their victims, including large numbers of women and children.

Writing his column in the *Amsterdam News*, March 20, 1965, NAACP executive secretary Roy Wilkins commented:

"They don't want just to keep segregation and inequality.

"*They want blood.* The die-hard Southern white element and many of those who hold office at its hands want blood.

"They got it last week and the week before in Alabama. They got James Jackson's blood during a march in Marion, Ala. They got it on Selma's Sunday, March 7, when they cracked heads, broke legs and curled bull whips around bodies in a vicious, hateful, shocking attack by fully armed state troopers against unarmed singing and praying men, women and children."

Wilkins' Urban League counterpart, Whitney Young, Jr., writing in the same edition of the *Amsterdam News*, called for the use of federal troops to protect the marchers, who were there to demonstrate for their right to vote: "The people and the soil of Alabama ought to be as precious to us as the people and the soil of Vietnam, where we have only in the past week dispatched 3,500 Marines to prevent aggression."

But sending federal soldiers into Alabama would be no simple chore. For one thing, Alabama's Governor George Wallace had, after a fashion, kept his threat to "stand in the schoolhouse door" a short time earlier to bar Negro children from entering all-white schoolrooms. Avoiding an impasse with Wallace was much more attractive than winning one.

Too, the troops and other commitments for the then quiet adventure in Vietnam were assured only through the favor of such as Georgia's Senator Richard Russell, chairman of the Senate Armed Services Committee; South Carolina's Congressman Mendel L. Rivers, chairman of the House Military Preparedness Committee; and Mississippi's Senator James Stennis, a ranking member of both the Senate Appropriations Committee and the Senate Armed Services Committee. All of these men represented states that are neighbors to Alabama, both geographically and in majority sentiment.

With just the right rationale, then, the President would avoid a confrontation with Governor Wallace. It was on such a note that the White House called a special meeting of the council, Friday, March 12, 1965.

The atmosphere in the Indian Treaty Room was tense and cautious. At the outset, the Vice President, distinctly strained, emphasized that the representatives were summoned on specific orders of President Johnson. With great care he also emphasized that the President would hold each man personally accountable for whatever views each expressed. He stationed David Filvaroff, secretary of the council, prominently at his left, and warned that each man's name would be written beside his remarks and submitted to the President.

Another massive march was being planned by Dr. King. The question put before the council: "What, if anything, should the President do in view of the threatened massacre of thousands of black, peaceful marchers?"

There were a few weak statements, such as Civil Service Commission director John Macy's suggestion that President Johnson should limit federal involvement to an expression "of moral concern." But there were also strong statements by such men as black FHA administrator Robert C. Weaver, Labor Secretary Wirtz, and numerous second-echelon officials engaged primarily in civil rights enforcement. Representing Shriver at the meeting, OEO assistant secretary Lisle C. Carter, Jr., expressed the sentiment of the council: "The federal government has no real choice but to provide support for Dr. King's movement." That became the council's recommendation to the President.

Eight days later, on March 20, President Johnson signed a proclamation citing the danger of domestic violence and took other actions federalizing the Alabama National Guard and authorizing use of whatever federal troops the Defense Secretary "may deem necessary" in the situation. The President said he had ordered 1,863 federalized guardsmen to the area, 500 regular Army military policemen to Maxwell Air Force Base in Montgomery, and 509 more MP's to Craig Field near Selma; 100 FBI agents and 75 to 100 U.S. marshals; 1,000 regular infantry troops had been alerted at Fort Benning, Georgia.

In taking the action, President Johnson said:

"It is not a welcome duty for the Federal Government to ever assume a state government's own responsibility for assuring the protection of citizens in the exercise of their constitutional rights. It has been rare in our history for the governor and the legislature of a sovereign state to decline to exercise their responsibility and to request that duty be assumed by the Federal Government. . . . I have responded both to their request, and to what I believe is the sure and certain duty of the Federal Government in the protection of constitutional rights of all American citizens."*

The strong recommendation of the council for the Alabama troop action could not have endeared it to the segregationist elements on Capitol Hill. But whatever was lacking in a North-South anti-civil rights coalition was abundantly supplied a few months later when education commissioner Francis Keppel took a sudden swing at *de facto* school segregation up North.

This was the second catalytic event that forged the coalition of Deep South Congressmen and governors with big Northern

* *The Negro Handbook*, compiled by the editors of *Ebony* (Chicago, Johnson Publishing Co., Inc., 1966) , p. 65.

city mayors. If, as Roy Wilkins said, Southern governers wanted blood, Northern mayors wanted no less than to be left alone.

In an unusual and startling action, Keppel and the Office of Education announced that some $90 million in federal education funds would be withheld from the Chicago school board for *de facto* segregation practices already documented in separate reports by sociologists Dr. Philip M. Hauser and Dr. Robert J. Havighurst. While there were some minor questions about meeting the technical requirements for cutting off funds, Keppel's announced action was taken under the enforcement provisions of Title VI of the Civil Rights Act of 1964. Although Title VI provides for cutting off federal aid, Keppel's action was political dynamite. The White House resoundingly reversed Keppel and ordered that school funds be promptly delivered to Chicago—without any relationship to *de facto* segregation or the lack thereof.

The Keppel reversal was a shocking psychological blow to the federal civil rights community, and there was no logic to explain either why Keppel so completely ignored political strategies by picking on Chicago and Mayor Daley first or why the preparation of his case against Chicago was, in the minds of many civil rights lawyers, so ill-prepared that it invited failure under the weight of the most meager technical challenges. That Keppel had consciously raked up a straw man for Daley and the segregationists seemed most unlikely, yet such suspicions were never satisfactorily laid to rest among some of the government's strongest civil rights advocates.

But most significant of all was the prompt demise of PCEO—almost certainly a direct result of Keppel's challenge to Daley. A few days later, one morning in October, the word came quite unceremoniously (from Filvaroff) that the President had rescinded the executive order, and the grand, coordinated federal attack on federally financed racism was no more. Its brief life of only eight months ended in record time for federal executive orders.

This sad, sudden death of the PCEO was a hurried retreat from a brief coordinated attack on federally financed racism. But more than that, it signified a resurgence of the entrenched

federal and local establishments, briefly threatened by a federally financed, federally directed move toward pacification, if
not liberation. The bosses of the system would not be content
with their mere victory of halting the brief federal stand for
civil rights; they would demand a reversal even of the basic
pacification thrust. The federal establishment itself would have
to be harnessed for a fast ride in the wrong direction.

The crash resulting from Keppel's ill-prepared attack on
Mayor Daley and the Chicago school system was only one kind
of reaction—swift and direct. The Democratic kingpin simply
got on the phone to Washington, and the show was over.

But other big-city establishments fought in subtler ways, ways
that belied the simple fact of the struggle between the establishment and the increasingly rebellious Blackpoor. Los Angeles,
under Mayor Sam Yorty, provides a graphic case in point. The
tactic was simply one of ignoring federal efforts to fund the
city's Blackpoor through newly formed community action
agencies. This was most effectively done by Yorty's forcing the
Community Action funds to pass City Hall first—and that's as
far as they got.

Yorty's tactic was detected early by Congressman Augustus
Hawkins, a Negro whose district includes the South Los Angeles
Watts section. A member of then Congressman Powell's Education and Labor Committee, Hawkins appealed to Shriver to
break the City Hall logjam that kept money sent to Los Angeles
from reaching the target areas. The stakes were high indeed; for
had Hawkins succeeded, he might well have at least delayed or
minimized the destructive Watts rebellion which occurred in
August, 1965.

What Mayor Yorty was doing, in effect, was "standing in the
ghetto door" to block money from entering the Los Angeles
ghettos just as Governor Wallace, more publicly, stood in the
schoolhouse door to block the entrance of black children who
legally sought to attend desegregated schools in Alabama.

For several months, Congressman Hawkins had tried unsuccessfully to confer personally with Shriver on Yorty's blocking
of federal funds. In late April, 1965, Hawkins finally managed
to send a message to Shriver by an OEO aide who met with

Hawkins in San Francisco. "Take a look at the Los Angeles situation," Hawkins pleaded to Shriver. Shriver sent back word that he would study the situation. Meanwhile, nothing was being done to keep Mayor Yorty from intercepting and placing in escrow OEO funds sent to Los Angeles for the poor. The mayor's argument was that an all-white, five-member group called the Youth Opportunity Board was sufficiently large to receive and disperse the funds. OEO regulations, however, called for handling by a more broadly representative group, a requirement of the Economic Opportunity Act which created OEO.

Spring rocked into summer, and by late summer, although more money (some $17 million) to fight poverty and deprivation had been sent to Los Angeles than to any other city, Hawkins' complaint was unresolved. Thus, in August, as South Los Angeles (Watts) seethed and burned from its legacy of neglect, the federal-state-city bureaucracy limped along at the mercy of political business as usual.

On July 27, just two weeks before the Watts explosion, Vice President Humphrey gave strategic reassurance to fretful mayors in an address in Detroit to the League of Cities convention.

"City government must play a key role in the Community Action Program," Humphrey told the mayors. "That role is assured."

The mayors had to be pleased when Humphrey specifically told them that poverty money would continue to come through city hall-dominated "umbrella" groups which would be designated the official Community Action Agencies (CAA's). "The great bulk of all community action funds are being routed through community action agencies," said the Vice President, "and in the future this will be even more so—as communities get organized and learn to take advantage of the priorities in the law extended to such agencies."

The direction of federal weight had shifted. In retrospect, the vaunted war on poverty had just surrendered to entrenched political powers, after the briefest skirmish.

Vice President Humphrey's strong reassurance to the mayors,

coming from the man President Johnson had personally designated to put a firmer hand on the problems of the OEO, was
confirmation of the surrender.

"I have had numerous discussions with the mayors of
America and with officials of the poverty program," he told the
convention. "And I can tell you that your important role is
assured—as it should be."

But on August 18, a week after the day the Watts rebellion
erupted, Shriver, beset by public demands to answer why OEO
had not reached Watts, issued a statement which sought to
minimize any friction between him and Yorty and to explain
what OEO had done in its skirmish with big city politicians:

> I have no fight or feud with Mayor Yorty. We have not used any
> strong-arm tactics against him or against anyone else. Our job is to
> help poor people out of poverty. That's what we have been doing
> for 10 months, and we have been helping communities everywhere
> to create and manage their own local campaigns against poverty.
>
> Five hundred twenty-three (523) cities, towns and counties have
> already organized effective local anti-poverty programs. Los
> Angeles, unfortunately, is the only major city in the United States
> which has failed to do this. . . . Unfortunately, a few local officials
> in Los Angeles have made it extremely difficult for the private
> agencies, minority groups and the poor to join in the war. . . . De-
> spite these difficulties, we have already sent $17 million to Los
> Angeles so that no poor person would be deprived of an available
> opportunity.

But in his effort to keep the blame in Yorty's court—not in
his—Shriver stated the new facts of life rather succinctly:

> We sent the Director of all of our Community Action Programs to
> Los Angeles five days ago. He has been meeting with city officials
> and with representatives of the groups which have previously been
> excluded from the local anti-poverty efforts. We hope he will be
> successful, but the final responsibility rests *not with us, but with the
> citizens and the leadership of Los Angeles.*

In that abdication, Shriver openly surrendered to City Hall
control. Thus, the poor, weak, and colored were again left to

the mercies of the rich, strong, and white. OEO, the agency established as partisan for the poor, had declared itself neutral. Actually, OEO's white flag started unfurling rather early in the "war." Shriver began preparing the senior staff for a *détente* shortly after the Eighty-ninth Congress returned from its 1965 spring recess. Even while they were in recess, some Congressmen had written or called Shriver about the ill effects OEO was having on their political fortunes.

"One Congressman laid it to me pretty straight," Shriver said with an unfunny laugh. "He said, 'Shriver, as you know, I voted for your bill, and I agreed with your talk about giving the poor a better break by helping them fight the system. But, Shriver, I just came back from home, and I must tell you that I found out back home that when poor people talk about fighting the system, they're talking about fighting me!! I don't need to tell you, Shriver, that it's nothing personal, but under these circumstances I can't support you anymore.' "

It got some laughs—but the story was true. And the punch of it was not lost on most members of the senior staff.

"And that's what we're going to have to start thinking about," Shriver said, ending the meeting and whatever there might have been of OEO's fight for the poor.

The direct approaches of Mayor Daley, the subtler tactics of Mayor Yorty, and the politically hazardous confrontation with Governor Wallace had each proved effective in controlling Washington-based efforts to aid the Blackpoor. Together they imposed an inescapable conclusion: The political-bureaucratic battle on behalf of the Blackpoor was, indeed, a losing battle.

The year 1965 is a logical time to mark the downturn of pacification, a brief civil rights boom that began moving toward a peak just five years earlier.

After one full year, many Blacks began to discover—or, at least suspect—that the so-called war against poverty was equally a war against the poor.

By then they were right. The Great Society pacification had failed.

# PART II:

# WAR, RACISM, RICE, AND SENIORITY

War and racism have common roots and objectives. Both begin in hate, fear, and suspicion, and both have as their objective a permanent advantage and domination of one's group or ideology over the other. The victor writes the history of the war and makes what he hopes will be the rules for all future endeavors.

Basic to racial exploitation—and war—are both need and greed. Natural law and social contract theorists, such as Thomas Hobbes, David Hume, John Locke, and Jean Jacques Rousseau, contended that when man emerged from his primeval and natural state, he agreed to enter a social contract with other men, giving up his individual absolute freedom both for group protection and to satisfy such other basic needs as food and shelter. Geography, however, played some part in the alliances formed by societal man, and a common geography seems to have influenced physical and other characteristics which amount to race. Consequently, alliances tended to follow racial or tribal lines.

More modern political theorists, such as the late American black intellectual W. E. B. DuBois, contended that war between races is a dominant theme of the twentieth century. Most certainly, race seems to have been a strong factor in tactical decisions made by the United States in its wars of this century, but the racial factor has counted even more heavily in the country's domestic wars than in the international sphere.

Actually, as John Locke pointed out, America, certainly since bringing slaves to these shores in 1619, has been in a perpetual state of war.*

* Wrote Locke: "And hence it is that he who attempts to get another man into his absolute power does thereby put himself into a state of war with him; it being to be understood as a declaration of a design upon his life. For I have reason to conclude that he who would get me into his power without my consent would use me as he pleased when he got me there, and destroy me too when he had a fancy to it; for nobody can desire to have me in his absolute power unless it be to compel me by force to that which is against the right of my freedom—i.e. make me a slave. To be free from such force is the only security of my preservation, and reason bids me look on him as an enemy to my preservation who would take away that freedom which is the fence to it; so that he who makes an attempt to enslave me thereby puts himself into a state of

Two things, psychic capability and grievance based on vested interests, seem minimal requirements for an aggressor to initiate war or for a defender to sustain his defense. Men identify with others who look like them, a natural inclination, since selfishness seems basic in man's nature. As Hobbes would contend, the selfish part of man's nature makes it impossible for him to take the life of another man—with two exceptions: (1) mental derangement, at least temporarily, tantamount to a capability for suicide, or (2) a psychic conditioning that dehumanizes—removes the natural self-identity from—the projected victim.

For the purpose of traditional war, the first exception becomes moot, at least with respect to the process and tactics. But the second exception, psychic conditioning that dehumanizes one's victim, relies heavily on racial contradistinctions. The aggressor must be able to see the victim as *unlike* himself. This explains why during World War II billboards along U.S. highways and in the cities carried large pictures depicting leaders of the Axis powers (hence their followers, too) as other forms of animal life. Adolph Hitler, leader of German Nazis, for example, was depicted as a rat; Japanese Emperor Hirohito was depicted as a snake; and Italy's Benito Mussolini was shown to be a Fascist pig.

Once these contradistinctions from ourselves were accepted, however tentatively, the rest was easy. We were then prepared psychologically to wage war without mercy—almost. There *were* racial exceptions, based on degrees of contradistinctions. Thus, the atomic bombs hit the Japanese, twice, but never the Germans or Italians. Also, U.S. citizens placed in concentration camps were of Japanese ancestry, not German or Italian.

---

war with me. He that in the state of nature would take away the freedom that belongs to any one in that state must necessarily be supposed to have a design to take away everything else, that freedom being the foundation of all the rest; as he that in the state of society would take away the freedom belonging to those of that society or commonwealth must be supposed to design to take away from them everything else, and so be looked on as in a state of war."—Sir Ernest Barker, ed., *Social Contract, Essays by Locke, Hume and Rousseau* (London, Oxford University Press, 1953) pp. 16–17.

Racial contradistinctions, greatly simplified and magnified by stark racial differences, accompanied black slaves to America. But they were not taken for granted. Slave traders and slave masters, with severest efforts from the outset, magnified and cemented every possible distinction. Language was both a crucial psychological and tactical factor. At penalty of death, slaves were neither permitted to speak their own language nor to master the language of their captors. Thus, gluttonous sharks followed slave ships from the West Coast of Africa all the way to Virginia, stuffing their gills with the black carcasses thrown overboard. The tongues of these black cargoes must have become a shark's delicacy, because when it either was not logistically feasible to separate slaves speaking the same language or was too expensive to throw them overboard to insure their muteness with one another, their tongues were frequently cut from their throats and pitched over the side.

Early slaveholders justified slavery on grounds that slaves were, after all, heathen—that is, neither did they have good command of English nor were they members of the Christian faith. In time, of course, these contradistinctions ameliorated to some degree, though not completely. The failure to command sophisticated grammar still denies federal assistance to the Blackpoor who cannot handle the paper work; and Muhammad Ali's adoption of the pacifistic Muslim religion and renunciation of his Christian name, Cassius Marcellus Clay, were adequate to deny him further draft deferments and strip from him his crown as Heavyweight Boxing Champion of the World. Color still remains the distinction upon which Blacks are denied housing, jobs, proper schooling, loans, protection of the laws, food assistance, and virtually every other necessity of survival.

The slavemaster's greed for rapidly produced slaves, and his rationalization of it, forced the black male into the role of superstud and the black woman into an image of immorality; the lingering legends of the black superstud are still mercilessly haunting the insecurities of many white males, prompting further rationalizations and contradistinctions.

A reasonable question is raised by this discussion: Who profits from all this, and why perpetrate wars against innocent people? A facile but true response: colonial domination of black colonies (ghettos) at home and neocolonialism abroad.

Highly significant is the fact that both the domestic and Asian wars are being waged without benefit of constitutional sanction. It is equally noteworthy (as discussed further in Chapter 6) that both the undeclared Korean conflict, beginning in 1950, and the undeclared Vietnam War, escalating into a national issue during the mid- and late 1960's, were accompanied by new repressive laws and threats of concentration camps to keep in check the legitimate concerns of citizens being robbed of their freedom to choose or reject war.

In the advent of both of these undeclared wars, there was also a marked drive by black Americans to secure citizenship rights and socioeconomic advancement. In other words, during those periods, Blacks have attempted to end the colonial existence of ghetto life, freeing themselves from economic and cultural exploitation. When such liberation movements are attempted abroad, they are usually labeled "communist threats"—as they are here at home—but there is less reluctance to say that a "war" is being fought abroad to put down the unrest.

In either case, however, the perpetration of those wars can proceed with popular support only when an adequate job of psychic conditioning has taken place. In modern America, propagandists for domestic and foreign wars tend to tie racial contradistinctions rather neatly into the vested interests of the dominant group, carefully labeling any and all attempts of the defender to survive and progress as threats to society and as manifestations of racially inferior characteristics.

A rationalization for U.S. involvement in Vietnam, therefore, would be that the indolence, backwardness, and venality, the failure of the South Vietnamese people to understand and appreciate freedom, and their unwillingness to fight for it require U.S. involvement. And secondly, their failure to secure their freedom threatens the freedom and national interests of Americans.

By the same illogic, the explanation for the war against Blacks here at home is that the Negro's slave legacy, alleged low I.Q. (hence, poor education), immorality, and criminal mentality (proclivity for drugs, rape, robbery, and murder) account for the need for new laws and military tactics to put down insurrection. Here, the vested interests are made ostensibly parallel to the public interests of maintaining law and order, reducing crime, and protecting the nation from internal enemies.

Thus, the psychic and vested interest factors are made "clear" to the domestic population majority and/or the manipulation of their will is achieved in order to wage race wars at home and abroad.

# Chapter 3

# The Psychic Preparation

Three doctrines were particularly instrumental during the 1960's in psychologically preparing Americans to mount a domestic pacification program, then escalate that pacification into a guiltless, exterminative war among themselves:

—*Puritanism,* a supramoralism, is perhaps the strongest pseudoethic in America. It claims moral virtue as the basis for all its acts, whatever their nature or consequences. It is as American as the Pilgrims.

—*Moynihanism* is a doctrine of "fault" psychology. It "documents" the basic faults and inferiorities of those being or about to be exploited. It is an old doctrine under new management.

—*Shriverism* is essentially a "good business" ethic. Like Puritanism, it, too, is as old and as American as the Boston Tea Party. As practiced in OEO—money going to big business and visibility going to the poor—Shriverism justifies free enterprise, even in pursuit of crucial social objectives. It offers the poor and defeated a chance to compete with the rich and triumphant on an "equal" basis, making sure that the poor do not take unfair advantage of the rich.

Puritanism was epitomized by John Calvin, a European moralist who thought it better to cut off a man's head than permit personal immorality or religious disagreement. But there were other aspects of Puritanism, or Calvinism, which were well suited to the needs of the colonial settlers in America. It required a rigid spiritual and physical regimen, demanded piety and hard work, and implied that while some men were born to die sinners, there was some correlation between one's regimen and his socioeconomic prosperity. The colonists found this useful for, indeed, they had to work hard and scheme well to persevere against the hardships they faced, not the least of which were taking from the Indian (actually, the original American) his hospitality, then his land, and eventually his existence as a people. The Indian was obsolete as soon as the colonists had survived a winter.

Similarly, the strong back and rugged constitution of black men were absolutely crucial to the white man's venture of mining wealth from the Indian's land. Impiety of deed did not erase the ponderous verbal piety of early America. Toil, a cardinal principle of Calvinism as practiced in America, was applied stringently to Blacks brought here from Africa; but the concomitant rewards were denied at all costs—with the enforced understanding that the black man's toil was legitimately performed solely for the white man's benefit, a convenience explainable under Calvinism's philosophy of fate. Obviously, the logic breaks down here. Puritanism is a false ethic, but it does help explain how colonists could fight a war for their independence soon after their arrival, while holding other men as slaves, and continue to deny the right of independence to that same group two centuries later.

With an overwhelming sense of virtue, many white Americans can rationalize this, and the OEO-related schemes of the 1960's required some modern interpretations of the basic Calvinist theme.

First, it was necessary for Americans themselves, especially the Blackpoor, to understand and accept their "fault"—that their failure to prosper under the system was due to some innate flaw, but a flaw which was being corrected via compensatory measures, such as special laws, programs, and other benevolences that the white guardians of morality and justice thoughtfully instituted. Hence, a massive civil rights program and a war on poverty, both federally sponsored, of course. This is standard Moynihan doctrine.

Secondly, the usual presumptions of the capitalists would

have to be insured: mainly, that they would profit economically from whatever modifications occurred, philosophically or otherwise. Crucial also was the clear understanding by all that such profits (and such arrangements as would guarantee them) were absolutely essential to correcting the basic flaws attributed to the Blackpoor. The cures could not come except by way of profits. Hence, "involvement of the private sector" in the implementation of new social legislation and programs—classic Shriverism. (Some might call this Republicanism of the Nixon variety, but it is characterized as Shriverism here because, during the Decisive Decade, this doctrine was most effectively espoused and implemented by businessman Shriver, a well-known Democrat.)

Moynihan was the establishment's chief broker for selling the fault psychology in the post-1960 era. It was his "The Negro Family," commonly called "The Moynihan Report," which, in 1965, "documented" the flabbiness of the black family fabric and provided the rationale for the Great Society's "rescue" of the Blackpoor via the education-and-training route.

A second brokerage was needed, however, to sell the cures that would come from the mandatory involvement of the public sector. The chief benefactors would be the fairly matured military-industrial complex and the education-industrial complex spawned and nourished by new technetronic educational experiments and the conglomerate giants, who, for a price, could be persuaded to assist their government in coming to the aid of society's downtrodden "misfits." The chief brokerage house, ironically, became the OEO establishment which enthusiastically handed out lucrative Job Corps contracts, while arguing at the same time that those trained under them must neither be permitted nor trained to compete with established white unionists and other privileged groups in the society.

Thus, Moynihanism and Shriverism came to represent two interdependent sales lines for neo-Calvinism (a form of racism in the technetronic society) and capitalism (a system whose foremost concerns are capital and business—money—with people running second, however close) .

Economist Moynihan prepared his report, with White House sanction, while he was Assistant Secretary of Labor during the early days of the OEO. It was to have been the basis for the 1966 White House conference "To Secure These Rights" (a forum for the Great Society pacifications), until black intellectuals were joined by some of their white colleagues in condemning the report as "benign racism." It was at least that.

The central point of fault he lays to the Negro as a group, then presses home his indictment of the black family: "At the heart of the deterioration of the fabric of Negro society is the deterioration of the Negro family."* Some might argue that this was a basic truth because it is true of the society in general. But Moynihan was not writing about the society in general, though introspection might have served better to uncover the real faults than this ostensibly objective investigation of the society's imitators and victims. But, to prove his allegation of black fault, Moynihan conjures up old sex theories and cites illegitimacy birth rates to demonstrate the weakness in the fabric of black family structure. In doing so, he gives no attention to the fact that the pseudopiety of early American Calvinism shredded black family structure by the systematic rape, kidnap, and forced division of black families during slavery and subsequently.

One facet of Moynihanism is to make any gains by the oppressed group appear to be magnanimity on the part of the oppressor. This is true regardless of how difficult the oppressor had made those gains. For example, in the central assertion of his chapter on "The Negro American Revolution," Moynihan wrote: "The award of the Nobel Peace Prize to Dr. Martin Luther King was as much an expression of the hope for the future, as it was recognition for past achievement."† Such phrasing belies the fact that the honor came to Dr. King *because* he fought against the oppressive forces in the society whom Moyni-

---

* *The Negro Family*, or "The Moynihan Report," Office of Policy Planning and Research, United States Department of Labor, Washington, D.C., March, 1965, p. 5.
† *Ibid.*, p. 1.

han implies were benefactors; it more than ignores the fact that Dr. King won the award because he opposed the slaughter in Indochina and the conspiracies that perpetuate black colonization at home.

After his insinuation that the federal government was in some way supporting Dr. King and the civil rights movement, Moynihan transfers the full weight of the movement onto the shoulders of the Johnson administration: "It is no less clear that carrying this [Negro] revolution forward to a successful conclusion is a first priority confronting the Great Society." Pacification, yes—revolution, no.

The Civil Rights Act of 1964 did little or nothing at all to break down the barriers at labor union halls that keep black men from getting a day's work and a day's fair pay. Nor did the Office of Economic Opportunity do anything materially to change the peonage of the mass of nonwhite citizens into a resource with economic viability of its own. The Voting Rights Act of 1965 did help add some 800,000 black voters to the rolls in the South in time for the 1968 elections, but beyond that gesture (at least 100 years late and incomplete), the Great Society pacifications failed on a grand scale. An establishment rationale for these failures hangs together only if people have been prepared to accept them through the dynamics of fault psychology, vested interest payoffs, and the successful dehumanization of exploited groups. These have been principal roles of neo-Calvinism, Shriverism, and Moynihanism. They are the essential philosophies which prepare a nation for guiltless war at home and abroad—all in the name of purity, good business, and altruism. Thus, when Moynihan wrote his "Negro lower class" memorandum* to President Nixon (dated January 3, 1969) shortly before the 1969 Presidential inauguration, Moynihan was simply extending his public disservice of dehumanizing the Blackpoor, paving the way for whatever "special" treatment seemed indicated in the decade of the 1970's.

---

* Newspapers unveiled this and other bits of Moynihan guidance in the early months of 1970 when persons inside the Nixon administration became concerned about trends and began to leak strategic notes to the press.

But the particularity of the treatment indicated was not left entirely for the President and others who would, likely by design, eventually read the Moynihan memos. The treatment was broadly prescribed in the description of the illness. First, in his January 3, 1969, memo, Moynihan reminds President Nixon that his election was a mandate to deal with the disruptions caused by new black demands for justice:

It is said that freedom lives in the interstices of authority. When the structure collapses, freedom disappears, and society is governed by relationships based on power.

Increasing numbers of Americans seem of late to have sensed this, and to have become actively concerned about the drift of events. Your election was in a sense the first major consequence of that mounting concern. Your Administration represents the first significant opportunity to change the direction in which events move.

Your task, then, is clear: To restore the authority of American institutions. Not, certainly, under that name, but with a clear sense that what is at issue is the continued acceptance by the great mass of people of the legitimacy and efficacy of the present arrangements of American society, and of our processes for changing those arrangements.

Next, Moynihan clearly labels those he wants identified as the source of the disruption, albeit with a gratuitous acknowledgment of "the true horror of the situation white America had forced on black America and the deep disabilities that came about in consequence." To him the current threat to the society comes from the "disabilities" of black people—the reasons for which being of minor immediate importance. Then comes some careful labeling, along with a passing dismissal of the causes:

The problem is not that one group in the population is beginning to react to centuries of barbarism by another group. The problem is that this cultural reaction among black militants is accompanied by the existence of a large, disorganized urban lower class which, like such groups everywhere, is unstable and essentially violent.

Once that crucial job of placing blame on the black villain is accomplished, Moynihan moves stealthily from fault psychology to five suggested remedies for the problem of a "disorganized urban lower class." Four of the suggestions peripherally relate to the one central theme of what to do with black people, whom he variously describes as "educated blacks," "militants," "black militants," "militant blacks," "lower class blacks," "black extremists," the "Negro community," and other euphemisms to hide the fact that eventually he means Blacks of whatever description.

The four peripheral remedies urged the President to:

—Maintain "the rate of economic expansion" which "steadily improved" the "lot of Negroes" during the 1960's, but which also keeps down white dissatisfaction at a time of black "cultural alienation."

—Keep black problems out of the news: "de-escalate the rhetoric of crisis about the internal state of the society in general. . . ."

—Avoid personal identification with Vietnam and keep establishment kids off your back by letting the Blackpoor do the fighting—overseas: "I fear the blunt truth is that ending the draft would be the single most important step you could take in this direction. The children of the upper middle class will not be conscripted." Children of the "Negro lower class" will be, by default if necessary, since it is the best employment they can find.

—Deny that the Blackpoor exist, thereby diminishing the legitimacy of the unrest: ". . . Stress those things Americans share in common, rather than those things that distinguish them one from the other; thus the war on poverty defined a large portion of the population as somehow living apart from the rest." (In February, 1970, a month before the memo became public, OEO chieftains ordered lower staff to drop use of the word "poor" in referring to people without money or power.)

Ominous as they were, those were remedies only related to

the central conclusion and recommendation that "the Negro lower class must be dissolved."

As written, the Moynihan memo's unusual use of the term "dissolved" ultimately gets around to meaning that enough jobs should be provided to move all Blacks above the lower class economically. While this interpretation requires a more generous view of the Nixon administration than any of its actions of the first year would justify, the best interpretation must be accepted as possible. However, the most generous interpretations possible do not remove the fact that the Blackpoor were identified as the major source of danger and unsuitability—a genuine threat and drag on the society—and, therefore, must be done away with one way or the other. They are, in a word, obsolete.

This is the central theme among Moynihan's five remedies:

Third, the Negro lower class must be dissolved. This is the work of a generation, but it is time it began to be understood as a clear national goal. By lower class I mean the low income, marginally employed, poorly educated, disorganized slum dwellers who have piled up in our central cities over the past quarter century. I would estimate they make up almost one half the total Negro population.

They are not going to become capitalists, nor even middle class functionaries. But it is fully reasonable to conceive of them being transformed into a stable working class population: Truck drivers, mail carriers, assembly line workers—people with dignity, purpose, and in the United States a very good standard of living indeed. Common justice, and common sense, demands that this be done.

It is the existence of this lower class, with its high rates of crime, dependency, and general disorderliness, that causes nearby whites (that is to say working class whites, the liberals are all in the suburbs) to fear Negroes and to seek by various ways to avoid and constrain them.

It is this group that black extremists use to threaten white society with the prospect of mass arson and pillage. It is also this group that terrorizes and plunders the stable elements of the Negro community—trapped by white prejudice in the slums, and forced to live cheek by jowl with a murderous slum population. Take the urban

lower class out of the picture and the Negro cultural revolution
becomes an exciting and constructive development.

Such memoranda by Moynihan (or anyone else, for that
matter) offer few plusses to decency and humanity, but there is
some candor in the January 3, 1969, memo that is useful in
underscoring the commonality of the race and rice wars perpetrated both in Southeast Asia and the southeastern United
States.

Wrote Moynihan:

> What has been pulling us apart? One wishes one knew. Yet there
> are a number of near- and long-term developments that can be
> discerned and surely contribute significantly to what is going on.
> Of the near-term events, the two most conspicuous are the Negro
> revolution and the war in Vietnam. Although seemingly unrelated,
> they have much in common as to origins, and even more as to the
> process by which they have brought on mounting levels of dis-
> unity. . . .
> Had the large-scale fighting by American forces been over by mid-
> 1967 (which is my impression of what Bundy anticipated in mid-
> 1965), had the children of the middle class accordingly continued
> to enjoy draft exemption, had there been no inflation, no surtax, no
> Tet offensive, then I very much fear there would be abroad at this
> point at most a modicum of moral outrage.
> But this is not what happened. The war has not gone well, and
> increasingly in an almost primitive reaction—to which modern
> societies are as much exposed as any Stone Age clan—it has been
> judged that this is because the gods are against it.
> In modern parlance this means that the evil military industrial
> complex has embarked on a racist colonialist adventure. (I have
> heard the head of S.N.C.C. state that we were in Vietnam "for the
> rice supplies.")

While Moynihan's purpose in mentioning rice in connection
with the Vietnam War was to deny any relationship, the opposite is nonetheless true: officials of several Cabinet departments
and a Congressional committee told me that rice markets influence U.S. involvement in Asia; also, the concerted actions of

Congressmen with vested interests in selling rice, getting elected, and colonizing segments of the home population prove it.

It is a part of the "free enterprise" or "good business" ethic as currently practiced, all done in the guise of helpfulness for a people who are "different." Rice is the main staple of Asia. It speaks directly to the rice grower's vested interest. Rice is food and, as such, is a weapon of war. Food—denied at home, but sold abroad—is adequate to explain both wars.

The colored people of Vietnam and Birmingham face different theaters of the same war.

# Chapter 4

# Memphis to Song My: The Common War

### A. *The Blackpoor Put It Together*

At the height of the Montgomery Bus Boycott, during 1956, a white Texas racist wrote a hate letter and addressed it simply: Nigger Preacher. It was promptly delivered to Dr. Martin Luther King, Jr. His name was already synonymous with the movement to feed and clothe the poor and restore dignity with justice to black people.

At the church where he later copastored with his father in Atlanta, Dr. King, at thirty-nine, looked ahead to "when I meet my day." He urged that the preacher of his funeral omit such extraneous details as his academic degrees, but he did want it remembered that he "tried to feed the hungry."

From the beginning of the Montgomery struggle in December, 1955, until the spring of 1967, freedom, justice, and equality for black Americans had been his major theme, although he drew constant, violent hate also by raising economic issues in the mid-1960's. On August 10, 1966, for example, he sent a lengthy letter to President Johnson, pleading the customary case for the Blackpoor:

Last January, numerous poor, homeless Mississippi Delta Negroes went to the empty Greenville Air Base seeking shelter from the winter cold. They were forcibly driven off by Federal troops. Some fled to Northern ghettoes. Some burdened already overcrowded Mississippi kinfolk. Others are trying desperately to survive today on 400 acres of land in Washington County without adequate permanent housing, jobs, education, on the verge of starvation, and with little hope. Another group of poor, evicted Mississippi Negroes at Tribbett, Washington County, Mississippi, struggled through the long winter in tents because of the Federal Government's failure to respond to their pleas for housing. They have no jobs and almost no food. Despite the fact that over 477,732 Mississippians are helped by food commodity and food stamp programs, these men, women, and children have been unable to get the food they so desperately need. Callous disregard of the Federal Government for their plight, and the plight of tens of thousands of other poor Mississippi Negroes makes a mockery of all the humanitarian ideals this Nation espouses throughout the world.

It was the kind of note sounded in that last sentence—his reference to "humanitarian ideals" espoused by the United States *"throughout the world"*—that increasingly alerted many of his supporters and enemies alike that Dr. King might over-step traditional concerns of the civil rights movement. The fear was that he might merge the movements of civil rights and peace. This, his enemies felt, would be the ultimate heresy; to some friends and supporters, it would not only be untactical, but the ultimate folly as well.*

The day did come when Dr. King saw the starvation in Mississippi and the Vietnam massacre as parts of the same war. That day was eloquently described in *Reader's Digest* (September, 1967) by columnist Carl T. Rowan:

On a crisp, clear evening last April 4, the Rev. Martin Luther King stood in New York City's Riverside Church and delivered the

---

* One of Dr. King's critics was the then Attorney General Ramsey Clark, who, in mid-1970, confessed that he had been wrong and Dr. King right. Reported *Jet* (July 23, 1970, p. 5) :

Echoing a conviction which he rejected when it was uttered several years ago by the late Rev. Dr. Martin Luther King, Jr., former U.S. Atty. Gen. Ramsey Clark told delegates to the annual NAACP convention in Cincinnati that "Martin Luther King told me once that the Vietnam war was a civil rights issue. I couldn't accept it then, but now I know he was right."

most scathing denunciation of U.S. involvement in Vietnam ever made by so prominent an American. He labeled the United States "the greatest purveyor of violence in the world today" and accused it of "cruel manipulation of the poor." He said that the people of Vietnam "watch as we poison their water, as we kill a million acres of their crops."

He stated that U.S. troops "may have killed a million South Vietnamese civilians—mostly children." He said that American soldiers "test out our latest weapons" on the peasants of South Vietnam "just as the Germans tested out new medicine and new tortures in the concentration camps in Europe." He accused President Johnson of lying about peace overtures from Hanoi, and urged Americans to become "conscientious objectors."*

The publicized massacres at My Lai and Song My were still a year away. At the time of their occurrence, garbage workers in Memphis were hungry, and Dr. King went there to help them. A single rifle shot ended his life—precisely on the first anniversary of his Riverside speech welding peace and civil rights into a single issue.

But, had he lived, Dr. King would have led a massive poor peoples' hunger march on Washington in the summer of 1968. His aim was to rub raw the nation's conscience on hunger. In his stead, Dr. Ralph David Abernathy, his friend and successor as head of the Southern Christian Leadership Conference (SCLC), led thousands of the nation's hungry—black, brown, and white—from the hollows of Georgia, the swamps of Mississippi, the hills of Tennessee, the plains of the West, the East Side barrios of New York, and the tenements of South Chicago on a Poor Peoples' Campaign in the nation's Capital.

In that rainy summer, Abernathy and his followers drove the stakes and set up the tents that symbolically became Resurrection City on the mall between the Washington Monument and the Lincoln Memorial. But their efforts got them little more than frustration, thousands of sightseers, thousands of news interviews, nights punctuated by District of Columbia policemen tossing tear gas cannisters in on them, rain and mud, internal strife, and eventually a routing from the area by police.

* *Reader's Digest*, September, 1967, p. 37.

They also got a $60,000 utilities bill, which they settled for $14,000. But they got no federal food help—the object of their journey.

As he drove the first tent stake, symbolizing the beginning of Resurrection City, Dr. Abernathy charged that people in the march were starving while Mississippi Senator James O. Eastland was receiving a $13,000 monthly farm subsidy for *not* planting cotton on 2,000 acres of his 5,000-acre plantation. It was hard to believe, but Courtney C. Pace, the Senator's administrative assistant, confirmed the figure, and added that the 3,000 acres still under cultivation are picked by machines. Asked whether poor Blacks still picked any of the Senator's cotton, Pace chuckled: "Why, no—they're all out in Resurrection City."

By almost any standard at all, the Resurrection City campaign did not go well. As a result, the following spring, mid-May, 1969, Dr. Abernathy returned with a band of 50 poor representatives who were determined to attempt it at least partly the other way: they would go directly to Capitol Hill and try to behave as lobbyists.

Even the bravest of the 1968 Resurrection City dwellers must have felt something cataclysmic about the downpours that mired in mud their efforts of a year earlier. So, when the new group of poor emerged from their prayer session at the Methodist Church headquarters at 100 Maryland Avenue, N.E., on Monday morning, May 12, 1969, some confessed to feeling a good omen in the bright sunlight.

There were toothy smiles from the multiracial group as they determinedly faced the sun two abreast and headed toward the U.S. Capitol. Two men—one black, the other white—hoisted a long, crudely constructed sign. It read: POOR PEOPLES CAMPAIGN, 2ND CHAPTER.

At the curb, they politely waited for the light to change before they started across the street to enter the Capitol grounds. Suddenly, Sergeant R. E. Nevitt of the U.S. Capitol police appeared in front of them and turned them around in the middle of the street.

"You all won't be able to come over with that sign," Nevitt

announced. "No form of demonstration on the Capitol grounds."

The rank and file poor didn't meet this first test gracefully. They began to grumble and hesitate in the middle of the street. "We're not here for a confrontation today," Abernathy announced, raising his hand messianically before the group. With that, they turned, walked back to the other side of the street and followed instructions—down to removing lapel buttons, union local hats, and any signs or insignia that smacked of demonstrations.

They had not come for a confrontation.

By 10:30 they were assembled behind closed doors with a group of about 20 Senators who described themselves as the "Senate leadership." The group included Senators Edward Kennedy (D-Mass.), Hugh Scott (R-Pa.), Winston Prouty (R-Vt.), Harold Hughes (D-Ia.), George McGovern (D-S.D.), Gordon Allott (R-Colo.), Charles Percy (R-Ill.), Walter Mondale (D-Minn.), Ralph Yarborough (D-Texas), Thomas Eagleton (D-Mo.), Clifford Case (R-N.J.), Philip Hart (D-Mich.), Charles Goodell (R-N.Y.), and Fred Harris (D-Okla.).

Abernathy was flanked by the Reverend Jesse Jackson, director of the SCLC's Operation Breadbasket in Chicago; the Reverend Walter Fauntroy, SCLC's Washington director and, until President Nixon replaced him, a member of the District of Columbia City Commission; and the Reverend Bernard Lafayette, coordinator of Phases I and II of the poor marches.

In a conciliatory tone, Abernathy opened one of their several Capitol Hill meetings by reading a ten-point set of "demands," but he left no doubt of where he placed the greatest emphasis: "Our highest priority demand is that hunger be wiped out in America now," he told the attentive Senators.

When he had finished his formal statement, Abernathy called on Mrs. Martha Grass, fifty-one, a quick-tongued, utterly bold member of the Ponca Indian Tribe of Marland, Oklahoma. A mother of eleven children, Mrs. Grass had been a resident of Resurrection City the year before. Dressed in Indian clothing, typical of the dress she wears on the Ponca Reservation, she stood and rattled the room with rhythmic oratory, lashing out verbally at the Senators:

You need to get out, instead of staying up here behind these shiny desks and in these beautiful buildings. You should be out seeing who you're suppose to help. We're sick and tired of being treated this way. Some of you should be getting sued for not doing your jobs. Why, I'm a poor woman. I don't even have an education. You should be ashamed of yourselves having me come back and forth over here to tell you your job. But I'm going to stay here until I get some answers.

You're just sitting here making trouble—trouble for the poor people in this country and in my state, and then going all over the world making trouble for other people with these wars. You ought to solve these problems or get out and let us poor people solve them. I hate to talk to you this way, but it's just come down to that. We've just got to say it like it is. We may not have the education and all, but you don't have to have education to know you're poor.

Mrs. Erma Gray, a black member of Chicago's affiliate of the National Welfare Rights Organization, warned that "People are ready to take matters into their own hands."

James Malone, a large, reddish man who said he was mixed Indian, white, and Negro, stated that in his home—the third Congressional District of Alabama—there is "a conspiracy going on to get federal money into that area for the poor, but to be used by the rich." In Alabama, his racial identification is "all Negro," he said.

The Reverend Jesse Jackson told the Senators that he would rather the Congress keep the money spent to help the poor, "and give us the money you spend for corruption—moon-landings and killing people overseas."

Senator Percy congratulated the marchers on their method of protest: "Everyone here has come to work through the process of government. Now it's our job to see that the process does work."

"When the system doesn't work, it organizes riots," Jackson interjected.

This first stop along Phase II was not unlike the several stops the group would make the rest of the week—except for Abernathy's sermon to an empty chair at the office of Agriculture Secretary Clifford Hardin, who refused to be present personally, and Abernathy's unhappy three-hour visit the next day with President Nixon at the White House.

On the morning following the White House meeting, Abernathy and one group appeared before Senator George McGovern and other members of the Senate Select Committee on Nutrition and Human Needs. Abernathy told the committee that he had personally asked President Nixon to come by and speak a word to the group of poor waiting in the Indian Treaty Room. But Nixon declined, because he had to work on a Vietnam speech, a White House aide stated. McGovern urged Abernathy to "review what happened at the White House."

Then Abernathy told his version of what happened:

"I stated to him our goals and demands. . . . The President made a beautiful, and charming statement. I asked him to let the poor people speak for themselves. He said he had another appointment. Then he made another statement. Then he got up to leave. I asked him to go in and speak with the poor people. He left us. He did not give any answers to any specifics."

Abernathy said the meeting was later chaired by Vice President Spiro T. Agnew.

"The Vice President said he didn't have the authority to instruct the Secretaries to see us." Then, said Abernathy, Agnew turned the chair over to Volpe and left. "Secretary Volpe made a wonderful statement," Abernathy told the McGovern committee. "Then we were interrupted by Mr. Moynihan, who said the people over in the Indian Treaty Room had said they were going to demonstrate if I didn't come back and give them some kind of report. . . . I asked the Secretaries if they would come over. Secretaries Romney and Volpe said they would go over to the room with us."

(Note: This was standard bureaucratic procedure. Neither Housing and Urban Development (HUD) Secretary George Romney nor Transportation Secretary John Volpe has any authority or responsibility for food programs. The men with such responsibility and authority, HEW Secretary Robert H. Finch and Agriculture Secretary Clifford Hardin, both refused to see the group beyond their "show" meeting with the President, which they did attend.)

Already, as Abernathy, painfully fatigued, and his followers sat before the largely sympathetic Select Committee, two facts grew increasingly obvious:

—The likelihood of a Phase III of the hunger march waned by the moment. The country had run out of time and space for the King-Abernathy peace marches, permeated with prayer and uncomfortable attempts at lobbying in the fashion required of power politics.

—No matter what pressure points the poor lobbyists had reached in recent years, they had not reached the right ones. With few exceptions, members of the McGovern committee were sympathetic to the cause of eliminating hunger and poverty in general, but they simply lacked the power to do it. And yet, sympathetic Congressmen became the most accessible, and the wrath of the hungry was vented upon them—not their enemies, those power brokers who really held the cards and the vested interest.

Shock and candor, nonetheless, remained the best shots in the poor people's arsenal. Following Abernathy's formal plea for help, the committee heard bearded, rotund, and dungareed Hosea Williams, the SCLC's chief field worker, move excitedly to the point of departure.

*"This starvation of black people,"* Williams shouted to the Senators, *"is a conspiracy—a form of genocide!"*

One or two of the Senators felt put upon by such accusations, and Abernathy moved in to try to salvage the occasion. "Do not hold our behavior against us," Abernathy said in a tired voice. "We are not responsible. We are poor and angry. We are products of the system which produced us.

"People have lost hope," Abernathy went on, "and they are dying from starvation and malnutrition, and they have turned to throwing bricks. As long as we have this climate of hunger and poverty they will continue to throw rocks, because they don't care how they die. It's frustrating, and I'm not going to

give up, but when officials won't listen—much less act—my task
of leading a nonviolent movement is much more difficult. . . .
Help us to win some nonviolent victories to show those who
have lost hope in the system."

As he spoke, Abernathy's tired eyes searched the panel of
Senators. They looked back at him—most of them sympatheti-
cally—but none was so bold as to guarantee action.

Actually, the committee* was more helpless than shocked. It
was not their first time seeing the hunger or hearing the anger,
the hopelessness, and the conviction among the Blackpoor that
their government was bent on extermination through starvation. Only a few months earlier, in March, 1969, the committee
heard testimony in Texas and Florida and had listened to
medical experts testify to the shock of death caused by
starvation.

In Immokalee, Florida, Marvin Davies, the NAACP Florida
field director and a former school teacher, had told how Collier
County had thwarted all attempts to bring in federally aided
food programs, such as surplus commodities and food stamps to
feed the hungry. In the schools, Davies said, "There were white
lips on black children, a sure sign of hunger. I witnessed 'pot
bellies' which made constant sounds of distress. . . . I have
reached the conclusion . . . that the 100,000 seasonal agricultural workers in the state of Florida are the victims of the most
extreme abuse and exploitation to be found anywhere in the
United States. In fact, it is my opinion that farm labor conditions in this state constitute a *serious national disgrace, if not a
deliberate conspiracy involving the U.S. Congress, U.S. government agencies, state, county and local business and public
officials*"† [Emphasis added.]

On Capitol Hill, however, Abernathy, trying to remain the

---

* Members of the committee: Democrats McGovern (chairman) ; Allen J. Ellen-
der, La.; Joseph S. Clark, Pa.; Herman E. Talmadge, Ga.; Ralph W. Yarborough,
Texas; Philip A. Hart, Mich.; Gaylord Nelson, Wisc.; and Walter F. Mondale,
Minn.; and Republicans Jacob K. Javits, N.Y.; Winston L. Prouty, Vt.; J. Caleb
Boggs, Del.; Charles H. Percy, Ill.; and Charles Goodell, N.Y.

† *Hearings Before the Select Committee on Nutrition and Human Needs of
the United States Senate*, Part 5A—Florida, March 10, 1969, p. 1491.

statesman, did not make direct reference to either conspiracies or to genocide. What he did say in a final plea to the Select Committee on May 14, 1969, however, raised questions logically answered only in conspiratorial and genocidal terms. Pleaded Abernathy:

I very much appreciate the opportunity to appear before you today. I want to commend you on behalf of the black, white, Mexican-American, Puerto Rican and Indian poor for your efforts on their behalf. I feel that this Committee's hearings and field trips have played a vital role in pointing up the shocking and degrading conditions in which millions of poor Americans are forced to live and their lack of the most basic need—food—in this country with the largest gross national product in the world.

It has been over two years since the Senate Poverty Subcommittee went to Mississippi and reported shocking instances of hunger. It has been over a year since we first came to Washington demanding an end to hunger in America. Yet the Congress still has not acted to provide adequate food programs for those who need them. The prior Administration ignored us. The present Administration has finally come up with a hunger program which asks the poor and the hungry to wait still another two years, until 1971, before being fed and even then to be content with half a loaf. We do not and cannot accept this. We are hungry now and we expect to be fed now.

Of what solace is it to the mother in the Mississippi Delta to promise her crying hungry baby who wants food for supper tonight that she'll have something for him next year or the year after that? Of what help is it to the growing school child who's poor and wants to eat lunch and who watches his richer classmates eating lunch, that in a year or two he may be able to get a free lunch? How can the unemployed father tell his children that they face another two years of gnawing hunger and denial instead of breakfast, lunch and dinner like other normal American children? How can this country think of asking people who have waited all their lives for a decent chance that they should wait still longer while we continue to pursue other ends far less just and compelling while ignoring the minds and bodies of our most precious possessions—our children, our men and women? How can we grudgingly request $1 billion for food and continue to spend $30 billion a year for an unjust and immoral war? What has happened to our values?

In the spring of 1968, a shot rang out in Memphis. In the same spring, thousands of shots rang out in Song My and My Lai and throughout scores of villages of South Vietnam, striking down hungry men, women, children, babies. It was as though the shots of Memphis and My Lai were fired from the same round. The shots did little to destroy *hunger;* they killed the *hungry,* instead.

In Memphis and in Song My, it was the same war.

**B.** *Starvation and Birth Control: The Ultimate Weapons*

There are other ways to kill a people or colonize them, but none is more certain than the denial or control of their food. This is true whether the colony being controlled is in South Carolina or in South Korea. Indeed, you are what you eat: if you eat nothing, you soon are nothing. Hunger kills.

In an interview during the first month of the Nixon administration, HEW Secretary Finch flatly denied the existence of hunger in the United States. Pressed on the question, he conceded that "there might be some instances of malnutrition," mainly due to ignorance of the kinds of foods to eat and how best to prepare them. But, hunger and starvation such as former Senator Joseph Clark of Pennsylvania and the late Senator Robert F. Kennedy of New York had reported from the Mississippi Delta in 1967?—No. Such hunger and starvation as the CBS documentary *Hunger in America* had already presented?—No. Finch would not accept them, implying that such reports were politically inspired. Asked what he himself would do as the new HEW Secretary to determine the validity or invalidity of such claims, he nonchalantly replied that he did not believe there was need "for any more bookkeeping" on the subject.

Two weeks later, Finch was to learn that considerable "bookkeeping" had been ongoing during the last year of the Johnson administration, and the results were presented before the McGovern committee by nutrition researcher Dr. Arnold E. Schaefer, of the U.S. Public Health Service. In a Senate speech on February 7, 1969, McGovern reported:

Mr. President, I rise today to speak for a national emergency far more grave than the spreading slick of oil that threatens the coast of California. Perhaps the main reason it is far graver is that it is less easy for America to see, and because it is harder to see, it is harder to deal with. I rise to speak about malnutrition and hunger that kills and cripples millions of our fellow citizens as surely as the oil in that ocean kills the fish and fowl. I rise to call for action, immediate action to feed our hungry people.

During the past month the Select Committee on Nutrition and Human Needs which I chair has received irrefutable testimony about hunger in this country, hunger that is painfully clear and hunger that is hidden from view in the form of malnutrition. We have heard expert witnesses whose testimony leaves no doubt that bad diets have created a public health emergency of serious proportions.

I shall briefly review that testimony, discuss its implications and suggest some immediate remedies.

First, let me highlight the findings of the National Nutrition Survey now being conducted by the Public Health Service of the United States Government. This survey is a scientific study of thousands of families in the lowest quarter income brackets in 10 states conducted by specially trained medical personnel. Its results are based on examinations of a large cross-sample of people living in diverse sections of the nation. The preliminary results from two of these states as explained by the director of the survey, Dr. Arnold E. Schaefer, indicate that hunger and malnutrition in this richest of all nations is as severe as in some of the poorer nations of the world.

Consider the human meaning of these findings by the National Nutrition Survey:

—34% of the pre-school children examined exhibit anemia which causes "fatigue, listlessness, an inability to perform . . . so serious that any doctor would pronounce its victims candidates for medical treatment."

—In Texas, goiter, a disease that can be prevented for 1/4 of a penny per person per year, and which we thought extinct in this country, is, by World Health Organization standards, endemic.

—Growth retardation, often companion to permanent brain damage, is common.

—Vitamin A deficiency, unknown to any child who simply drinks enough milk, afflicts 33% of our children under 6.

—Children in this country have rickets and scurvy and beriberi, marasmus and kwashiorkor, diseases common in developing countries and usually associated with famine.

What do these and other findings of the survey really mean? The Committee has learned from expert testimony that present nutritional deficiencies result in:

—Children born with their brains already damaged because their mothers are severely undernourished and haven't seen a physician or even a mid-wife until delivery.

—Premature babies, 50% of whom may grow up to have "intellectual competence significantly below that which would be expected" in full-term infants.

—Decreased learning ability, body growth, rate of maturation, ultimate size and productivity throughout life.

—Lastly, early death.*

McGovern obviously hoped that publicizing such statistics would put public pressure on the Nixon administration to adopt a new set of priorities. "Our President wants to lavish $7 billion to protect two missile sites with dubious military hardware," McGovern said in a statement two weeks later. "We can purchase with half that an end to hunger in America. . . . So long as hunger, poverty, and racism continue to afflict our country, it does not matter how many missiles we have. Not a single one of us as an individual, or all of us as a nation, will be secure."

Representative Charles E. Bennett of Florida, one of a few Southern Congressmen active in the antihunger fight, introduced for a second consecutive year a bill he believed would "cut through the governmental red tape and bureaucracy which permits children to starve in America. My bill directs the Secretary of Health, Education and Welfare to meet the responsibility and challenge of death from hunger in America."† But

* From a statement released to the press by Senator McGovern, February 7, 1969.

† From a statement released to the press by Congressman Bennett, February 6, 1969.

the quite deliberate governmental red tape was keeping the hungry from being fed—and also threatening the life of the McGovern committee which insisted on keeping the issue before the public.

In 1968, the committee had requested $115,000 but was given only $25,000 by the Senate Rules Committee, chaired by Senator B. Everett Jordan, a North Carolina Democrat. Out of funds early in 1969, the McGovern committee had the blessings of fifty other Senators in asking for an extension of its life plus a budget of $250,000. Eventually, the McGovern committee received $100,000, but the pressure against the mere survival of the committee indicated the depth of the hunger strategy.

First, the resolution to continue and expand the funding of the committee was supported by all of its thirteen members except two—Louisiana Democrat Allen J. Ellender and Georgia Democrat Herman E. Talmadge. Although their own states were subject to committee investigations, there was more to their opposition than parochial political consideration. Both men are well known for their opposition to civil rights, but their use of political power in the hunger arena is equally strong. As chairman of the Senate Agriculture and Forestry Committee and a ranking member of the Senate Appropriations Committee, Ellender has an interest in food denial that is international as well as domestic, a fact discussed more fully later in this chapter.

Talmadge, also a member of the Senate Agriculture and Forestry Committee and the Senate Finance Committee, is a stalwart in the anti-civil rights forces of the South and had cruelly tied the entire hunger proposition into the issue of school desegregation. Cleverly, Talmadge continued to pursue the school segregation objective in several ways:

—As a member of the Finance Committee, he attached an amendment to the HEW appropriation which would have nullified the cutoff of funds to segregated schools as provided under Title VI of the Civil Rights Act of 1964. The administration sponsored a bill essentially supportive of the Talmadge objective, but McGovern countered with an opposition bill. The result was a decisive Talmadge victory. The basis of the

Talmadge victory was the fact that no matter what happened to school funds, food distributed by the Department of Agriculture was not affected. Thus, the USDA retained the control and the kind of flexibility it has used for years to starve black children. The second part of the Talmadge victory was a provision of the administration bill which emerged as a compromise. It continued Title I funds of the Elementary and Secondary Education Act (ESEA) of 1965 *through the states,* rather than through some supervisory arm of the federal government or as grants directly to the schools. This multi-billion-dollar ESEA block grant to the states continued the guarantee of control by the political machinery in the states, a machinery which had consistently misused ESEA funds since the enactment of Title I. The effect was that the states would continue to spend this poverty-targeted money for middle- and upper-middle-class whims—but not for food when racial politics dictated otherwise. That they almost always *did* dictate otherwise was emphasized in a report jointly sponsored by the Washington Research Project of the Southern Center for Studies in Public Policy and the NAACP Legal Defense and Educational Fund, Inc. Made public on November 9, 1969, the report covered an in-depth study of how Title I funds were being used. The report stated:

In this report we have tried to spell out Title I requirements and match them against what is actually happening in many districts. We found that although Title I is not general aid to education but categorical aid for children from poor families who have educational handicaps, funds appropriated under the Act are being used for general school purposes; to initiate systemwide programs; to buy books and supplies for all school children in the system; to pay general overhead and operating expenses; to meet new teacher contracts which call for higher salaries; and to equip superintendents' offices with paneling, wall-to-wall carpeting and color televisions.

Though Title I funds are supplemental to regular money, there are numerous cases where regular classroom teachers, teacher aides, librarians, and janitors are paid solely from Title I funds. New school construction and equipment, mobile classrooms, and regular classroom construction and equipment are common costs charged to local Title I budgets which should be paid for out of regular school budgets.

Title I funds are not to supplant other Federal program funds. But the extent to which Title I funds have been used to feed educationally deprived children, to purchase library facilities and books, to provide vocational education for disadvantaged students, raises serious questions as to whether Title I funds are being used to supplant National School Lunch, Child Nutrition Act, Title II ESEA and Vocational Education Act funds. . . .

And Title I funds are not to equalize racially segregated schools. Yet many Southern school systems which have steadfastly refused to comply with the Constitutional mandate to desegregate use Title I funds to make black schools equal to their white counterparts. *These funds are sometimes used to actually frustrate desegregation by providing black children benefits such as free food, medical care, shoes and clothes that are available to them only so long as they remain in an all-black school.* [Emphasis added.]

—In a clever propaganda move, Talmadge introduced, on April 18, 1969, S. 1864, "A Bill to amend the Food Stamp Act of 1964." Ostensibly, this bill was designed, as Talmadge explained it in a statement on March 11, 1969, "to eliminate an outrageous aspect of federal enforcement of the provisions of Title VI of the Civil Rights Act of 1964." While this was clearly an attack on Title VI, it was more than that. This was a move to call attention to the fact that black parents had two simple choices for their children: they could eat or integrate—but not both. As *worded,* the bill would have exempted federal food aid from HEW's Title VI cutoffs when a school district refused to desegregate. But its aim and effect were different, indeed. As Talmadge must have known when he submitted the bill to Senator James O. Eastland's Judiciary Committee for action, the bill would either die there—as it did—or languish there until the two Deep South Senators decided just when and what would become of it. But the aims of the bill were clear and effective.

* *Title I of ESEA: Is It Helping Poor Children?* A report of the Southern Center for Studies in Public Policy and the NAACP Legal Defense and Educational Fund, Inc., released November 9, 1969, in Washington, D.C., pp. 104–6.

(a) It portrayed Title VI as the villain in the struggle against hunger, and (b) it helped manage the delay of cutoff of funds from segregated schools, while the issue was pursued through more sympathetic courts which reversed the cutoff order.

While the stated aims of the Talmadge Bill would normally be misleading as to the true aims, the real intent of the series of Talmadge actions are more clear from a letter he sent HEW Secretary Finch on February 27, 1969, regarding the schools in Washington County, Georgia: *

Dear Mr. Secretary:

It has come to my attention that you are presently considering withholding federal financial assistance from the School System of Washington County, Georgia.

I believe you are well aware of my position on the school desegregation guidelines issued by the Office of Education during the past Administration. I have strenuously objected to the hard-line approach taken by Mr. Howe and the former Secretary in the enforcement of these guidelines, which I regard as unreasonable and impractical. I have had high hopes that the Department of Health, Education and Welfare would abandon its heavy-handed tactics of the past and assume a more rational stance in dealing with desegregation problems.

My purpose, however, for this letter is to call your attention to the fact that the withdrawal of federal funds from such school systems as that of Washington County, Georgia, will result in great human suffering, especially insofar as hungry children are concerned. Because many poor families are unable to afford even the small price of a school lunch, approximately 2,200 children—almost half the total enrollment—in the Washington County School System are now receiving food under the free School Lunch Program every day. Termination of federal financial support would deprive these children of probably the only nutritious meal they receive each day. . . .

I, of course, do not pretend to know all of the answers to the problem of hunger and malnutrition in the South or in the United

* See *Hearings Before the Select Committee on Nutrition and Human Needs of the United States Senate*, Part 8—The Nixon Administration Program, May 7, 1969, pp. 2532–33.

States, but I do know that we are not going to make any progress by denying school systems federal assistance that is necessary to maintain the continuance of free lunches to extremely needy children, both black and white.

I hope that you will seriously consider these facts in your examination of the Washington County situation. Should the Department of Health, Education and Welfare precipitously cut off all federal funds to Washington County schools, it must then bear the responsibility for many hundreds of school age children being denied nourishment and food for an indeterminate period of time.

I regard this as a very serious matter that merits your close attention, and I would appreciate very much hearing from you at your earliest opportunity concerning this case. . . .

On April 1, 1969, Leon Panetta, Finch's civil rights director, responded to the Talmadge letter, in part:

We are deeply concerned, as you are, about the impact of the termination of Federal financial assistance to Washington County—or any other school system. I certainly would agree with you that "the withdrawal of Federal funds from such school systems as that of Washington County, Georgia, will result in great human suffering, especially insofar as hungry children are concerned." However, we do have the mandate of Congress to uphold.

You are, no doubt, aware that the failure of a school district to comply educationally with the nondiscrimination requirements of Title VI of the Act does not affect the participation of a school district in the Department of Agriculture school lunch programs. The Department of Agriculture, not HEW, would be responsible under Title VI to see that discriminatory practices in its programs were discontinued, and existence of a dual school system does not affect that program.

Nonetheless, the Georgia Republican Party chairman was writing White House aide Harry Dent (a former aide to South Carolina's Senator J. Strom Thurmond) about "wealthy" persons who would contribute to the Republican Party if the Washington County cutoff could be reversed. Under such pressures, the 1969–70 desegregation deadlines for Washington

County were postponed, funds were continued, and the entire matter was sent back to the courts for new arguments.

As for Panetta, those same pressures forced his firing in February, 1970.

While McGovern was having his troubles from within his committee from Ellender and Talmadge, opposition to the inquiry of the committee was by no means limited to committee members.

For example, the National Nutrition Survey being conducted by Dr. Schaefer was covering ten states, including Texas, Louisiana, Kentucky, and New York—but not Mississippi. At a committee hearing McGovern asked Schaefer why Mississippi was not included. Schaefer admitted that he dropped Mississippi from the plan after FBI agents—sent by Mississippi's redoubtable Congressman Jamie L. Whitten, chairman of the House Agriculture Appropriations Subcommittee—had questioned him on the purpose of the study. In an interview, Whitten admitted that he had, indeed, asked the FBI to look into the matter, but only in the interest of getting pictorial documentation of the hunger reported by CBS and Senators Robert Kennedy and Joseph Clark.

Nonetheless, the public concern aroused by Schaefer's testimony and the work of the McGovern committee did succeed in forcing the Nixon administration to take a public stance against hunger.

Despite the fact that the President's communications director, Herbert G. Klein, had criticized the McGovern group for "traipsing around the country with television cameras,"* by early May, 1969, the President found himself sending a message on hunger to the Congress. In the message, the President stated in classic neo-Calvinism: "America has come to the aid of one starving people after another. But the moment is at hand to put an end to hunger in America itself for all time."

But then, in characteristic Shriverism, the President turned for advice—not to the hungry—but to those who might profit financially from dealing with it:

* Washington *Post*, March 16, 1969.

I shall shortly announce a White House Conference on Food and Nutrition, involving the executives from the Nation's leading food processing and food distribution companies and trade unions. I shall ask these men to advise me on how the private food market might be used to improve the nutritional status of all Americans, and how the government food programs could be improved. I shall also call on these men to work with the advertising industry and the Advertising Council, to develop an educational advertising and packaging campaign to publicize the importance of good food habits.*

The White House conference itself, December 2–4, 1969, was worse than a farce. Not only did it dash the hopes of the hungry in a way almost unprecedented, it also succeeded in advancing— against strong sentiments of the poor at the conference—the administration's own program of imposing birth control on the Blackpoor.

The fighting backstage of the conference was furious, but it mainly involved such questions as which contender would ultimately win the President's ear—conference coordinator Dr. Jean Mayer, who favored prompt feeding of all the hungry, or Moynihan, who favored more research and eventually a guaranteed income which would substitute the food commodity and food stamp programs for the existing welfare program.

Mayer and the poor lost all efforts at immediate relief.

Moynihan won, at least on his advice to the President to take the long view: say nothing concrete at the opening plenary session and study the problem further. Thus, Mayer returned to Harvard and Moynihan experienced another raise in personal stock at the White House.

In his December 2 speech opening the conference, President Nixon dashed the hopes of many by not proposing any specific measures for immediate relief of hunger. His primary concern obviously was toward reducing the number of the *hungry*—not hunger itself—for it was on how to reduce the hungry that he had specific recommendations and specific action.

The most emphatic of his three recommendations to the

* Washington *Post*, May 7, 1969, p. A-17.

conference urged that the conferees support his birth control proposals to Congress.* This had to be a strange emphasis at a conference which ostensibly had been called to deal with those hungry. But for six months beforehand, one of the conference's dozens of committees of technical experts—those doing the policy work on which the conferees would be asked to give tacit or explicit approval—had been working toward some absolutely fantastic proposals.

There appeared inadvertently in the press room during the first morning of the conference a working paper of the panel on

* In his address to the 4,000 conferees at Washington's Sheraton-Park Hotel, President Nixon prefaced his three recommendations with a concession which, for his administration, was a reversal of philosophy: "We can argue its extent. But hunger exists. We can argue its severity, but malnutrition exists. The plain fact is that a great many Americans are not eating well enough to sustain health."

Then his recommendations: "In this connection, I urge each of you to enlist yourself in the effort to win passage of three landmark pieces of legislation I have already recommended to Congress.

"One of these is what many observers consider to be the most important piece of domestic legislation proposed in the past 50 years, the establishment of a floor under the income of every American family."

While Moynihan has made his liberal reputation almost solely on the strength of favoring a guaranteed minimum income, the "floor" of $1,600 proposed by President Nixon would, as Senator George McGovern pointed out, actually leave many poor persons with less than they already receive under the existing welfare system, and would, for many, guarantee a perpetual existence in poverty, while living under the illusion of federal help.

"The second measure I would especially urge your support for," the President told the conference, "is the reform and expansion of the food stamp program, which I requested in my May 6 message on hunger. This has been designed to complement the welfare reform."

Again, as proposed, the poor would have less food and less purchasing ability than already provided.

"A third measure for which I would ask your support"—and this is the only one the government has *really* tried to have reach the poor—"is the Commission on Population Growth and the American Future which I have proposed to Congress, and which has been most cordially received there, as well as by church and civic organizations throughout the nation. America, I believe, has come to see how necessary it is to be responsibly concerned with this subject. In proposing the Commission I also declared that it would be the goal of this administration to provide 'adequate family planning services within the next five years to all those who want them but cannot afford them.' There are some five million women in low income families who are in that situation. But *I can report that the steps to meet that goal have already been taken within the administration, and the program is underway.*" [Emphasis added.]

"Pregnant and Nursing Women and Infants," which was the first panel under a section titled "Establishing Guidelines for the Nutrition of Vulnerable Groups (With Special Reference to the Poor)."

From those titles, one certainly had reason to suppose that this panel, headed by Dr. Charles U. Lowe, of HEW's National Institutes of Health, would deal with the questions of how best to get food to pregnant women and newborn babies. This supposition was strengthened by the fact that Dr. Lowe had testified before the McGovern committee and had told the Senators that "severe malnutrition suffered during childhood affects learning ability, body growth, rate of maturation, ultimate size, and if prolonged, productivity throughout life."

Dr. Lowe had further told the committee: "In effect, the quality and quantity of nutrition given during the first formative years of life may have the effect of programming the individual for all the years of his life. Malnutrition during the last trimester of pregnancy and certainly during the first months of life may seriously compromise ultimate intellectual achievement."

Another member of the panel, Dr. Herbert Birch, chairman of the Department of Pediatrics at Albert Einstein Medical School at Yeshiva University, had told the committee: "A serious consideration of available health information leaves little or no doubt that children who are economically and socially disadvantaged and in an ethnic group exposed to discrimination, are exposed to massively excessive risks for maldevelopment."

Surely, with this kind of knowledge, that panel of physicians at the White House conference might have been first and foremost concerned with how to get food to Blackpoor mothers, expectant mothers, and young children. But this was by no means the case. First and foremost, that panel was following the same wish most devoutly expressed by the President, himself: birth control.

What this medical panel concocted for tacit approval and adoption by the conference of poor and hungry people was a cleverly phrased recommendation that Congress pass a law providing for:

—Making birth control information and devices available to any and all girls over the age of 13 who requested them, with or without the approval of parents.

—*Mandatory* abortion for any such unmarried girl found to be pregnant and within the first three months of that pregnancy.

—*Mandatory* sterilization of any such girl giving birth out of wedlock for a second time.

Asked whether these proposals would not constitute a form of genocide, Dr. Lowe insisted that his major concern was for the safety of the young girl giving birth out of wedlock and at an unhealthy early age and for the newborn who, under the circumstances of poverty, would not be well nourished. A luncheon was agreed upon, at which Dr. Lowe and two members of his panel would continue to explain the finer points of their proposals. At the luncheon with Dr. Lowe were Dr. Howard N. Jacobson, of the Harvard School of Medicine, the vice-chairman of the panel, and Robert W. Harkins, director of research at the Ross Laboratories, Columbus, Ohio.

On the afternoon of the second day of the conference, Dr. Lowe was asked how the proposals were going in the panel sessions. He answered that formulation was complete and passage had been virtually assured from the strong support given in the panel by Dr. Alan F. Guttmacher, of the Population Council. A look at the panel itself showed only one black person present, a woman who admitted that she hadn't really recognized the proposal for what it was when it was presented. She didn't really understand it, she said, but hadn't wanted to hold up proceedings by asking "stupid" questions.

Mrs. Fannie Lou Hamer, the brave black civil rights lady of Ruleville, Mississippi, still ailing and lame from police beatings over the years, was resting on a bench in the lobby of the Sheraton-Park Hotel. Asked whether she would favor such birth control measures as those proposed by Dr. Lowe's panel, she responded with shock and grave disappointment. "What?!" she exclaimed. "What are you talking about? Birth control? I didn't come here to talk about birth control. I came here to get some food to feed poor, hungry people. Where are they carrying on that kind of talk?"

Hearing the location, and without another word, the gallant lady pulled herself up on a cane and headed for the panel's meeting room. Along the way, she spotted certain black men whom she summoned to follow her. She arrived at the room with about half a dozen bold black men who walked to the front of the room and stood like soldiers. Mrs. Hamer followed them to the front and stood in the center of the panel leaders, demanding to be heard.

Dr. Lowe yielded.

She then demanded that the birth control proposal, which had just been adopted, be reconsidered. After a ten-minute oration, spelling out the horror of such a law in the hands of public officials she had known, the resolution was obliterated. After a promise from Dr. Lowe and the panelists that no such resolution would be further entertained, Mrs. Hamer and her black male aides marched out as directly as they had come.

Quite apparently, a major objective of what was originally called "The White House Conference on Hunger" had failed. However, that tentative failure by no means obscured from the poor a clear attitude which the government would seek to implement as law and policy: *The solution to the hunger problem would not be more food to feed the hungry, but fewer hungry persons to be fed.*

Nowhere is this attitude more a fact of life than in the U.S. Rice Cup, the nation's center of power and prejudice.

## C. The U.S. Rice Cup: Center of Power and Prejudice

William Robert (Bob) Poage was born three days after Christmas in 1899. He grew up in his home town, Waco, Texas, and spent much of his childhood on a ranch. He is an active member of the American Legion and a lawyer by trade. In 1936, he was elected to the Seventy-fifth Congress and reelected to every succeeding one. By reasons of longevity and seniority, he happens to be chairman of the House Committee on Agriculture.

Congressman Poage believes that the owner of a big farm should get unlimited subsidies for not farming the land, but he fears that a poor man receiving $30 a month to buy food stamps under federal family assistance would likely spend the money on "liquor, or for pot, or for those sort of things." He also speaks out against Socialism and Communism.

On October 31, 1969, just a month before the White House conference on hunger, Chairman Poage conducted hearings on the federal food stamp program. The chairman is suspicious that free or low-cost food to the hungry would take away their incentive to work. He put the question to one witness, Stephen Kurzman, a lawyer with the Urban Coalition: "Do you think we can just continue to make it just as profitable to sit under the tree as it is to work, and expect to find as many people working as we have today?"

Responded Kurzman: "I am afraid, Mr. Chairman, that we disagree on very basic premises. I think there is very little evidence that any significant proportion of those who receive food stamps or any other kind of food assistance are choosing to do so, so as to elect not to work."

But Chairman Poage was by no means persuaded by Kurzman or anyone else who said food wouldn't make poor people lazy. So, the chairman gave Kurzman a little lecture on what ought to be done. It concluded like this:

> Now, if you ask me to help that fellow have a better life down at the pool hall, why I am just not interested in helping him. I am interested in helping that family, but I am not interested in helping that bird who could work just as well as I can. Are you? . . .
>
> The point I am making is I have not understood why you and others, who have appeared before this Committee, who have a legitimate and proper as I see it concern for the needy are also so concerned in maintaining a bunch of drones.
>
> You know what happens in the beehive. They kill those drones.

That is what happens in most primitive societies. Maybe we have just gotten too far away from the situation of primitive man.

Reporting that discussion, the *Action Report,* a publication of the National Council on Hunger and Malnutrition in the United States, headlined it, "Sick Humor: A Modest Proposal to Kill the Hungry . . ." and raised the question: "Genocide, anyone?"

Obviously, because of his chairmanship, Congressman Poage is one of the men of power in Congress, but he is more than that. He is a man of particular power, special interests, and a point of view. He is a member of the "Rice Empire"—a group of Congressmen, who, because of their seniority and chairmanships, wield inordinate power and who represent the five states which make up this country's "Rice Cup."

The five Rice Cup states are Arkansas, Louisiana, Mississippi, Texas, and California. This terminology—Rice Cup—suggests a comparative relationship to the Asian Rice Bowl countries of Indochina—Vietnam, Thailand, Burma, Laos, and Cambodia. These countries have traditionally been called the Rice Bowl because they consume a large proportion of the world's rice and because, prior to 1960, they had raised most of it inside their own borders.

These Rice Cup representatives hold the reins of power and racial prejudice here at home and profit most from wars both against racial minorities in America and against the rice-eating colored populations in Asia. The key remains food. In Asia, that means rice. In the Rice Cup, it means several things: high subsidies paid to farmers *not* to grow certain crops; high price supports guaranteed them for the crops they do grow, such as rice; and the *obsolescence* of black cotton-choppers resulting from government policies and from the mechanization of farming. No longer productive, as Chairman Poage defined the situation, black erstwhile cotton-choppers no longer deserve to eat —that is, to live.

While the Blackpoor are nonproductive and obsolete, and while such Congressmen as Chairman Poage consider it socialistic or communistic to help them, Senator Eastland and thousands of other wealthy farmers are paid *not* to be productive. Eastland and Poage are both from the Rice Cup. Mississippi and Texas farmers sell rice to Asians.

The psychic key is race, but the economic key, the vested interest, is rice. The holders of the keys are a close-knit Congressional clique who represent the Rice Cup states. The key to their strength is the seniority system which gives them chairmanships over the crucial Congressional committees which run the legislative branch of government, and to that extent they exercise extraordinary influence over the other two branches as well. It is with these chairmanships that they become the elements of political control in the country, and their sentiments become the controlling sentiments of the country, both at home and abroad.

To reach a quick understanding of this power and its dynamics, one is tempted to state flatly that U.S. troops are fighting in Vietnam merely to satisfy the vested interests of the Rice Cup clique. The same would be said of the war against colonized Blacks at home, nearly half of them still residing in the five Rice Cup and neighboring states. But rather than state this flatly, a discussion of the facts will arrive at a more reasoned conclusion.

In 1969, Congressman Paul Findley, an Illinois Republican and newspaper publisher, made a valiant attempt to limit to $20,000 the welfare payments to wealthy, nonproductive farmers. The saving—some $400 million—he argued, could be diverted to feed the poor. House Minority Leader Gerald Ford engineered the defeat of Findley's amendment to the Agriculture Appropriations bill, but Findley's research of vested interests and incredible unfairness was made public.

On May 12, 1969, Findley placed in the *Congressional Record* a tabulation of the counties which reject federal food assistance to the poor but themselves gobble up massive payments for imposing a scarcity of food by not farming. While Findley's speech inserting the tabulation failed to override the big-farm lobbies, he clearly showed the vested interests the Rice

Cup elite have in starvation at home and "defoliated" crops abroad.

Findley told the House:

According to President Nixon, there are over 400 counties in the United States which are not now participating in any Federal food-aid program for the poor. The President very commendably has stated his determination that by next July a food-aid program will exist in each of these counties. It is important to recall that Lyndon Johnson, while President, expressed a similar determination but did not succeed.

For some reason, these counties have proved to be strangely but effectively resistant to Federal food aid to their poor, and perhaps their resistance will tend to thwart President Nixon's promise to the poor and hungry. Indeed, Agriculture Secretary Hardin, in testifying last week on the administration's food-aid program, stated:

"I want to emphasize—as strongly as I can—that the success or failure of our Federal efforts to eliminate hunger and poverty-induced malnutrition depends heavily on the level of concern and action by states and local communities."

The statistics I am today placing in the Record concerning the non-food-program counties—425 are actually listed—are revealing. They give important dimensions to the problem and at the same time suggest a way to meet part of the food-aid costs.

They also lead to the embarrassing conclusion that Federal food aid to poor families is deliberately excluded from the very counties where farm production is curbed at extremely high cost to the taxpayer.

Deliberate exclusion of Federal food aid by these counties is a fact. Although limitations exist in the availability to additional counties of the food-stamp program, the direct distribution program, under which 22 items of food can be distributed free to the poor, is immediately available to any county in the United States and has been for years.

That farm production is curbed at high cost in these counties is evident from farm program payments made to farmers. For the most part these payments are made in exchange for agreement not to grow feed grains, wheat, and cotton. . . .

But what makes this practice truly astonishing, and directly contrary to that of Biblical days, is that it is so extensive in the very counties which bar poor people from access to free or low-cost food from the Federal largess. It is incredible that these counties, with tax bases swollen by Federal aid capitalized into the wealthy farmers' land values, flatly refuse Federal aid to their poor people. *Why does this incredible practice exist?* [Emphasis added.]

Surely not because of a local philosophical aversion to welfare, even Federal welfare. After all, Federal farm payments cannot possibly be explained or justified except as a means of providing income support. Income support is but another interchangeable expression for welfare. And let there be no mistake as to which farmers are receiving the most income support—or welfare—from Federal farm programs. It is not the little farmer. Nor is it the average farmer. Rather, it is the large, often wealthy farmer who receives most of the benefits from farm programs. The top 15 percent of the farmers, with sales in excess of $20,000 per year, receive almost one-half of the $3 billion plus in Government payments each year.

Plainly, the political leadership of these counties finds Federal handouts to wealthy farmers something they can live with, but Federal handouts to hard-core poor something else.

I would hate to think that this deplorable situation is to be explained as reflecting an aversion to poor people themselves. Surely the local leadership in denying Federal food benefits does not purposefully take this means to encourage poor people to move on and take their troubles elsewhere. Out of sight, out of mind, the saying goes.

Nor would I want to think that in areas where poor people are predominately Negro, it might reflect a *racial bias*. . . .

Of the non-food-aid counties, the one whose farmers received the largest total in Federal payments is Lynn County, Tex., with $8,903,000.

This is especially noteworthy because Lynn showed a population of only 10,914 with 2,282—nearly 25 percent—classified as hard-core poor.

The number of Lynn County families directly benefiting from the farm payments happens to be about the same as those classified as hard-core poor. Their income from farm payments alone, however, is more than three times the gross income of the poor. This estimate is based on $1,200 as the national average income of the hard-core poor.

[In Texas] . . . farm payments totaled more than $2 million each in 14 [counties], and more than $1 million each in 14 others. Put another way, 28 were million-dollar-plus counties but hardly so viewed by poor people.

Actually, Texas leads the Nation in size of farm payments and in total poor people without access to a Federal food-aid program.

Of $3 billion in direct payments in 1967 nationally, Texas farmers received $457 million, which was 15 percent of the Nation's total and more than twice as much as its nearest competitor, Kansas. . . .

While Texas has 53 farmers who got over $100,000 each, and 278 who got between $50,000 and $99,999 each, Kansas had no farmers in the first category and only nine in the second.*

The stark immorality of this farm subsidy arrangement is further indicated by the fact that some of the payments for *not* producing go as high as nearly $3 million per farmer per year. It is impossible that one farmer's nonproduction is that much more valuable than that of the day laborer or a man who spends his weeks and months in an unsuccessful search for work.

Nonetheless, based on 1967 figures as submitted by Congressman Findley, three California farmers, for example, shared a bounty of $8,259,579 for *not* farming. Five other California farmers split nonproducing "earnings" of $3,552,019. Farmers in other Rice Cup states did quite well also, while setting records for denying the federal government the permission to establish food-aid programs for the poor in their states.

Nonproducing Texas farmers, for example, received a total of $457,205,685 in 1967, while rejecting federal food aid for the poor in 99 of their counties. Louisiana rejected such poor aid in 7 parishes, while the state's big farmers were given $55,463,315 *not* to farm.

Perhaps most decent Americans would not believe that such an immoral system could operate in the company of the men of high integrity and purpose they believe they send to Congress every two or six years. In fact, to insure that their men *are* men of high character and moral conscience, on election day many districts tend to recall their representatives in favor of what the

* *Congressional Record,* May 12, 1969, pp. H-3531–H-3532.

voters regard as better people. This happens in many districts but not in all of them. It is, in fact, the longevity and seniority of the most immoral and venal Congressmen that enable them to thwart the best efforts of the others. Good men, of course, also get elected for long periods to Congress. Yet it is true that conscientious voters replace their Representatives periodically, while other voters, especially in the Deep South, retain their same Representatives for generations. It happens, then, that often the repeaters who get the seniority and, hence, the chairmanships, come from the least innovative, most repressive areas of the country.

The slightest examination of the Congressional committees and their hierarchy shows this to be true when the Nixon administration came to power. Rice becomes an important factor in this when it is recalled that Arkansas, Louisiana, Texas, California, and Mississippi produce the bulk of the commercial rice grown in the United States; their Congressmen, together with their colleagues from neighboring states, control virtually every key committee in both houses of Congress.

One of the Rice Cup states, California, has no committee chairman in the Senate and only one in the House. The other Rice Cup states are located in the Deep South, and theirs is the most formidable power bloc in Congress. Of the 16 standing committees of the Senate, for example, seven chairmen are from the four Deep South states of the Rice Cup, while three other chairmen (Senators Richard B. Russell of Georgia, John Sparkman of Alabama, and B. Everett Jordan of North Carolina) are Deep Southerners whose views are known to be equally conservative. In effect, the Rice Cup sentiment controls 10 of the 16 standing committees of the Senate.

In the House, seven chairmen of the 21 standing committees represent the four Deep South Rice Cup states. Excluding comparatively noncritical committees, such as the committees on House Administration and on Merchant Marine and Fisheries, the Rice Cup states then command 7 of 11 of the most important House committees.

In both the House and Senate, the *most* crucial committees are commanded by Rice Cup Congressmen. For example, the Senate Agriculture and Forestry Committee, which controls subsidies to rich farmers, has Louisiana's Ellender as its chairman, and his backup men are Senators Spessard Holland of Florida, Eastland (who, himself, gets an unconscionable welfare subsidy), Georgia's Talmadge, and Jordan of North Carolina. Similarly, the Appropriations Committee, on whose action the financial operation of the entire federal government depends, has Georgia's Senator Russell as chairman, but the line of succession is Ellender and Arkansas' McClellan, and includes Mississippi's John Stennis, who is chairman of the militarily powerful Armed Services Committee.

The extent to which these ranking members stand in line to succeed one another is just another indication of their hammerlock on the political trading process and of the extent to which they can control the direction and even the *existence* of legislation. No bill, for example, can reach the Senate floor for debate and action without approval by the Senate Judiciary Committee. Judiciary chairman is Mississippi's Eastland, whose backup is another Rice Cupper, McClellan, who happens to be the number one man on the Government Operations Committee which holds the reins on how the bureaucracy operates.

To a lesser degree, the same is true in the House where there are 335 more members and five more committees than in the Senate. The most casual look at the lineup of chairmanships in the House gives instant proof of the fact that Texans ride most high in the financial saddle. The Constitution restricts the origination of tax revenue bills to the House of Representatives. The committee in the House controlling such matters is the Ways and Means Committee, chaired by Arkansas banker Wilbur Mills. But Mills's fellow Rice Cupper, Wright Patman, is chairman of Banking and Currency, while another Texan, George Mahon, is chairman of the omnipotent House Appropriations Committee.

Not all Rice Cup Congressmen, of course, are rabid racists or zealots for the Indochina war. Exceptions are rare, however, with freshman Senator Alan Cranston, a Democrat of California, and Texas's Democratic Senator Ralph Yarborough being most notable among the exceptions in the Senate. However, Yarborough, who was serving as chairman of the Senate Labor and Public Welfare Committee, opposed the war in Indochina and supported civil rights and was defeated in a 1970 primary bid to retain his Senate seat.

Arkansas' Senator J. William Fulbright, who as chairman of the Senate Foreign Relations Committee was in a position to have fought effectively against escalations in Indochina, merely talked against them after giving them a crucial boost with his support of the Gulf of Tonkin Resolution. A clearer explanation of why he was able to oppose the war and still maintain his Senate seat in 1968 is indicated by his views on civil rights.

Shortly before the Nixon inaugural, HEW Secretary Finch returned to California for a visit and told a news conference that because Blacks had not voted for President Nixon, the Nixon administration could afford to deal more "candidly" with black problems. He said also, regarding school desegregation, that each community in the nation is a "different slice of pie" and would be treated differently, and that, therefore, there would be no consistent civil rights enforcement on school desegregation. This, of course, made many segregationists happy, including Fulbright. There were others less happy about it, among them Indiana's Senator Vance Hartke, who, like Fulbright, is a member of the Senate Finance Committee before which Finch appeared on January 14, 1969, seeking confirmation in the HEW job. In response to Hartke's questioning, Finch repeated the "different slice" doctrine. When it was Fulbright's turn to question Finch, Fulbright was full of compliments, but seeking reassurance that Finch would not go soft on school desegregation:

Fulbright: I . . . want to compliment you on what to me was a very perceptive comment made to the Senator from Indiana about each community having a chemistry of its own. Many people who have become immersed in the Washington bureau forget that. They

assume naturally that all communities are the same, but they are not. I hope you do not lose your views that you expressed so well.
Finch: I will keep a certain amount of chauvinism.
Fulbright: . . . You said it so well. . . . Well, thank you very much, and I have great hopes for your appointment. I know of your experience, and from what you said, you have made a very good impression.

Confirming the "right" appointees is only one of the power-ful prerogatives of the Rice Cup Senators who achieve seniority rank on key committees. The adjoining chart of the committee chairmanships for the first session of the Ninety-first Congress (beginning March 3, 1969) graphically shows the inordinate concentration of power and prejudice in the hands of the U.S. Rice Cup.

Congressional Chairmanships, Ninety-first Congress
(Rice Cup Representatives in bold type; their allies in *italics*.)

*Senate*

1. Aeronautical and Space Sciences
   Clinton P. Anderson
   (N. Mex.)
   *Richard B. Russell* (Ga.)
2. Agriculture and Forestry
   **Allen J. Ellender** (La.)
   *Spessard L. Holland* (Fla.)
   **James O. Eastland** (Miss.)
3. Appropriations
   *Richard B. Russell* (Ga.)
   **Allen J. Ellender** (La.)
   **John L. McClellan** (Ark.)
4. Armed Services
   **John C. Stennis** (Miss.)
   *Richard B. Russell* (Ga.)
5. Banking and Currency
   *John Sparkman* (Ala.)
6. Commerce
   Warren G. Magnuson (Wash.)
7. District of Columbia
   *Joseph D. Tydings* (Md.)

*House*

1. Agriculture
   **W. R. (Bob) Poage** (Tex.)
   *John L. McMillan* (S.C.)
   **Thomas G. Abernethy** (Miss.)
2. Appropriations
   George Mahon (Tex.)
   Michael J. Kirwan (Ohio)
   **Jamie L. Whitten** (Miss.)
3. Armed Services
   *L. Mendel Rivers* (S.C.)
   Philip J. Philbin (Mass.)
   **F. Edward Hébert** (La.)
4. Banking and Currency
   **Wright Patman** (Tex.)
5. District of Columbia
   *John L. McMillan* (S.C.)
   **Thomas G. Abernethy** (Miss.)
6. Education and Labor
   Carl D. Perkins (Ky.)
7. Foreign Affairs
   Thomas E. Morgan (Pa.)

8. Finance
   **Russell B. Long** (La.)
9. Foreign Relations
   **J. William Fulbright** (Ark.)
   *John Sparkman* (Ala.)
10. Government Operations
    **John L. McClellan** (Ark.)
11. Interior and Insular Affairs
    Henry M. Jackson (Wash.)
12. Judiciary
    James O. Eastland (Miss.)
    **John L. McClellan** (Ark.)
13. Labor and Public Welfare
    **Ralph Yarborough** (Tex.)
14. Post Office and Civil Service
    Gale W. McGee (Wyo.)
    **Ralph Yarborough** (Tex.)
15. Public Works
    Jennings Randolph (W. Va.)
16. Rules and Administration
    *B. Everett Jordan* (N.C.)

8. Government Operations
   William L. Dawson (Ill.)
9. House Administration
   Samuel N. Friedel (Md.)
10. Interior and Insular Affairs
    Wayne N. Aspinall (Colo.)
11. Interstate and Foreign Commerce
    Harley O. Staggers (W. Va.)
12. Judiciary
    Emanuel Celler (N.Y.)
13. Merchant Marine and Fisheries
    Edward A. Garmatz (Md.)
14. Post Office and Civil Service
    Thaddeus J. Dulski (N.Y.)
15. Public Works
    George H. Fallon (Md.)
16. Rules
    **William M. Colmer** (Miss.)
17. Science and Astronautics
    **George P. Miller** (Calif.)
18. Standard of Official Conduct
    Melvin Price (Ill.)
19. Un-American Activities
    *Richard H. Ichord* (Mo.)
20. Veterans' Affairs
    **Olin E. Teague** (Tex.)
21. Ways and Means
    **Wilbur D. Mills** (Ark.)

The rice elite in Congress require that Asians buy U.S. rice. They do this in precisely the same way colonized Blacks in South Africa and in the United States are always required to buy from someone else—at the other party's price—in order to survive, however shabbily, however tentatively.

The colony principle is a patented feature of the ghetto life in America: perpetual economic and cultural rape. In Dayton, Ohio, during the early 1960's, a black man sitting in the front row before the start of a meeting of the City Plan Board was hailed by a board member who thought the black man was wearing a Masonic ring. When Park Wineland, who had been a member of the board for thirty-four years, finally got the black man's attention, they discovered that Wineland had been mistaken about the ring.

"Well," said Wineland, not the least discouraged, "you ought to join—there's a Masonic temple right near where you live."

"Have we met before?" asked the black man, attending his first board meeting.

"No, not that I know of," confessed Wineland.

"Then," asked the black man, "how did you know where I live?"

"Aw, come on!" Wineland begged off good-naturedly, then acknowledged that the man's *color* was enough to indicate where in Dayton the black man lived.

Wineland was right: The black man lived only two blocks off Germantown Street, the street on which the Prince Hall Temple Masonic Lodge stood, exactly 1.2 miles from the black man's doorstep. What the veteran city planner knew was what *everyone* in Dayton knew: If a man was Black, whenever he came to Dayton, he simply had no alternative to going across the Third Street bridge to find living quarters somewhere between the Miami River on the east, Wolf Creek on the north, Nicholas Road on the south, and Gettysburg Avenue on the west. There were *no* exceptions. Thus, all the real estate broker had to do was stand at the bridge and wait, with 100 percent assurance that he could rent the new black arrival an apartment or sell him a house under whatever conditions and price the broker chose.

As in other communities across the United States, the power elite in Dayton guaranteed this exploitation at whatever expense or insanity was required. For example, when the issue of Blacks not being able to buy or build a home outside the Westside colony became a public issue in 1962, every banking institution in town went on record acknowledging the fact that they would flatly reject any loan request to any black person who wanted to buy or build outside the Westside colony. Bankers were quick to explain, however, that the policy was for the good of the entire city, including the victims.

"The goodness" of the policy was that racial and economic segregation facilitated every conceivable exploitation. The failure of a city bond issue, for example, meant a cutback in city services. What would be more convenient than having all victims of the cutback in one place? How better to insure that certain groups always bear the brunt of any public dislocation and that selected other groups still make whatever profit there is to be made?

Balancing the city budget despite the failure of a bond issue was made easier by the concentration of all Blacks in a Westside colony. The failure of a bond issue would not deprive other sections of the city of such adequate facilities as fire protection, street, traffic, and other safety improvements, and educational expansion. Nor would the lack of these things increase fire insurance rates, create safety hazards, or further cripple educational services in any area of the city except on the Westside. Only the carefully designed colony would suffer these disadvantages. Segregation was an invaluable tool of colonization and exploitation.

Herman Miller's revelation* of the 1960's that the poor pay more is now an unshocking truism. And when they pay more, they pay it to the colonizers—to the real estate broker in Dayton and to the Lynn County farmer who sells rice to Asians, collects millions from his own government in subsidies and price supports, and denies federal food aid to the "human scrap heap" outside the gate. There is ample evidence that the colonized poor pay more, and that ruthless, irrational action meets any attempt to break away from the colony.†

* Herman P. Miller, *Rich Man, Poor Man* (New York, Thomas Y. Crowell Company, 1964).

† Under the headline "Poor Pay 60% More, FTC Study Finds," the April, 1968, edition of *Law in Action*, a monthly publication of OEO's Legal Services Program, reported the following:

Furniture and appliance retailers that cater to the poor in Washington, D.C., charge an average of 60% more for merchandise than stores dealing with the general public, according to a large-scale study by the Federal Trade Commission.

The survey of 96 retailers with estimated sales of at least $100,000 in 1966 found that those who purchased at low-income stores paid heavily for the cost of "easy credit," door-to-door selling, and collecting on installment contracts.

In late 1969, for example, when a group of black people who call themselves Muslims bought cattle and land in St. Clair County, Alabama, and attempted to produce their own food, colonial insanity broke out. In a page-one banner story, the December 2, 1969, edition of the Washington *Afro-American* reported:

A group of angry white St. Clair County residents, estimated at 2,200 or more, met in a local school last Friday night to decide what action should be taken to regain land legally sold to the Chicago-based Black Muslims.

The land in question, over 900 acres, was purchased in cash for over $300,000 by the Muslims and will be used as the site of a $2.5 million industrial-agricultural complex.

---

The survey disclosed that without exception low-income market retailers had high average markups and prices. On the average, goods purchased for $100 at wholesale sold for $255 in the low-income market stores, compared with $159 in general market stores.

The retailers studied had combined sales of $226 million or 85% of the sales of furniture, appliance and department store retailers in the District of Columbia.

Chairman Paul Rand Dixon of the FTC said that the agency would have found much the same situation "if we had studied Philadelphia, Louisville, or San Francisco."

The report called for a requirement that finance charges be clearly and conspicuously stated but said this was only part of the solution. . . .

The report found that a small group of the low-income market retailers used the courts extensively to collect on installment contracts. Eleven of 18 low-income retailers obtained 2,690 judgments that resulted in 1,568 garnishments and 306 repossessions. They obtained one judgment for every $2,200 in sales.

The FTC noted that creditors could seek both repossession and payment of deficiencies including penalties. It suggested that creditors be required to choose one or the other of these remedies, and not be permitted to pursue both courses at the same time. . . .

Contrasts between the markup policies of low-income and general market retailers are most apparent when specific products are compared. Retailers surveyed were asked to give the wholesale and retail prices for their two best-selling models in each product line. These price data are typical of the large volume of products sold by each class of retailer.

For every product specified, low-income market retailers had the highest average gross margins reported. When similar makes and models are compared, the differences are striking. For example, the wholesale cost of a portable TV set was about $109 to both a low-income market and a general market retailer. The general market retailer sold the set for $129.95, whereas the low-income market retailer charged $219.95 for the same set. Another example is a dryer, wholesaling at about $115, which was sold for $150 by a general market retailer and for $300 by a low-income market retailer.

Among other facilities, they plan to have a cement manufacturing plant, a lumber yard, a slaughter house and a meat-processing plant which will employ local black non-Muslims and some local whites.

The Muslims were attacked in speeches as being anti-Christian and a threat to the local community. The white conservatives said they [the Muslims] are seeking to use the land as a guerrilla warfare training base for black revolutionaries. . . .

Spokesmen for the whites said that the fight [to oust the Muslims] would be channelled through the courts.

*With the support of the governor, Albert Brewer, state Atty. Gen. McDonald Gallion and U.S. Rep. William Nichols, D-Ala., seven court suits have been filed to date.* [Emphasis added.]

Four suits contest the legality of the Muslim organization and its non-compliance with Alabama State law which requires Muslims, Communists and Nazis to register after spending five consecutive days in the state.

Three civil suits challenge the legality of the land title. . . .

A worker who showed up at the farm last week was arrested under the Alabama law that requires Black Muslims, Communists, Nazis and others deemed subversive, to register after five days. . . .

It is one of many properties owned by the Muslims who are among the most peaceful citizens anywhere.

When they bought land in Missouri, there was some tension for a time by white residents, but now they appear to be welcome and they operate one of the most modern and productive dairy farms in the state. . . .

The sect's leader, Elijah Muhammad, teaches his members to work hard to own *something for themselves and to try to build an economic base for black people.* [Emphasis added.]

The court suits against the Muslims failed. However, despite the Muslims' insistence that they had come merely to provide for themselves economically, the county's 20,000 whites (60% majority) were not through. They were determined that such an effort must fail. So, in mid-March of 1970, the Muslims found scores of their cattle lying dead in the pastures, victims of poison which authorities said was cyanide. With that, the Muslims put the poisoned land up for sale, loaded up what live cattle remained and, under threats to their own lives, departed St. Clair County.

The economic measures attempted by the Muslims threatened the economic value of the black colony by making it self-reliant and independent of the colonizers. The extreme steps taken to prevent this makes predictable the dangers Blacks in Dayton would face with any similar efforts to break away from the bankers, real estate brokers, and merchants who colonize them. The economic (and constabulary) importance of such acts of war are urgent and quite analogous to U.S. "altruism" in Asia, for example. In fact, it is the same thing: the preservation or establishment of colonies for economic and political exploitation. Although race is a contributory factor, the economic vested interests alone are sufficient to create the ultimate predicament. Those who are the objects of such exploitation by superior and corrupt forces have two simple choices—accommodate or die.

At whatever expense, inconvenience, or irrational and immoral behavior, these colonies, at home and abroad, are being preserved. The imminent danger to Blacks in the United States is that they are no longer willing to accommodate, or even tolerate, colonial occupation.* In Dayton, colonial domination included denying loans to otherwise well-qualified citizens whose simple wish was to buy a home outside the colony, thereby partially escaping colonization. In Indochina, it includes denying the right of the South Vietnamese to buy rice more cheaply and conveniently from an Asian neighbor, Taiwan (Formosa) or Thailand.

---

* This being the essence of Black Power: "Black power means black people coming together to form a political force and either electing representatives or forcing their representatives to speak their needs. It's an economic and physical bloc that can exercise its strength in the black community instead of letting the job to the Democratic or Republican parties or a white-controlled black man set up as a puppet to represent black people. We pick the brother and make sure he fulfills *our* needs. Black power doesn't mean anti-white, violence, separatism or any other racist things the press says it means. It's saying, 'Look, buddy, we're not laying a vote on you unless you lay so many schools, hospitals, playgrounds and jobs on us.' "—Stokely Carmichael, 1967, as quoted in *Life*, December 26, 1969, pp. 104–105.

*When the Decisive Decade—the 1960's—began, the United States was not a leader among the world's rice growers, exporters, or consumers. At the close of the decade, the United States still was not a big rice consumer, nor even a major rice grower. But, as an exporter, the United States was number one, despite a "Green Revolution" that dramatically increased rice yields in the Philippines, India, Pakistan, and South Vietnam— all customers for U.S. rice. As the decade closed, the United States still produced less than 1 percent of the world's rice but was, incredibly, the world's leading rice exporter, consuming only 35 percent of its rice produced, selling the other 65 percent abroad to a hundred countries, but mainly to South Korea and South Vietnam.*

In 1963, at the time of the death of President Kennedy in Texas, military involvement in Vietnam had already begun, though on a relatively small "advisory" scale. Thailand, a key country in Asia's Rice Bowl community, was by far the world's biggest exporter of rice, selling to many of her neighbors, including South Vietnam. For two years, President Kennedy had had agonizing doubts about the intrusion of U.S. forces and matériel in Vietnam, and, in fact—shortly before his death—had acceded to the persistence of Senate Majority Leader Mike Mansfield (Democrat of Montana) and agreed to a pullout. The President's condition, however, was that the pullout would have to wait until after the 1964 elections so that he would not be branded as militarily soft and soft on Communism, thus running an increased risk of defeat. So, in early October, 1963, he ordered Defense Secretary McNamara to tell the press that 1,000 of the then 16,000 U.S. troops in Vietnam would be withdrawn immediately, with the likelihood that the entire force would be withdrawn by the end of 1965. That President Kennedy's assassination was related to his plan to withdraw U.S. presence from Vietnam was broadly hinted in memoirs by Kenneth O'Donnell, a JFK intimate and confidant.*

In 1965—the year President Kennedy had secretly planned to

* See "LBJ and the Kennedys," *Life,* August 7, 1970, pp. 45–56.

complete the pullout from Vietnam—his successor, President Johnson, a Texan, secretly began a massive buildup of U.S. troops and munitions there. This buildup was—in direct contradiction of President Johnson's campaign pledges—accompanied by "tactical defoliation" of Vietnam jungles and rice paddies. In that same period, U.S. rice growers tripled their production from the 1960 volume, and the United States had replaced Thailand as the world's number one exporter. In less than a decade, the world's biggest rice-growing community of nations had reverted from a rice-surplus area to an area of severe dependency, buying rice from one of the world's smallest producers: the United States of America.

In the 1968–69 rice season, South Vietnam enjoyed a record-high rice yield, owing to the new strain of high-yield IRS-8 (international rice strain number 8) and a good-weather year. The country might well have become rice-independent except, as a U.S. intelligence source stated in 1969: "South Vietnam did have a good rice crop, but it didn't get into Saigon." This he attributed to "the fortunes of war." In other words, there was difficulty getting the rice from the defoliated rice fields to the market places. A staff member of Senator Ellender's Agriculture and Forestry Committee explained it further: "They could have a big crop, and can't ship because of 'enemy activity.' "

Such defoliations and enemy activity are the same activities that chased the Muslims from St. Clair County, Alabama, with cyanide-poisoned cattle, defoliated pastures, and threats to the lives of the peaceful black owners. No tactic was too irrational to be employed by the colonizers, and the forces of law were used to support the colonizers rather than the peaceful, law-abiding citizens.

A basic tactic in the food-war syndrome came to light in 1969 when South Vietnam sought to resist U.S. rice colonization by shopping in other markets—Taiwan or Thailand.

In the fall of 1969, word began leaking out of the State Department that South Vietnam was buying 40,000 tons of rice from her southeastern neighbor, Taiwan. That word came as particularly bad news to USDA Secretary Clifford Hardin, who saw in this the possible loss of an outlet for U.S. surplus rice for which the USDA was guaranteeing price supports to U.S. rice growers. Hardin was also in the process of setting rice acreage allotments for U.S. rice growers, which, because of increasing world production, had dwindled from 2.4 million acres in 1968 to 2.1 million acres in 1969. While U.S. rice acreage shrank by about 10 percent, U.S. rice production had fallen about 15 percent—from 105 million hundred weight (cwt.) to 90 million cwt.

Added to this predicament of a dwindling demand for U.S. rice, then, was the shocking news that South Vietnam, a country whom the "fortunes of war" had made increasingly dependent on imports (despite increased production), might turn, nonetheless, to a non-U.S. source for rice. U.S. rice growers, in the meantime, had been assured a large shipment to South Vietnam through P.L. 480, the foreign aid gimmick by which the United States customarily ships surpluses to needy countries in exchange for military and diplomatic favors or repayment on long-term bases. (The U.S. taxpayer pays for these surpluses, however, via price supports to the growers.)

Hardin promptly went to the State Department's Agency for International Development (AID), which administers P.L. 480, but was unable to get immediate confirmation of the sale or to influence the arrangements in any way. This required Hardin's trump card—a call on the rice empire on Capitol Hill, where foreign aid was being debated. This set the stage for an unprecedented look at the Rice Cup, vested interests, and the secret uses of food as a military and diplomatic weapon.

"It was a mess between AID and Ag [USDA]," a spokesman for Senate Agriculture and Forestry Chairman Ellender said. "AID had okayed this sale and refused to let Ag know so that we could get this stuff [rice] bought from our sources. . . . The AID bill is going to be cut back substantially. We're supporting Vietnam entirely; we send them every dollar they've got over there, and to turn around and buy something like that from one of our friends is a slap in the face."*

* Interview, December 17, 1969.

In addition to organizing a quick campaign to block the Taiwan rice sale, the rice state representatives on Capitol Hill sought to retaliate against the Nixon administration for "permitting" it. Not only had U.S. rice growers anticipated sales to South Korea (the biggest single U.S. rice customer) and South Vietnam (among the hundred countries who buy U.S. rice) but, depending on the "fortunes of war," there was the chance also that Thailand, once the world's largest exporter, might need U.S. rice.

As Senate Agriculture Chairman Ellender stated in an interview, December 18, 1969: "We in this country increased the production of rice for the expressed purpose of trying to meet their [South Vietnam's] demands, and instead of buying from us, they buy from Taiwan, and we're going to try to reduce grants made to them in order to improve their economy. South Vietnam, and Thailand, if necessary, were the countries we were to provide rice for. It was thought that *if Thailand was attacked from the north, they might be without rice."*

Senator Ellender didn't explain exactly whom he expected to attack Thailand from the north, but he left no doubt at all that war, from whatever source, would disrupt the accessibility of rice for the people, and U.S. rice sales would be enhanced accordingly.*

---

* Assessing motives and separating them from happenstance cause and effect is difficult in these matters. So, in this circumstance, it seems fair to include the most favorable explanation I've read for Ellender's role. Richard Wilson, not a notably liberal columnist, discussed these dynamics in the context of Ellender's lack of sympathy for the poor who fail to sign up for the Food Stamp program because they lack the $18 or $20 required in advance to do so.

Wrote Wilson, in the *Evening Star*, February 26, 1969, p. A-19:

"Now, Ellender is not a wicked man. He is a compassionate man but he, his colleagues on the Senate and House Agriculture Committees, and officials of the Department of Agriculture have dedicated themselves to a single purpose, the welfare of the producers of farm commodities. The reason for the existence of the food distribution program is not to be found primarily in the hungry bellies of the poor, but in the programs adopted in Congress to dispose of farm surpluses and thus sustain what is deemed to be a fair level of farm prices.

"Economic objectives and humanitarian aims are often in conflict. One pertinent example: the Agriculture Department drags its feet on the development of low-cost, highly fortified foods for domestic use for the obvious reason that they will compete with natural processed foods.

In any event, the failure of Thailand to meet with the expected adversity only placed greater pressure on the Rice Cup delegation on Capitol Hill to undo the Taiwan sale and to make its point with the Nixon administration to guard against future "mistakes." Beyond that, the rice Congressmen would work to insure acreage and price support protection for their rice-growing constituents.

These three jobs were divided along the rice power lines in the House and Senate. Senator Ellender would handle the foreign policy aspects. Meanwhile, the domestic politics would be engineered by Louisiana Congressman Edwin W. Edwards, a member and past president of the International Rice Association, the elected whip of the Louisiana-Mississippi delegation in the House, and a member of the House Judiciary and House Internal Security* committees.

Ellender's rationale and strategy were simple enough: "If they [South Vietnam] use the cash we gave them, we'll just take it back from them. That's what I'm trying to do."

Ellender was well situated for the attempt. On November 26, 1969, the administration's foreign aid bill was being debated, and Joseph A. Mendenhall, assistant administrator of AID's

---

"But that is not the only conflict. The idea of helping the poor is not given high priority in four of the most conservative committees of Congress which control the destiny of the multibillion dollar agricultural programs. These are the House and Senate Agriculture Committees and the House and Senate subcommittees on appropriations for agriculture.

"The doctrine in these old-line conservative citadels of Congress is that the commodity distribution and food stamp program is 'a food program, not a welfare program.' This type of reasoning is perfectly compatible with policies which caused the Department of Agriculture to turn back to the Treasury $277 million which could have been used for food for the poor last year while paying incredible subsidies rising as high as $3 and $4 millions each to big farm operating companies.

"The Nixon administration is now face to face with the realities of hunger in America and its intolerable embarrassment to the free enterprise system while enormous subsidies are being paid out to sustain prices through reduction of production. This screaming contradiction in policy can be corrected by recognizing that helping the poor get enough to eat is a welfare imperative. The way to do that is to end control over the programs by agencies, committees and officials whose primary concern is the prosperity of commercial agriculture."

* This is the committee which, in 1968, recommended concentration camps for black "guerrillas" and protesters against the war.

Vietnam Bureau, was appearing as a witness before the Foreign Operations Subcommittee of the Senate Appropriations Committee. Sitting across from witness Mendenhall: Ellender, architect of rice protectionism.

Mendenhall's role was to absolve the State Department of softness toward rice-independence for South Vietnam and to defend the administration generally against punishment by Ellender, who insisted that the State Department could—and, indeed, *should*—have prevented the sale of the 40,000 tons of rice to South Vietnam by Taiwan.

The following are excerpts taken directly from the subcommittee transcript of the Mendenhall-Ellender exchange:

Senator Ellender:  All right. I just want to know.
Respecting this stabilization program which you, mentioned, did you say that the imports have increased greatly?
Mr. Mendenhall:  Yes, sir.
Senator Ellender:  Why is that?
Mr. Mendenhall:  They increased basically because of the rise in military expenditures by the Vietnamese Government in the past couple of years, and the resultant increased budgetary deficit which has forced piasters into the economy means that demand is generated for goods. Part of that demand falls on imports.
Senator Ellender:  What countries primarily export to Vietnam?
Mr. Mendenhall:  Under our commercial import program we are furnishing over 62 percent of the total imports from the United States. The balance is almost completely furnished by countries such as Taiwan, Korea, and Singapore. Petroleum products for example, come from Singapore. This balance of about 37 or 38 percent comes from less-developed countries, the principal ones of which I have mentioned under either barter arrangements or under special letter of credit arrangements which require the recipient country to spend those funds in the United States.
In other words, we have made special arrangements in connection with the balance of our purchases for Vietnam to avoid adverse effects on the balance of payments of the United States.
Senator Ellender:  The 62 percent you speak of, did I understand you to say that that includes not only exports from us but exports from Taiwan?

Mr. Mendenhall: In fiscal year 1969, 62.7 percent came from the United States only.

Senator Ellender: So that 38 percent is from Taiwan and Thailand, I presume?

Mr. Mendenhall: Taiwan, Singapore, Korea, those are the big ones. There are a few other small ones.

Senator Ellender: Do you supervise that?

Mr. Mendenhall: Yes, sir.

Senator Ellender: Do you see to it that the funds that we furnish for that purpose are used wisely.

Mr. Mendenhall: Yes, sir.

Senator Ellender: Two years ago the Department of Agriculture asked that rice production in this country be increased by 17 percent in order to have rice available to feed the South Vietnamese. I understand that AID bought rice from Taiwan instead of the United States. Will you explain why?

Mr. Mendenhall: I think I know the transaction you are talking about.

Senator Ellender: This is why I am asking this because it is a very serious thing.

Mr. Mendenhall: May I explain this to you?

Senator Ellender: Just a minute. I want first to give you a little background. I happen to be chairman of the Senate Committee on Agriculture and Forestry. Agriculture is getting kicked around by every Member of the House except the few who depend on the farmers for their votes. It has been very expensive, I admit. But some of these expenses were incurred because we were asked to procure food, in this case for Vietnam, 17 percent increase in acreage production, so as to produce this rice.

I understand that a couple of days ago, maybe this week, instead of buying this rice which we now have on hand—it really does not belong to the Government but the Government has a big interest in it—you folks through the State Department have permitted the sale of rice by Taiwan to South Vietnam.

Now explain it to me.

Mr. Mendenhall: May I say first that I completely share your interest in the farmer. I was born on the farm and my father is still a farmer.

Senator Ellender: I am not interested in that. I am interested in finding out why it is that you people, who are trying to do a good job here as you have just said, in the circumstances I have outlined, are permitting dollars that we are now appropriating to be used to buy rice from Taiwan. I understand you are also going to permit the purchase of rice from Thailand.

Mr. Mendenhall: Senator, no AID dollars are being used or going to be used to finance the purchase of rice from Thailand or Taiwan. I would like to explain to you what has happened, but there are no AID dollars involved in this at all.

As I said, I have a great deal of sympathy for the rice growers here in the United States. I am also interested in the United States balance of payments provision. I want to see us sell commodities wherever we can.

What has happened in Vietnam is this: A sudden emergency has arisen in connection with the rice market in Saigon. Starting with the adoption of the austerity taxes about October 20, there was a 25 percent increase in rice prices to the consumer in Saigon. Even though these taxes had no direct effect on the price of rice and only modest indirect effect by increasing the price of gasoline, the price of rice zoomed up.

This led to a great increase, very suddenly, in the drawdown of the rice stocks of the Vietnamese Government. Now, those stocks normally are drawn down at the rate of about 700 tons a day. As a result of this, the drawdown tripled by going up to 2,000 tons per day.

Now, when this first started, everybody expected and hoped this was simply something that had occurred suddenly and that the panic would quickly subside. Obviously the price went up because people were beginning to hoard rice—they were buying it and hoarding it. It was hoped that this would stop. But it has continued.

When this first started, the Vietnamese Government in early November indicated to us that they felt they were going to have to go to a neighboring country to buy some rice to meet this emergency because their stocks might well be exhaused. You can well realize what a terrible thing exhaustion of rice stocks would be. We initially urged them not to buy rice from another Asian country because we hoped this drawdown wouldn't continue at this rate. But it did continue.

Last week the Vietnamese Government told us that they were going to have to go ahead and buy 40,000 tons of rice from Taiwan, or Thailand. They said they would have to buy it there because these were the only places from which they could get it soon enough into Vietnam to meet the problem in case their stocks were exhausted.

Senator Ellender: What moneys are they using to buy the rice?

Mr. Mendenhall: They are using their own foreign exchange earnings.

Senator Ellender: Yes, sir. The dollars.

Mr. Mendenhall: Yes, sir; in dollars.

Senator Ellender: Money we furnished them indirectly.

Mr. Mendenhall: I agree—money they earned from the U.S. Department of Defense.

Senator Ellender: No doubt about it. That is why I cannot understand, that you are using $240 million to stabilize the economy of Vietnam.

Mr. Mendenhall: But there is no alternative under the circumstances to this rice transaction in the area. I don't like to see it any more than you do. I have to agree there is no alternative.

Senator Ellender: I do not know how much it will cost to do this, how much we will lose by it, but I shall try to take it from your request for this stabilization fund, because somebody has to pay for it. I am sick and tired of having the farmer kicked around in our country, as in this case, when the farmers are trying to assist by growing food for Vietnam. That means there will be a curtailment of rice production next year in our own country and it is going to mean also the surplus which we now have will dangle over the market and keep the price down. That is how we get kicked around. I am sick and tired of it.

Mr. Mendenhall: I have complete sympathy.

Senator Ellender: We have to do something about it. You and the Ambassadors are the men to get that off our hands. As I said, somebody is going to have to pay for the surplus we now have on hand. Otherwise, the cost of the farm program is going to increase more than we anticipated, and we are innocent folks; we are not responsible for it.

* * *

Senator Ellender: You folks do not seem to consider the effect that all of this is having on our own economy. I wish we had someone to make a case for our balance of payments as you have made it for South Vietnam. You people come here and ask for this and do not seem to have any idea of what it is going to mean for our own economy.

Mr. Mendenhall: I completely share your interest in our balance-of-payments problem, Senator Ellender. If we could have avoided this we would have.

Senator Ellender: That does not help a bit, just to feel that way. It strikes me that our AID people should be able in some manner to alleviate the circumstances, because we are putting up all the funds for South Vietnam. Imagine the huge amount of money that our soldiers are spending in South Vietnam, which has a tendency of bettering their economy. All of that comes from your own country, your own country.

Mr. Mendenhall: Yes, sir.

(Discussion off the record.)

Senator Ellender: You cannot rectify this rice condition?

Mr. Mendenhall: Because of the emergency, Senator.

Senator Ellender: Why is there an emergency?

Mr. Mendenhall: I explained it to you.

Senator Ellender: You explained it but why did you not know about it?

Mr. Mendenhall: No one could have predicted that as a result of the austerity taxes you would get a dramatic increase in rice prices and this would lead to such hoarding. No one could have predicted that there would be such an increase in purchases and hoarding that the Government stocks would be drawn down to the point where they might run out. I am as sorry for it as you are.

\* \* \*

Senator Ellender: I was in Russia for 6 days. I did not go to Saigon or Thailand because of the war. I knew I could not get anything there to be of assistance to the study I was making because of the presence of war. I am now sorry that I did not go. I was in South Vietnam five times. My last visit was in 1962, just before Diem was assassinated. We had been spending there quite a bit of money. I tried to curtail it to a large extent but without any success. What was that you were smiling about? Something I said?

Mr. Mendenhall: No.

Senator Ellender: I was there in 1962, and I was there in 1961. I was there in 1955 or 1956. When was Diem sworn in, do you remember?

Mr. Mendenhall: 1954.

Senator Ellender: I was there in 1954–1955, anyhow five times.

Mr. Chairman, I do not wish to clutter the record any more because you have covered it very well. And I have another appointment to make. But I am hopeful that, when you go back to your office, you, in particular, Mr. Ambassador—I was informed that the Department of Agriculture did all they could to sell this rice instead of having it purchased from Taiwan—I understand that you are now going to buy some from Thailand.

Mr. Mendenhall: May I say it is not we who are buying the rice, it is the Government of Vietnam.

Senator Ellender: You can tell them what they ought to do in view of all we are giving them. I am going to examine your requests in an effort to determine how they can best be reduced to cover the cost of rice surplus occasioned by the increased production which the Government requested as an accommodation for the South Vietnamese.

(Discussion off the record.)

Senator [Gale] McGee: I would agree that this never should have happened. I hope we would not create another mistake by trying to get even with one. I have been so carried away with how much there is to do there now. We ought to learn from this one by not doing it again. I hope the Senator will not follow through by suggesting we knock out this program to achieve that. Maybe we can find some other way. Maybe we can assign it to the Pentagon.

Senator Ellender: I tell you I was successful in doing what we desired to do in South Korea by telling Mr. Syngman Rhee. He wanted to impose a tax on all of the goods that came from our country to help South Korea. He was insisting on that; he needed the money. The Ambassador was all worked up about the situation; he could not talk to the old man. I talked to Mr. Rhee and told him simply:

Mr. Rhee, I understand you want to impose a tax on goods that come from our country for use in your country.

Yes, sir, we need the money.

All right. I have no objection, but remember every dollar of tax you collect we will take it off your foreign aid.

He did not impose a tax. That is what I would like to pass on to the people in South Vietnam, that there is a way for us to protect our interests. In other words, they ought to deal with us since this product was produced for their use.

Mr. Mendenhall: Senator, the Vietnamese Government was very reluctant to do this. The only reason they did it was that it was the only way they could get the rice in time because of the difference in shipping time.

Senator Ellender: You have enough rice there to feed them for almost a year. It is just an excuse they give you. If you folks use the little power that you have there and tell them what you will do if they do not do this, you will have some control. I have found that we are too easy with them. We do not exert ourselves enough.

Mr. Mendenhall: We have gone into the figures on their stock position and what they are expecting to have. There is a very real risk that they could run out by the middle of December at the present rate of drawdown on the stocks. I completely share your view.

\* \* \*

Senator Ellender: We will find some way to get that back in this bill.

\* \* \*

Senator [Milton] Young: Mr. Chairman, if I may say, I share fully sentiment expressed by the Senator from Louisiana. With all the money we are pouring into their country, to say nothing about the lives that are lost, if they can't buy from us when we have surpluses like we have, it just doesn't make sense.

Senator Ellender: Especially when this was produced for them. We increased our rice acreage by 17 percent to help these people out. Here we have the dangling over the market and facing a big cut in rice, and then it is going to hurt our farm program.

Senator McGee: I agree in our total effort that we ought to honor this commitment.

Senator Ellender: If it is not, I am going to find some way to get it out of this and you let the administration know about that.

Senator McGee: I just don't think we need any more problems than we already have. This is one. I think if we are going to Vietnamize we are going to get some other lumps in this process. It sounds a lot easier than it is going to be, in fact. If you are going to Vietnamize it, you are not going to Americanize it. It can't go both ways at the same time. It is going to be rough and hard to take. We have to roll with it gracefully and protect the commitment that we have made here that can totally wreck this thing.

We ought to take the measures to protect it and not wreck the program in trying to protect it. I think we have that capability and ought to initiate it. I will back the Senator in trying to do that.

Senator Ellender: My dear sir, the effect that it has had on wheat, Senator Young knows that Mr. Freeman made an error, thought there would be a shortage of wheat. We have a big surplus now. Are they buying from us? No. They get it a little cheaper and we are putting up all the money.

*   *   *

Senator McGee: To get rice from the States would have taken much longer than getting it from Taiwan or Thailand. Twice as long in terms of shipping time.

Senator Young: The difference would not be over 2 weeks, would it?

Mr. Mendenhall: It would be about a month.

Senator McGee: I think this makes some rationale for it. It does not eliminate the kind of problem that Senator Ellender has focused on here. I would hope that even this committee could recommend or put some heat on trying to compensate for this rather serious error. I don't think you are going to do it without costing us still more by taking it out of the program.

Senator Ellender: That is all right. We will find some way. I did it in South Korea and I will do it again in South Vietnam.

You are going to telephone the Ambassador about that?

Mr. [William H.] Sullivan: Yes, sir.

Mr. Mendenhall: I think it should be understood clearly that 32,000 tons has already been bought from Taiwan. That is a concluded deal.

Senator Ellender: We will take it out of this program right here. I promise you that. I will be darned if I am going to sit here and on the Agriculture Committee and sweat out the programs and then be confronted with a thing of this kind. I know that something could be done.

I have nothing else to say.

Senator McGee: Senator Young.

Senator Young: I have nothing else.

Senator McGee: I have no additional questions at this point. If anything else pops we will be back at you. I appreciate your patience in probing these matters with us in a very considerate way. It is very helpful and it has made a strong record. I hope that AID can find some graceful way around this last problem because there is no point in opening up new problems in retribution against an old problem, a crisis which has already been here and gone and the consequences are already expressed.

This just is not the way to run a store. I am not about to be a part on this committee of creating a new one, but I want to lend my energies in trying to adjust, to ameliorate this very understandable distortion of an expectation in the rice picture. I repeat that if we are going to Vietnamize, we had better quit talking out of both sides of our mouths and work at it.

Thank you very much. It is good to see you again.

Mr. Mendenhall: Thank you, Mr. Chairman.*

In an interview, Senator Ellender stoutly defended his role and attitude regarding the continued dependency of Asian countries on U.S. rice and other products and said that he "spoke for all the Senators in the rice-producing states."

Just as Senator Ellender spoke unanimously for the rice industry representatives in the Senate, Congressman Edwards was pleased with his role as spokesman for the powerful group of rice protectionists in the House. Edwards' dedication to the role is strongly attested to by his credentials in the rice industry and also by the fact that he quite openly continues to lobby for the rice industry—even on his Congressionally franked stationery. At the lower left-hand corner of Edwards' official envelopes is a design showing stalks of rice and a cornucopia-type barrel with sacks of potatoes rolling out. The legend across the design exhorts: "For appeal in every meal use Louisiana rice and yams."

Edwards' thrust is by no means all rhetoric. In concert with Ellender and others in position to effect it, Edwards moved to dump the anticipated U.S. rice surplus on South Korea, using such persuasives as P.L. 480 and other firm-but-gentle pressures.

* *Senate Hearings Before the Committee on Appropriations, Foreign Assistance, and Related Programs Appropriations,* Ninety-first Congress, First Session, pp. 315–25. This testimony occurred before the Senate Appropriations Committee, November 26, 1969.

So pleased was Edwards with his efforts that he outlined them in a press release on December 11, 1969, two days after the House rice group held a massive strategy session with Agriculture Secretary Hardin:

—Agriculture officials have taken action and are optimistic that money will be budgeted to dispose of rice stocks under the provisions of Title II, P.L. 480. No funds had been scheduled for use under this Title prior to our meeting. We pointed out that $10 million per year over a three-year period would exhaust the 6.2 million hundred-weight (cwt.) now held by USDA in CCC takeover stocks. Title II of the Act relates to government use of grains in schools, prisons, worldwide volunteer and other institutions.

—USDA, Bureau of the Budget and other agencies are making a concentrated effort to obtain a large Title I, P.L. 480 order from Korea. Korea has indicated an interest in four to five hundred thousand tons of rice; however, P.L. 480 funds are limited and Japan has offered the rice to Korea on very favorable credit terms and at low prices. USDA is now moving to capture all or a large part of the order. If we succeed, most California and Southern medium grain stocks could be moved and this would greatly increase our chances for little or no acreage cuts for 1970. . . .

—Additionally, Congressmen representing the industy argued that an additional 4.5 million cwt. could be disposed of through Title I, P.L. 480 sales which have not but could be budgeted if proper effort were made to do so. This would reduce the total estimated carryover from an industry standpoint of 8.8 million cwt. . . .

—The overall poor situation with reference to the industry was emphasized by the large group of Congressmen who attended the meeting, including W. R. Poage (Tex.), Chairman of the House Committee on Agriculture; Wilbur Mills (Ark.), Chairman of Ways and Means; Hale Boggs, House Democratic Whip; all Members of the Louisiana and Arkansas Delegations; six Congressmen from Texas, five from California and two from Mississippi. The Congressmen present presented a unified argument and firmly recommended to the Secretary that acreage levels not be cut in 1970 unless absolutely necessary under existing regulations and based upon known and intended disappearance for 1970. Additionally, it was pointed out by all present that a need for an increase in support prices was clearly indicated and the Secretary was urged to make an immediate study to justify ordering an increase in support from 65% to 75% of parity. . . .

—This meeting was attended by the most political muscle I have ever witnessed at a rice meeting and I frankly state that the Secretary of Agriculture was impressed by facts and figures advanced by our Delegations and I am cautiously optimistic that the end result will not be as damaging to the industry in 1970 as had been predicted only six weeks ago. In the meantime, we will continue our efforts on a Washington level to move additional stocks of rice through and in applicable government programs as this appears to be the only way to substantially decrease existing stocks and keep the industry on a sound basis and in a healthy condition. It is expected that a firm announcement will be made by the Department as to 1970 acreage levels and 1970 support price levels sometime between Christmas and New Year's Day and in the meantime we will continue pressing for consummation of the Korean order now under consideration which will have a dramatic effect on the ultimate decision to be made by the Secretary in the last week of this year.

The result of all this attempt by colonized Asian countries to become independent of U.S. rice barons was Ellender's promised slice of $658 million from the administration's foreign aid to such countries, plus a scurry by USDA Secretary Hardin to raise both price supports and acreage allotments for the heavily subsidized U.S. rice farmers. Considering the unequaled power of the Rice Cup Congressmen, it would be extremely difficult for them to lose such an undertaking.

There remained, however, the matter that Thailand, still a big rice exporter, might also sell 20,000 tons of rice to her neighbor, South Vietnam. But Rice Cup Congressmen, with their hands firmly on the U.S. military machine, had a solution for that possibility, too, as reported by *Newsweek:*

Even less vengeful members of the Appropriations Committee argued that Saigon had acted hastily [in the Taiwan rice deal]. Said Sen. Gale McGee of Wyoming: "This never should have happened." And to complete their vengeance, rice-state politicians are attempting to dump whatever U.S. surplus there may be on South Korea and Indonesia. This would neatly slap the Thais for trying to move in on the Vietnamese market, since Indonesia is a big importer of rice from Thailand. (But this maneuver may fail, since the Japanese are also hard at work trying to dispose of their surplus rice in Indonesia and Korea.)

Malice: All this left the Thais understandably grumpy. The U.S., huffed Thailand's Minister of Economics, doesn't understand the problems of developing nations. From Saigon, a U.S. aide replied that it was "absurd and regrettable to think there was malice aforethought" in the U.S. crackdown. But malice or no, the United States had used a considerable amount of muscle to keep Thai rice out of Saigon markets—and that boded ill for the day when the rice glut hits Asia in full force, and South Vietnam joins Thailand, Taiwan and Japan in competing for export markets. "The U.S. has some say in what [the South Vietnamese] will do or not do, because it's all U.S.-financed," explained an aide to Ellender's Senate Agriculture Committee. *"And Thailand is our buddy, too. We've got troops there now."* [Emphasis added.]*

Similarly, and ostensibly for altruistic purposes, the United States would soon have troops in neutral Cambodia—an invasion of Vietcong "sanctuaries," President Nixon said, to protect the lives of U.S. servicemen as they withdrew from Vietnam. This two-month military excursion into Cambodia to protect American lives lost the lives of hundreds of U.S. servicemen, and the shifting reasons given for the invasion were as unclear as what U.S. servicemen actually *did* in Cambodia.

Looking to the June 30, 1970, deadline, the date President Nixon had set for having U.S. ground troops out of Cambodia, columnist Jack Anderson reported what seemed to have been a significant, if not a major, assignment of U.S. servicemen in "friendly" Cambodia:

In their haste to get out of Cambodia on schedule, U.S. troops are burning captured rice that is urgently needed to feed hungry Vietnamese refugees.

* *Newsweek,* January 12, 1970, p. 60.

The U.S. publicity machine has been grinding out stories about the capture of 2,500 tons of Vietcong rice and its humanitarian use to feed the refugees. But my associate Les Whitten, writing from the combat zone, reports:

"Despite the artificial winds stirred up by the propagandists, the rice is one place and the refugees another. To be sure, about 37, perhaps 40 tons a day have been trucked or otherwise transported to the refugees who need at least 40 tons a day.

"But at this rate, the Army can't move the rice out of Cambodia fast enough to meet the July 1 withdrawal deadline. A maximum of 1,600 tons can be shipped across the Cambodian border in time. This would leave 900 tons of food to be destroyed."

*U.S. troops are solving the problem, states Whitten, by burning the rice.* [Emphasis added.]*

In Indochina, such chores are handled by the U.S. Marines and other members of the uniformed military service. Back home, the National Guard, the state police, sheriff's patrols, and civil disturbance units stood ready for duty in Lynn County, Texas, St. Clair County, Alabama, South Side Chicago, and Memphis, Tennessee—for those, too, are sites of U.S. altruism, good business, and fault psychology. They all are scenes in a common war.

## D. *The Blackpoor Soldier: A Mercenary Suicide*

Few aspects of the Blackpoor experience are more cruelly ironic than the fact that young black men are required—by their poverty and Blackness—to give their lives ostensibly in pursuit of freedom, while actually denying it to themselves and to their military victims elsewhere around the world.

A black Vietnam veteran, still out of work six months after returning to Washington, D.C., had to face the fact that citizens of the nation's Capital—70 percent of them black—do not have the same right to vote he thought he was obtaining for the South Vietnamese.

Pathetically, he faced also the fact of being a mercenary:

* "The Washington Merry-Go-Round," Washington *Post*, May 27, 1970, p. D-11.

I did my thing, now I'm waiting for the Man to do his.
I wiped out entire villages for him. It wasn't my war; my cause is here in America right here. It's a carpet-baggers' war.
I shot little kids, like the little kids who shine shoes. And that hurt me, man. . . . Everybody feels guilty about shooting kids.
We've gone on patrol, search and destroy, I've seen the Man give commands to wipe out the entire village. We don't know if these people are VC or not. We burned the village out. This is wrong.
It's not a question of what we're going to do now. It's what the Man is going to do. We've done ours for him. He pumped a bunch of lies into us about communism. Those people over there are just trying to survive. I feel like we did the same thing to the VC that the Man has been doing to us. . . .
I feel as though I've been cheated, taken, like me and my people have been taken all our lives.*

Part of the same cruel irony is the fact that the Job Corps—ballyhooed as the instrument to correct whatever was wrong in the chemistry of the young Black and his deliberately bad public school system—was, in fact, little more than an express vehicle to Vietnam.

But this was quite in accordance with the concealed designs of the Moynihans, McNamaras, and Shrivers at the outset of the so-called war on poverty. This was part of the Moynihan contribution as a member of the OEO Task Force in 1964, during the period of his formulation of the "Moynihan Report," or "The Negro Family."

In the report, Moynihan bemoaned what he regarded as a low representation of Blacks in the armed services:

In 1964 Negroes constituted 11.8 percent of the population, but probably remain at 8 percent of the Armed Forces.
The significance of Negro under-representation in the Armed Forces is greater than might at first be supposed. If Negroes were represented in the same proportions in the military as they are in the population, they would number 300,000 plus. This would be over 100,000 more than at present (using 1964 strength figures) . If

* Washington *Post*, Potomac, June 8, 1969, p. 32.

the more than 100,000 unemployed Negro men were to have gone into the military the Negro male unemployment rate would have been 7.0 percent in 1964 instead of 9.1 percent.

In 1963 the Civil Rights Commission commented on the occupational aspect of military service for Negroes. "Negro enlisted men enjoy relatively better opportunities in the Armed Forces than in the civilian economy in every clerical, technical, and skilled field for which the data permit comparison."

There is, however, an even more important issue involved in military service for Negroes. Service in the United States Armed Forces is the *only* [emphasis original] experience open to the Negro American in which he is truly treated as an equal: not as a Negro equal to a white, but as one man equal to any other man in a world where the category "Negro" and "white" do not exist. If this is a statement of the ideal rather than reality, it is an ideal that is close to realization. In food, dress, housing, pay, work—the Negro in the Armed Forces *is* [emphasis original] equal and is treated that way.

There is another special quality about military service for Negro men: it is an utterly masculine world. Given the strains of the disorganized and matrifocal family life in which so many Negro youth come of age, the Armed Forces are a dramatic and desperately needed change: a world away from women, a world run by strong men of unquestioned authority, where discipline, if harsh, is nonetheless orderly and predictable, and where rewards, if limited, are granted on the basis of performance.*

The ultimate condemnation of U.S. society, of course, is the acknowledgment that civilian life is so unjust, so unfulfilling, so impossible to survive that black citizens are best advised to seek refuge in the utterly unnatural institution of military life.

Any unhappiness Moynihan and others might have had about black underrepresentation at ground-zero in the nation's war machine should have vanished soon after the Job Corps began to operate in early 1965. During the 1968 Presidential campaign, the late Senator Robert F. Kennedy told college students

* *The Negro Family,* Office of Policy Planning and Research, United States Department of Labor, Washington, D.C., March, 1965, p. 42.

in Omaha: "If you look at any regiment or division of para-troopers in Vietnam, 45 percent of them are black."*

Attempting to "correct" the record, the *Christian Science Monitor* reported: "There are no airborne regiments in the active Army, but a survey of brigades and divisions serving in Vietnam discloses an average Negro assignment rate of 17 per-cent. Last year Negro percentages in airborne units in some cases ran above 20 percent, but there has been an apparent decline.†

But the question is not whether black men should be in Vietnam on a proportional (11 percent) rate but rather whether black or white men should be there at all. That obviously was the feeling of one Air Force veteran, Lewis Dixon, who resigned from the Love County, Oklahoma, draft board, saying: "I will not draft another American boy to be murdered by a bunch of rich lobbyists in Washington." Dixon further complained that the war was being prolonged by people in Washington "who want to keep this thing going for the next 20 years just to feather their own nests."**

During the early days of OEO, statistics that would have proved or disproved that Job Corps enrollees—essentially black boys—were being readied not so much for civilian jobs but for Vietnam were consistently denied. However, even before the Job Corps was fully organized, Congress amended the Economic Opportunity Act solely "to prevent Job Corps programs from displacing presently employed workers or impairing existing contracts for services."‡ This slightly euphemistic language simply meant that boys successfully completing Job Corps train-ing were not to press for union memberships or in any way

---

* George W. Ashworth, "Ratio of U.S. Negro Troops Declines," *Christian Science Monitor,* May 18, 1968.
  † *Ibid.*
  ** Washington *Daily News,* April 24, 1969, p. 3.
  ‡ This is the actual language used in OEO's official "section-by-section analysis" of the Economic Opportunity Amendments of 1965, as passed by the Eighty-ninth Congress, October 9, 1965. This particular amendment was to Title I, Section 2 of the EOA of 1964.

jeopardize the profit-making of any contractor who was already profiteering from the boys' encampment.

Eventually the agency itself had to justify to Congressional hawks how well it was feeding the war machine. Indeed, so well was Job Corps doing that the Defense Department, whose education budget was bigger even than that of the U.S. Office of Education, invaded this area already carved out by Job Corps. On August 23, 1966, Defense Secretary McNamara provoked national debate by telling a Veterans of Foreign Wars (VFW) convention in New York of his immediate plan to take into the Army 40,000 boys deprived educationally and economically and who failed to pass the regular qualifications test given enlistees. That 40,000 would just be a beginner, he said. In subsequent years, this new "educational" program would take in 100,000 such poor boys annually.

McNamara told the veterans:

Fully one-third of the nation's youth currently do not qualify for military service under Department of Defense fitness standards. Six hundred thousand young men a year are rejected.

. . . The vast majority of these 600,000 young men are the victims of faulty education or of inadequate health services. They have been born and raised in the richest nation on earth—but below the participation line. They are part of America's subterranean poor. . . .

After studying the matter in close detail, I am convinced that at least 100,000 men a year who are currently being rejected for military service, including tens of thousands who volunteer, can be accepted.

To make this possible, we need only to use fully and imaginatively the resources at hand—the Defense Department today is the largest single educational complex that the world has ever possessed.*

This challenge—that the Defense Department could better prepare poor black boys for the military machine than the Job

* New York *Times,* August 24, 1966.

Corps—drew a testy response *the same day* from OEO director
Shriver, who issued a press release, saying:

Two years ago the "experts" scoffed when we said exactly what
the Secretary of Defense said today. But now that such a distinguished leader of our military endorses our position so eloquently I
am sure that public opinion will change. In fact, I predict that all
the conservatives, in and out of Congress, who have attacked Job
Corps Centers when managed by American industrial corporations,
educational institutions, private foundations, and the government
itself will suddenly approve of a similar program run by military
authorities. These conservatives will also cry out that the Job Corps
is no longer needed now because the Army can do a better job with
the same youngsters. . . .
*Job Corps has also done well in preparing youth for military
service. Always 30% of all enrollees, upon graduation, enter the
military service, even though the vast majority were totally ineli-
gible before.*\* [Emphasis added.]

The question that cries out through all this, of course, is: If
these thousands of young black and poor men could be so
effectively prepared for a life in the military, why are they
found so inept for life *out*side the military or paramilitary
institutions such as the Army or Job Corps?

One answer must be that racism and war, like capitalism,
require institutional victims—a class of expendables.

"We are willing to make the Negro 100 per cent of a citizen
in warfare, but reduce him to 50 per cent of a citizen on
American soil," Dr. King said, joining four U.S. Senators in a
peace rally in Beverly Hills, California, February 25, 1967.
"Half of all Negroes live in substandard housing and he has half
the income as whites. There is twice as much unemployment
and infant mortality among Negroes. There were twice as many
Negroes in combat in Vietnam at the beginning of 1967, and
twice as many died in action—20.6 per cent—in proportion to
their numbers in the population as whites."†

It is not easy to perceive or believe the deliberation and skill

---

\* From an OEO press release, August 23, 1966.
† Gladwin Hill, "Dr. King Advocates Quitting Vietnam," New York *Times,*
February 26, 1967.

that go into the institutionalization of racism, war profiteering, and socioeconomic dependency and exploitation. But a scheme offered a Congressional committee by OEO's Shriver is an appropriate case in point. On March 23, 1967, one month after Dr. King's speech at Beverly Hills, Shriver testified before the Senate Subcommittee on Employment, Manpower, and Poverty, which was considering military draft legislation.

The first of Shriver's several proposals was that the draft deferments be abolished: "I've never seen or read of a deferment system yet which did not operate to provide a haven for slackers and slicksters. As Burke Marshall testified yesterday, anyone can avoid the draft today who has 'the will, the intelligence and the means.' "*

Events strongly supported Marshall's observation.†

Secondly, however, Shriver began to unravel a bombshell:

I favor the registration and testing of all young Americans at age 16—females as well as males. The Peace Corps and VISTA and Job Corps have all proven—once again—that women are just as courageous and patriotic and hard working as men. Thousands, possibly millions, of young women would like a chance to help their country by performing recognized national service and such service should *not* be restricted to combatant military service. It's an archaic sentimentalism which excludes young women from selective service in the generic sense of those words. Moreover, if we registered and tested all youngsters at age 16, we would know who needs what help early enough to do something—time to perform significant remedial physical fitness, academic education, and motivational training. . . .

Finally, let me make one statistical statement and one modest proposal:

There are today 900,000 young men and women who are the children of yesterday's poor and the irony of today's affluent society;

* From prepared text of testimony, released by the Office of Economic Opportunity, March 23, 1967.

† "Dozens, perhaps hundreds of young American men are finding out every day that the easiest way to beat the draft is to be abroad on their 18th birthday," James Goldsborough wrote from Paris. "A little-known loophole in the draft law in effect exempts from induction men who have registered for the draft abroad. They are safe as long as they stay abroad."—Washington *Post*, February 9, 1969, p. A-30.

900,000 young men and women who are in grave danger of *never* becoming productive members of society.

For we can almost take it for granted that if they cannot pass the minimum mental requirements for the Armed Forces, they are not trained and equipped for the labor market either.

But the *dimensions* of the problem are sadly familiar. The question is, what are we going to do about it?

What I propose, Mr. Chairman, is not a total solution; but it is, I believe, a meaningful step in the right direction: the *establishment of a national and continuing census of America's youth resources, coupled with a national referral network.* [Emphasis added.] Let me explain what I mean.

We know *where* these 900,000 young people are, to a large extent *why* they are there, and *what* they are doing or not doing. What we *don't* know in many instances is *who* they are. Our most elaborate manpower studies cannot lead us to one young woman in poverty who might find her way through Job Corps, or a myriad of other training programs possibly available to her. Nor do we now have a precise mechanism to identify and refer to possible help those young men who were never tested by the Armed Forces System. . . .

The census I am proposing would test every American between the ages of 16 and 18, boys *and* girls, immediately identifying the total manpower pool available for Selective Service—and, at the same time, showing us who the young men and women are who are in need of some form of help to prepare them to leave behind their heritage of deprivation and poverty.

Once the census identifies those young people whose limitations are below those required to cope with existing manpower needs, the national referral network would take over. The lost legion would be sought out, placed in both public and private training programs, and perhaps in some of the five million new jobs that could exist through public employment, according to the report of the National Commission on Technology, Automation and Economic Progress. . . .

At the Federal level we have in the Job Corps a model that could be vastly expanded if we had a precise method of locating every young man and woman who could escape poverty through its training. If we could pinpoint our Job Corps recruiting to individuals, we could probably add 25,000 "day corpsmen" to our urban Job Corps Centers—corpsmen who would commute from their homes to our local centers at a substantial reduction in present costs. The total cost per year for each "day corpsman" would be only about $300 per year. . . .

This, painted in the broadest possible strokes, is the program I propose. It is not a panacea; but I believe it represents a necessary and feasible adjunct to our Selective Service system.*

However engagingly phrased, such a proposal, if ever adopted, would subject the Blackpoor to a permanent military cycle, beginning as teenagers. Fortunately, members of the subcommittee were more stunned than receptive. But that may not always be the case. If such a system were ever adopted as a practical matter, it would work like this:

As Shriver proposed, *all* 16-year-olds would sign up and be tested when they reached that age. *But,* only the *deprived* (those needing educational and medical repairs) would then be taken into these encampments proposed by Shriver. Meanwhile, the privileged—the educationally and economically elite—would pursue their normal lives. The result would, undoubtedly, be called a Volunteer Army, a likely pattern for the 1970's, in view of the black soldier's overrepresentation in Southeast Asia during the 1960's.

As the decade closed, there was increasing evidence that more stringent measures would have to be used to get Blacks to fight future Vietnams, particularly as U.S. foreign policy turns increasingly toward Africa. "It is no accident that the U.S. government is sending all those black troops to Vietnam," wrote Eldridge Cleaver, in 1968. "Some people think that America's point in sending 16 per cent troops to Vietnam is to kill off the cream of black youth. But it has another important result. By turning her black troops into butchers of the Vietnamese people, America is spreading hate against the black race throughout Asia. Even black Africans find it hard not to hate black Americans for being so stupid as to allow themselves to be used to slaughter another people who are fighting to be free. Black Americans are considered to be the world's biggest fools

---

* From prepared text of testimony, released by the Office of Economic Opportunity, March 23, 1967.

to go to another country to fight for something they don't have for themselves."*

In the year of Cleaver's best-seller, 1968, there was important evidence that the view expressed by Cleaver was being felt by black servicemen.† And as the decade closed, established leaders regarded as less radical than Cleaver were openly calling on black men to abstain from the war. For example, on November 12, 1969, Ivan Brandon, of the Washington *Post,* reported on an antiwar rally sponsored by the Black Coalition:

About 200 persons attended a black anti-war rally yesterday to hear local and national black leaders denounce the Vietnam war and call for its end.

"We have to put an end to that war because that war is blowing up our future," said the Rev. Andrew Young, executive vice president of the Southern Christian Leadership Conference.

Mr. Young said the United States talks with white Communists in Europe while "When we deal with colored Communists, we kill them.

"Do we kill them because they are Communists or because they are colored," he asked. . . .

R. H. Booker, chairman of the Emergency Committee on the Transportation Crisis, said the Vietnam war is "designed to kill off unemployed black males in this country."

"Black people are losing their lives in a senseless war in Vietnam when they should be losing their lives in Watts, Harlem, and 7th Street and Florida Avenue," Booker said.

It is the cruelest of paradoxes that a black youth must go from America to the farthest corner of the earth ostensibly to secure freedom for another people. He must bear arms under the incredible logic that it is for the welfare of the Vietnamese people that he must aid in scorching their land with incendiaries, roasting their bodies with napalm, mortar shelling the quaint villages, and leveling in flames the little huts where

---

* Eldridge Cleaver, *Soul on Ice* (New York, Dell Publishing Co., Inc., 1968) , p. 127.

† "Last month, the Department of Defense issued a statistical sheet showing the severe drop in Negro re-enlistment rates. For the Army alone, the rate dropped from 66.5 per cent for all first-term Negro soldiers in 1966 to only 31.7 per cent the next year. Other services showed similar drops—although not as dramatic." —Washington *Post,* September 12, 1968, p. F-2.

starving, screaming children suffer the shock and horror of his acts. Then, too, this black boy from Birmingham—prevented at great cost and intimidation from receiving a meaningful education at home, but hurriedly taught to kill abroad—must block from his mind, if he can, the fact that his victims abroad, like himself, are nonwhites seeking to escape a yoke of white oppression.

That same December 2, 1969, edition of the Washington *Afro-American* which reported the plight of Muslims trying to farm peacefully in Alabama reported also a news conference by black Congressman Augustus Hawkins, the representative of the Watts district of Los Angeles. According to Hawkins black fighters receive little credit. Reported the *Afro-American:*

Congressman Augustus F. Hawkins, D-Cal., expressed concern about the great emphasis being placed on the so-called silent majority. In a recent press conference in his Washington office he said: "Many speak for what they want to believe is the silent majority but few speak for the very real silent minority, our black fighting men in Vietnam.

"They bleed, they die, and hunger for home but their voices are not really heard. They ask such questions as these: 'How fair was the draft board that tapped me on the shoulder and sent me away?

" 'Am I in Vietnam only because I am black and poor?

" 'Is there no sound of my voice in high places where policy is made and destiny determined, in the President's Cabinet or at the Pentagon?'

"He hardly had an opportunity to raise such questions in unfamiliar and often unfriendly induction centers nor would the answers have satisfied him."

\* \* \*

"The statistics, had he known them, would have revealed: Had he come from Mississippi, the odds that he would face a black member on his draft board was one in three hundred.

"In any one of three other states (Alabama, Arkansas, and Louisiana) not a single black face would have participated in the judgment to draft him," he continued, "although in these states, black people constitute almost a third of the total population.

"And the same 100 percent exclusion of blacks from draft boards would have been true in 20 other states. As a matter of fact, in only three states would the percentage of black people on draft boards have been higher than three percent. Even in California it adds up to a mere 1.6 percent.

"What about the Pentagon where policy is made and the military conducts the war?," he asked. "Only three black people are included in the 523 super-grade positions and this silent black trio are like prisoners 'inside the walls but not a part of the establishment.'

"So," he said, "the black fighting silent minority servicemen in Vietnam fight on . . . a little weary perhaps but with still other unanswered questions on his mind.

"Why doesn't the President speak out against the injustice against him? When will the Congress get around to real draft reform and making things better back home? And if he is really fighting for self-determination for others in far away places, why not for himself?"

He concluded, "And so our brave fighting man goes on with the answers, in jungles whose names he never heard in the all-black schools he attended . . . silently fighting for a freedom he himself never enjoyed."

But what alternative is the system offering black men?

Virtually none.

Fighting unjust wars against oppressed people at home and abroad is one of the few remaining barriers between black men and total obsolescence. Thus, the black soldier at home and abroad is forced to engage in the purposeful genocide of himself and his victim—all "in the public interest."

His refusal either to join police forces or the armed services is particularly reprehensible to the colonizers, as this is destructive of the colonial scheme. Understandably, then, immediate liquidation of Blacks is a more favorable alternative than their refusal to be purposefully engaged in their own liquidation over a longer period.

Locked out in peace but licensed in war, a black soldier is expendable in war but obsolete in peace. He is forever a candidate for extinction. It is compensatory suicide. A thousand men's suicide is another man's genocide.

# PART III:

# THE CHOICE: GENOCIDE?

# Chapter 5

# The Threat and Tactics

"The scripture predicted that this day of separation would come," the tall, classically handsome black man told his mixed audience of several hundred. "And here it is in 1970."

"Why is this problem worse in America?" he asked rhetorically. "Because it is a 400-year-old problem. In this moon age, the problem is getting worse.

"Black people have done sit in, prayed in, laid in, crawled in—done everything but get in, and still getting their heads whipped in," he summarized ungrammatically.

"Now," he said, mainly to the whites in his audience, "you have some 20 million frankensteins walking around. Frankenstein was not created to be equal with the master in the house. We weren't brought here to be equal to whites. We were brought here to work."

Then, to his black listeners, he said with a strange enthusiasm: "All of us black folks are going to have to die for *something*. We've been dying for America, and for other people's freedom. So, what's wrong with dying for our own freedom?"

The speaker was a fighter—the world's best, in fact. Under his given name, Cassius Marcellus Clay, he won an Olympic Gold Medal for his country and then went on to win the world's heavyweight boxing championship. But the championship title was lifted from him—outside the ring—after he chose another name and new religious beliefs.

Many in his audience remembered him, though, in prime rhyme as well as prime time. He did not disappoint them, as he talked about the white treatment of the black man in America:

> You had him wait 'til he dies
> to git his in the sky.
> But we're hip to that lie.
> We want something sound
> right here on the ground
> *While we're still around.*

Nor did he fail—even in light poetry—to deal with the main thrust of his message: the lives of black Americans are in jeopardy.

The unbeaten champion, draft resister, and Muslim minister was speaking at the Bloomington campus of Indiana University as part of the "Nairobi Series," a group of weekend programs devised by black students to exchange ideas on what they regarded as the plight of black people in America in the new decade.

Earlier in the day, February 21, 1970, an avowed black nationalist had spoken far more ominously of what perils he felt black Americans face:

We ain't nothing but twentieth-century slaves. Before, we were slaves to the most casual observer. But now the cracker's got us to where most of us don't even know that we're slaves.

For one thing, we don't make nothing. That's bad. The cracker ain't going to *let* us make nothing. We used to make babies, but we don't even make that anymore.

You know, if you had a headache, and went to the drug store for an aspirin, you can't get it free; you have to take that cracker some cash. But if you wanted to kill some black babies, the planned parenthood people will kill them for you free of charge. Free of charge.

If every nigger in America had a million dollars, would that solve our problem? No, indeed. That white cracker would charge us a million dollars and a penny for a loaf of bread. We don't control nothing. Nothing.

Do you *really* want to know how bad off we are?

The Jews in Germany controlled the economic structure of Germany, but 6 million of them went to the gas chamber before they got themselves together. With all that money, the Jews made the biggest mistake of all by not controlling the military, and when they went to the gas chamber, that was German gas, German law, and a German jury.

And in this country, when we go to the chamber, it's going to be this cracker's gas, this cracker's law, and this cracker's jury. We don't control nothing. We niggers ain't nothing but twentieth-century slaves. This cracker is getting it ready for us.

So, you don't think so?

Remember hearing about those 500 sheep that got killed out in Colorado last summer? What do you think that was all about? *Really?* Don't you know that cracker is getting it ready? It was gas. Gas.

Remember?

And then you read that after that gas-killing-sheep accident that they had to move that stuff to the ocean to dump it. Remember? Yeah, dig this cracker, jim. He says he's got to take that stuff to the ocean, so instead of going 250 miles down to the Gulf of Mexico, or a thousand miles out to the Pacific, he brings that stuff 2,200 miles all the way back East to the Atlantic. Do you hear that jive-ass cracker? Why did he bring that gas all the way back East?

You don't really know?

Well, then, I'll tell you.

That cracker told you in his jive newspapers and television that he had to stop along the way for "repairs" and to "check on the safety" of that stuff. Dig that crap! Where did he stop? Yeah—where did he stop? He stopped in Omaha, Chicago, Cleveland, Washington, Baltimore—he stopped in 37 cities that have the biggest number of niggers. *That's* where he stopped.

And if you *still* ain't got the picture, go over to Chicago and look at that new precinct house they're building on the Southside. Sure, you'd better believe they dropped off gas there. But did you ever hear of railroads under the jailhouse before? Sure you did! Can you dig it? Remember how Hitler had those railroads running underneath those Nazi station houses? That's how they carted all those Jews out to meet that gas, jim, and don't you niggers forget it, 'cause that's just where this cracker's heading, and we got to get ourselves together.

The cracker is ready.

Back in the Pentagon, he's got a pickup list with a million niggers on it. All he's got to do is push a button, and in nine seconds he got a telegram landing on the chief of police's desk telling where you're at. The concentration camps are waiting. And when that cracker gets done with this 1970 census, he's got all the jive he needs— where you live, what your pad's made of, whether you're using gas or electricity, how big your door is, and if he blows up your place whether any crackers would get hurt. . . .

To be sure, one's own nature rebelled against such revelations. But everywhere there was more confirmation than contrary evidence. Irrepressible and disturbing indications of serious danger emerged as the '70's drew near.

On March 4, 1968, just a month before the day of Dr. King's assassination, the Senate was debating the latest in a series of civil rights laws. House Majority Leader Mike Mansfield, Republican veteran Senator Jacob Javits of New York, and others moved to cut off what amounted to a filibuster. Mansfield, well noted for his frugality with words, warned his colleagues: "The nation is in the most difficult period in its history, and I include the Civil War in that statement."*

The Associated Press reported further that Mansfield "said it was not a time for apprehension but a time for understanding, reminding his colleagues that this is 'a conglomerate nation' made up of many different races and peoples." The need for such a reminder coupled with the danger warning was not reassuring.

During the same period, H. Rap Brown, Stokely Carmichael's successor as head of the Student Nonviolent Coordinating Committee (SNCC), had understated this reminder in his book *Die Nigger Die*: "Me and Carmichael can't fill all them [concentration] camps. They must be planning on taking somebody else."†

But this was by no means a solitary warning. Indeed, clear soundings on this theme had begun to appear in "respectable" media as early as 1967, though from persons often labeled as unrespectable or irresponsible. By mid-1968, however, "respect-

* Associated Press item #85, March 4, 1968.
† H. Rap Brown, *Die Nigger Die* (New York, Dial Press, 1969), p. 138.

able" observers began issuing learned, dispassionate warnings.

For example, Charles V. Hamilton, a black political science professor at Roosevelt University and coauthor with Stokely Carmichael of the book *Black Power,* wrote the first of four articles on the subject for the August 3, 1968, edition of the Chicago *Daily Defender.* The question posed by the *Defender* editors: "Is Genocide Possible in America?"

Wrote Hamilton:

The clear answer to this question must be "yes." Then one must proceed to explain why and under what conditions the answer is "yes."

I deal with the question in terms of black Americans and their relationship to a dominant white society. That relationship has been one of subordinance and deliberate deprivation. The statistics show this; the "official reports" show this—but, above all, the everyday lives of masses of black people clearly show this. This condition has been deliberately imposed; it has not been one unconsciously achieved or one that accidentally happened.

Therefore, calmly and quietly and unemotionally, we must conclude that the oppression of blacks is not a result of unintended consequences or a result of some prevalent defect in the character of black people.

The fact that this is the case is frequently confused by rhetoric pointing to "progress" in race relations, and by rhetoric of trusting people that "it couldn't happen here;" it is confused by the clear fact that some black people have attained "high" positions of visibility in the public and private sectors. It is obscured by the fact that many black people live in quite comfortable communities like Chatham Park and Baldwin Hills [in Los Angeles] and Collier Heights [in Atlanta] and attended universities and ride first-class and carry attache cases. Many people will point to these things as evidence that blacks are "making progress." And yet, all these things confuse what is deliberately happening to masses—millions— of black people.

When the masses, in increasing numbers, begin to object to their depressed status, and when they begin to protest and make demands which challenge their condition, the various decision-making centers are required to respond.

More likely than not, and inevitably, those demands will exceed the ability of "the system" to respond positively. These demands and the unwillingness and inability of the dominant society to meet those demands will create stress and strain and tension. Notwithstanding the fact that the demands are legitimate, we can no longer assume the rationality of white America.

We simply must remember that the oppression is not accidental. It is deliberate.

We cannot assume—as John Locke, the English political philosopher, did—that white, Western man is rational.

On matters of race, he might well be irrational. Therefore, when he is confronted with legitimate demands which challenge his presumed superiority and his conception of his self-interest he might well react in a further oppressive manner—even to the point of genocide.

This might well be thinking about the unthinkable. This might well be the ultimate culmination of a reactionary "backlash." But, however we characterize it, candor requires that we answer the opening question with a "yes." The American Indians know this. Japanese-Americans are aware of this.

What all this means, I suspect, is that black Americans must not be naive about the "inevitability of progress." It means that black demands and white responses are operating in an environment quite unpredictable as to consequences. The demands should, and must, continue. . . .

A month later, United Press International carried a story based on an interview with sociologist Dr. Philip M. Hauser. Hauser narrowed the nation's choices to two:

It is easy to understand the "why" of the colored rebellion in America.

It is even easy to suggest what ought to be done about it.

What is not easy, according to Dr. Philip M. Hauser, is how to make the break with our past which must be made before the obvious solutions can be undertaken.

Hauser is director of the Population Reference Bureau.

What he says makes grim reading. As he sees it America has two choices:

It can make the heavy "investment in people" which will have to be made to transform the underprivileged into responsible citizens; or

It can suppress its rebellious minorites.

"If we are not prepared to make the investment in human resources that is required," according to Hauser, "we will be forced to increase our investment in the Police, National Guard, and the Army.

"And possibly—it can happen here—we may be forced to resort to concentration camps and even genocide."*

In politics, the survival fears reached the "little people" who have reaped little of the society's harvest, and a pervasive fear also reached black elected officials who had whatever reason there was to be confident and hopeful. "I don't know that we can talk about the civil rights movement in this country in any relevant or legal sense any longer," said Richard Gordon Hatcher, the newly elected mayor of Gary, Indiana. "It has now become a struggle for survival between civil rights and 'law and order' philosophies." Hatcher added that rumors that the Nixon administration was preparing concentration camps "can lead one to several conclusions, the most frightening of which is that such camps are being prepared for dissidents, maybe Black and white."†

The fear of genocide grew among black Americans as the Decisive Decade drew to a close, but what had been just a widespread uneasiness became a near epidemic during President Nixon's first year in the White House. Virtually every act of his administration was broadly interpreted—even by Blacks not usually regarded as militant or particularly paranoiac—as a move toward some eventual harm. His public statements and even the semiprivate statements of Cabinet members were scrutinized for traces of deepest malevolence.

Among black journalists, the President's credibility was not helped by the fact that the White House rearranged the seating

* Joseph L. Myler, UPI senior editor, writing in the Washington *Afro-American,* September 7, 1968, p. 1.
† Chicago *Daily Defender,* June 19, 1969.

at press conferences in a way that virtually excluded black newsmen—as they always had been prior to the election of President Kennedy. Some accommodation was finally worked out, but the President's own words at press conferences led black journalists to be leery of the President's motives.

Writing in the June 26, 1969, edition of the Chicago *Daily Defender,* columnist Ethel L. Payne provided a case in point:

President Nixon somehow managed to lose or drop 11 million blacks from the population at his press conference last Thursday evening. He had just, in his own words, made a "Freudian slip" when he referred to Governor Nelson Rockefeller of New York as "President."

Mr. Nixon was downplaying the demonstrations accompanying Governor Rockefeller on his recent South American fact-finding trip. Said he, "We must not interpret these demonstrations as reflecting the will of the people of Latin America. The few demonstrators, violent as they are, in Latin America no more represent the 200 million people of Latin America than the Black Panthers represent the 11 million law abiding Negro citizens of this country. That is what we have to get across."

That was the second "Freudian slip" within a sentence and inadvertently, the President either chopped the black population in half, which might have been a sub-conscious desire to, or else he made 11 million more black ultra militants than there are on record in the CIA and FBI files.

This, of course, showed deep suspicion about the motives of a President whose "slips" might have been attributed either to his newness in the office or a slightly jumbled reference to the black population of about 11 percent.

But questioning of the administration's statements and motives regarding the lives and welfare of the black population was by no means limited to the black press. In that same first summer of the Nixon administration, the Washington *Post,* recalling some odd counsel from the Justice Department, was critical of the administration's ousting of Clifford Alexander, Jr., as chairman of the Equal Employment Opportunity Commission. Editorialized the *Post:*

"You'd be better informed," Attorney General Mitchell told a group of black Southerners who came to the Department of Justice a month or so ago to protest against administration complacency about racial discrimination, "if instead of listening to what we say, you watch what we do." We have been watching ever since, and we are not reassured.

. . . If this [the support of a weaker enforcement law by Alexander's successor] were an isolated phenomenon, one might put it down to an aberration on the part of the new EEOC chairman or to a singular concession on the administration's part toward the reactionary wing of the GOP. But looked at in conjunction with the administration hostility toward extension of the Voting Rights Act and the administration default on school guidelines one can hardly escape discerning a pattern of apathy about civil rights that speaks far louder than any presidential protestation to the contrary. What the administration does in this area makes it difficult to credit what it says.*

If the Washington *Post* had reason to distrust the motives and pronouncements of the Nixon administration, consider the anguish of the SCLC, which had just completed another outstandingly unsuccessful hunger campaign in Washington. Viewing the hostility of administration officials and the possibility that further efforts might provide an excuse for rash police action, the SCLC abandoned national demonstrations as a tactic.

At the SCLC national convention in Charleston, South Carolina, Andrew Young, the executive vice-president, concluded that black people "have no friends in power" in the Nixon administration, and, therefore, national protests were useless. "There can be no general dramatizing of the problem in hopes that the nation will respond," Young continued. "They won't. They may promise, they may play games, but there will be no concessions granted; they must be taken."†

Young explained that by "taking" he meant that black voters and office holders would have to do the job themselves, by getting elected as had been done in Greene County, Alabama. A

---

* Washington *Post*, August 15, 1969, p. A-20.
† Washington *Post*, August 18, 1969, p. A-5.

far larger point loomed here, however. The SCLC was an organization whose tactics had been based largely on conscience and the persuasive power of First Amendment remedies—essentially, freedom of speech, the press, religion (conscience), and assembly. This considered judgment by SCLC that further reliance on appeals to a national conscience was useless acknowledged a frightening new realization. It said that there was no longer a national conscience to which the SCLC felt Blacks might successfully appeal. This logic attributed the meanest of motives to the controlling sentiments in the nation.

The time had come when the threat to black survival was so meticulously hinged to an unwillingness to continue as twentieth-century slaves that the ablest black lecturers began urging black masses, especially students, to understand the relationship and the alternatives, however uninviting. In his baccalaureate address at black Hampton Institute, June 1, 1969, black educator Dr. Samuel DeWitt Proctor* urged:

"We are at our best when we hold up before this nation her own character, her own commitments, her own code of justice, her own proud proclamation of the divine origin of the rights of man. Don't turn her loose! Hold her to it! Don't cop out with impulsive and profane alternatives that will leave our young people shot down in streets by the National Guard. *Don't give our enemies the excuse they want to cart us off in great big feed wagons to a new Auschwitz or a new Dachau.* [Emphasis added.] Let us make our case so plain that their altars will burn with the incense of our just claims for dignity, and their courts will pound out verdict after verdict that will complete our emancipation."

But even as Proctor eloquently pleaded for further reliance on the courts, the Nixon administration had managed the resignation of liberal Justice Abe Fortas from the Supreme Court and was offering in his place Judges Clement Haynsworth of South Carolina and Harrold Carswell of Florida. Liberal Senators, led by Birch Bayh (Democrat of Indiana),

---

* Dr. Proctor was president of North Carolina A & T College in 1960 when four of his students started the "sit-in" movement.

defeated the nomination of Haynsworth on charges of racism and stock manipulation. Carswell, the second Nixon nominee, tried to conceal but finally acknowledged a campaign statement he made in 1948: "I believe that segregation of the races is proper and the only and correct way of life in our state. I have always so believed and I shall always so act. I shall be the last to submit to any attempt on the part of anyone to break down and to weaken this firmly established policy of our people. If my own brother were to advocate such a program, I would be compelled to take issue with and to oppose him to the limit of my ability. I yield to no man as a fellow candidate or as a fellow citizen in the firm, vigorous belief in the principles of white supremacy and I shall always be so governed."*

In the fall of 1969, the nation would hear about Chicago's Judge Julius Hoffman and his conduct of the conspiracy trial of the "Chicago 8." The nation saw the spectacle of the black defendant, Bobby Seale, being bound and gagged in the court-room to shut off his insistence on his constitutional right to defend himself in the illness and absence of his chosen lawyer.

So filled was that season with threats to life and constitutional due process that black freshman Congressman William L. Clay of St. Louis wrote in his weekly column about the danger and existence both of concentration camps and concentration camp laws. Congressman Clay did not try to hide or disguise his fear. Citing the existence of the McCarran Act, Clay wrote: "The implications of this detention provision for black people seem clear. The temper of our times and the posture of the present administration make it imperative that our efforts to repeal Title II succeed. . . . No one can predict when this nation may see fit to seize upon a witch hunt. Those of us who are sensitive to the nature of protest and to the hasty and violent reactions to dissent feel warranted in our anxiety."†

Increasingly, black people in certain quarters were speaking openly and candidly about such basic concerns. They were, however, confined largely to politicians, some radical writers,

---

* Washington *Post*, January 22, 1970, p. A-8.
† St. Louis *Sentinel*, August 30, 1969, p. 3.

and those generally regarded as members of extremist groups. But in mid-1970, the patience and confidence of more reserved groups and individuals were clearly exhausted. Stunning evidence of the breakdown of diplomacy under the weight of onrushing repression came at the end of June in uncommonly strong language from the board chairman of the due-process-oriented NAACP. In his keynote address to the sixty-first annual convention in Cincinnati, Bishop Stephen G. Spottswood startled the Nixon administration by declaring:

For the first time since Woodrow Wilson, we have a national Administration that can be rightly characterized as anti-Negro.

This is the first time since 1920 that the national Administration has made it a matter of calculated policy to work against the needs and aspirations of the largest minority of its citizens.

. . . On April 9, after the rejection of his nominee, Judge Carswell, for the Supreme Court, the President described the ideal judge as "someone who believed in the strict construction of the Constitution, as I do—a judge who will not use the power of the Court to seek social change by freely interpreting the law or constitutional clauses." This is the Administration's expressed opposition to the equal protection clauses of the 14th amendment.

The effect of this has been exactly what was predicted. It has given encouragement to the Southern racists whose fullpage advertisements have exposed their radical retreat to the calendar level of the 1870's, such as produced by Senator [John C.] Stennis of Mississippi and Gov. [John J.] McKeithen of Louisiana, to say nothing of the melodramatic pose of Florida's Gov. [Claude R.] Kirk in defying the Federal court's orders to desegregate the Public schools of the Everglades state.

. . . If American democracy is to survive, we shall be one society, as the Declaration of Independence visioned and the Constitution declares.

Even as lynching was the Roman holiday sport of the 19th century America, killing black Americans promiscuously has been the 20th century pastime of our police, whose primary duty is law enforcement and keeping the peace.

I'm thinking of the six Negroes killed in Augusta, Ga., all shot in the back; of the Panthers slain in their beds in Chicago; of the students slain at Jackson State College; of the almost daily news stories of the indiscriminate, ruthless slaying of black Americans by police and civilians, under the guise of "law and order," but actually fulfilling the guidelines of a bitter, white majority, whose vain effort to keep us "in our place" leads them to resort to the policeman's pistol and kangaroo court trials. . . .

No major problem afflicting black Americans can be solved except by solving them for all Americans.

We have worked too long and too hard, made too many sacrifices, spent too much money, shed too much blood, lost too many lives fighting to vindicate our manhood as full participants in the American system to allow our victories to be nullified by phony liberals, die-hard racists, discouraged and demoralized Negroes and power-seeking politicians.*

That unprecedented NAACP charge that the Nixon administration was anti-Negro brought a bitter denial the next day from President Nixon's minority group liaison, Leonard Garment. In a lengthy telegram from the White House, Garment purported a point-by-point rebuttal and closed the communiqué to the NAACP by saying:

It is one thing to criticize, to give voice to deeply-felt concerns and to articulate real disappointments. Everyone benefits from such a debate. It is an entirely different thing to search out ways to portray the actions of this Administration in the worst possible light, to rally every fear, and reinforce every anxiety. Such a message, painting a false picture of what the Administration has done, is doing, and hopes to do, sows distrust and makes our commonly-agreed-on goals more difficult to achieve.

I note that even now, as speakers at your convention are attacking every aspect of the Administration's record in this area, and doing so without a balancing word, members of the Administration are working with many of your colleagues on important projects of mutual concern.

The President and the Administration are committed to achieving equal opportunity for every American, and are determined to maintain their efforts to reach that goal.†

* New York *Times*, June 30, 1970, pp. 1, 24.
† New York *Times*, July 1, 1970, pp. 1, 34.

If the Nixon administration's response to the NAACP assessment was designed to dissipate pessimism or at least placate so-called moderate Negroes, the effort was an immediate failure. The following week, on July 6, the New York *Times* reported the results of a survey it conducted among Blacks "within the system." In a page-one story by Thomas A. Johnson, the *Times* reported:

"There has been some progress, yes, but there is more resistance to Negro aspirations today than at any time in recent history," said Gloster B. Current, director of field administration for the NAACP's 1,700 branches across the country.

This judgment by Mr. Current, who is considered a racial moderate on the black American scale of activism, reflects the strong concerns of scores of other black Americans interviewed in the last three weeks.

All of those questioned are working somewhere "within the system," subject to periods of frustration and doubt but not yet ready to break away and work from outside.

But by early July, 1970, not even all "system" Blacks were willing to continue their faith and trust in the system as it existed. What some called for, in fact, was a "Black Declaration of Independence" whose implications were deliberately similar to its 194-year-old predecessor. In a full-page ad in the July 3, 1970, New York *Times,* 40 signatories and sponsors of the ad issued the declaration "by Order and in behalf of Black People" and as representatives of the National Committee of Black Churchmen, Inc., headquartered in New York City. Stated the declaration:

In the Black Community, July 4, 1970 a Declaration by concerned Black Citizens of the United States of America in Black Churches, Schools, Homes, Community Organizations and Institutions assembled:

When in the course of Human Events, it becomes necessary for a People who were stolen from the lands of their Fathers, transported under the most ruthless and brutal circumstances 5,000 miles to a strange land, sold into dehumanizing slavery, emasculated, subjugated, exploited and discriminated against for 351 years, to call, with finality, a halt to such indignities and genocidal practices—by virtue of the Laws of Nature and of Nature's God, a decent respect to the Opinions of Mankind requires that they should declare their just grievances and the urgent and necessary redress thereof.

We hold these truths to be self-evident, that all Men are not *only* created equal and endowed by their Creator with certain unalienable rights among which are Life, Liberty and the Pursuit of Happiness, but that when this equality and these rights are deliberately and consistently refused, withheld or abnegated, men are bound by self-respect and honor to rise up in righteous indignation to secure them. Whenever any Form of Government, or any variety of established traditions and systems of the Majority becomes destructive of Freedom and of legitimate Human Rights, it is the Right of the Minorities to use every necessary and accessible means to protest and to disrupt the machinery of Oppression, and so to bring such general distress and discomfort upon the oppressor as to the offended Minorities shall seem most appropriate and most likely to effect a proper adjustment of the society.

Prudence, indeed, will dictate that such bold tactics should not be initiated for light and transient Causes; and, accordingly, the Experience of White America has been that the descendants of the African citizens brought forcibly to these shores, and to the shores of the Caribbean Islands, as slaves, have been patient long past what can be expected of any human beings so affronted. But when a long train of Abuses and Violence, pursuing invariably the same Object, manifests a Design to reduce them under Absolute Racist Domination and Injustice, it is their Duty radically to confront such Government or system of traditions, and to provide, under the aegis of Legitimate Minority Power and Self Determination, for their present Relief and future Security. Such has been the patient Sufferance of Black People in the United States of America; and such is now the Necessity which constrains them to address this Declaration to Despotic White Power, and to give due notice of their determined refusal to be any longer silenced by fear or flattery, or to be denied justice. The history of the treatment of Black People in the United States is a history having in direct Object the Establishment and Maintenance of Racist Tyranny over this People. To prove this, let Facts be submitted to a candid World.

The United States has evaded Compliance to laws the most wholesome and necessary for our Children's education.

The United States has caused us to be isolated in the most dilapidated and unhealthful sections of all cities.

The United States has allowed election districts to be so gerrymandered that Black People find the right to Representation in the Legislatures almost impossible of attainment.

The United States has allowed the dissolution of school districts controlled by Blacks when Blacks opposed with manly Firmness the white man's Invasions on the Rights of our People.

The United States has erected a Multitude of Public Agencies and Offices, and sent into our ghettos Swarms of Social Workers, Officers and Investigators to harass our People, and eat out their Substance to feed the Bureaucracies.

The United States has kept in our ghettos, in Times of Peace, Standing Armies of Police, State Troopers and National Guardsmen, without the consent of our People.

The United States has imposed Taxes upon us without protecting our Constitutional Rights.

The United States has constrained our Black sons taken Captive in its Armies, to bear arms against their black, brown and yellow Brothers, to be the Executioners of these Friends and Brethren, or to fall themselves by their Hands.

The Exploitation and Injustice of the United States have incited domestic Insurrections among us, and the United States has endeavored to bring on the Inhabitants of our ghettos, the merciless Military Establishment, whose known Rule of control is an undistinguished shooting of all Ages, Sexes and Conditions of Black People:

For being lynched, burned, tortured, harried, harassed and imprisoned without Just Cause.

For being gunned down in the streets, in our churches, in our homes, in our apartments and on our campuses, by Policemen and Troops who are protected by a mock Trial, from Punishment for any Murders which they commit on the Inhabitants of our Communities.

For creating, through Racism and bigotry, an unrelenting Economic Depression in the Black Community which wreaks havoc upon our men and disheartens our youth.

For denying to most of us equal access to the better Housing and Education of the land.

For having desecráted and torn down our humblest dwelling places, under the Pretense of Urban Renewal, without replacing them at costs which we can afford.

The United States has denied our personhood by refusing to teach our heritage, and the magnificent contributions to the life, wealth and growth of this Nation which have been made by Black People.

In every stage of these Oppressions we have Petitioned for Redress in the most humble terms: Our repeated Petitions have been answered mainly by repeated Injury. A Nation, whose Character is thus marked by every act which may define a Racially Oppressive Regime, is unfit to receive the respect of a Free People.

Nor have we been wanting in attentions to our White Brethren. We have warned them from time to time of Attempts by their Structures of Power to extend an unwarranted, Repressive Control over us. We have reminded them of the Circumstances of our Captivity and Settlement here. We have appealed to their vaunted Justice and Magnanimity, and we have abjured them by the Ties of our Common Humanity to disavow these Injustices, which, would inevitably interrupt our Connections and Correspondence. They have been deaf to the voice of Justice and of Humanity. We must, therefore, acquiesce in the Necessity, which hereby announces our Most Firm Commitment to the Liberation of Black People, and hold the Institutions, Traditions and Systems of the United States as we hold the rest of the societies of Mankind, Enemies when Unjust and Tyrannical; when Just and Free, Friends.

We, therefore, the Black People of the United States of America, in all parts of this Nation, appealing to the Supreme Judge of the World for the Rectitude of our intentions, do, in the Name of our good People and our own Black Heroes—Richard Allen, James Varick, Absalom Jones, Nat Turner, Frederick Douglass, Marcus Garvey, Malcolm X, Martin Luther King, Jr., and all Black People past and present, great and small—Solemnly Publish and Declare, that we shall be, and of Right ought to be, FREE AND INDE-PENDENT FROM THE INJUSTICE, EXPLOITATIVE CON-TROL, INSTITUTIONALIZED VIOLENCE AND RACISM OF WHITE AMERICA, that unless we receive full Redress and Relief from these Inhumanities we will move to renounce all Allegiance to this Nation, and will refuse, in every way, to cooperate with the

Evil which is Perpetrated upon ourselves and our Communities. And for the support of this Declaration, with a firm Reliance on the Protection of divine Providence, we mutually pledge to each other our Lives, our Fortunes, and our sacred Honor.

To be sure, there was parody—even a touch of satire—in that Black Declaration of Independence. But, taken in its context, along with the statements of Bishop Spottswood and field director Current of the NAACP, this Black Declaration of Independence left no doubt whatever of the extreme danger and hopelessness in which black Americans had begun to view their predicament.

Nor was the fear of impending destruction limited to black people, who feel especially vulnerable. Perceptive Blacks occasionally make the case that black Americans would not have survived the '60's had it not been for the intervention of the "hippies," who served as lightning rods—drawing the fire momentarily away from Blacks—or as insulation between the Blacks and the ruling parents of the hippies. Evidence that this kind of substitution was a real and present danger to those regarded as hippies was provided in a series of articles by James S. Kunen, author of *The Strawberry Statement.**

* From the Washington *Post,* August 17, 1969, p. B-5:

"From Albuquerque, I headed for Taos, N.M., via Santa Fe. As it turned out, the Santa Fe Exterminator was awaiting me in a cafe. I was talking with the man behind the counter when the S.F.E. asked me who gave me rides, considering my 'hippie-esque physique.'

"The counterman countered, 'He's not a hippie, or I wouldn't be talking with him. He's clean.'

"I know he's 'clean,' said the Exterminator. 'I said hippie-esque.'

"It's really funny, sitting around while total strangers discuss your personal hygiene.

"A Diseased Appendix

"THE EXTERMINATOR, a middle-aged, middle-class man, said that if I refused the draft, I would be a second-class citizen and no longer have any rights. If I could break the law, why couldn't he break the law and murder me, which he said he might like to do?

"At first I thought the murder thing was an *ad absurden* formal argument, but we talked for an hour and he happens to be strongly in favor of exterminating all hippies. He said they contribute nothing, have in fact descended from the human race and should be slaughtered like pigs.

"In Russia or China they would be killed, he said. Therefore, since they are

While the hippies have been more generally identified with the antiwar protests than with civil rights for Afro-Americans, one of the final, and lasting, contributions of Dr. King was to integrate the two issues. This has lent fuel to claims that the civil rights movement and Dr. King died together. What may be more true is that by the time he died, the civil rights issue had simply become a part of a wider, more pervasive struggle for world peace with justice.

James Baldwin, the black writer and expatriate, viewed the Afro-American crisis from Istanbul, Turkey, at the end of 1969 and concluded that black and white Americans are on a collision course:

What we called the civil rights struggle can be said to have been buried with Martin Luther King. Because as of that event . . . and with the arrival of the new administration, it began to be very clear to black people in the United States that what *Time* magazine [*sic. Newsweek,* October 6, 1969] calls "the troubled American" is not going to listen, does not want to know, does not want to hear the truth about the situation of the American black.

I know America has gotten itself into a place it does not know how to get out of. It's been coming for a very long time. Now here we are. What happens is anyone's guess. . . . It seems very unlikely to me that there is enough moral energy left in most white Americans to accomplish the miracle which is now demanded. I hope I am wrong.*

One aspect of the threat Americans increasingly envisioned at the outset of the '70's is the similarity of alarm by those, such as Baldwin, who viewed the nation's course in an historical context. The year-end 1969 meeting of the American Historical

---

not sufficiently grateful to this country for letting them live, they should be killed. The Exterminator's brother was killed during World War II fighting, as I pointed out, so that Americans should not have to live in a totalitarian country.

" 'This country will go the way of the Roman Empire,' retorted the S.F.E., unless we purge ourselves of this diseased portion of the body politic. He went on at length about what you do with an infected appendix.

"With the usual I respect your opinions, hope you respect mine, I asked him to please think about what a bad thing it is to kill people, and left."

* The Washington *Post,* December 14, 1969, p. E-8.

Association in Washington, D.C., was punctuated with learned warnings and incessant parallels drawn between the United States in 1970 and the Germany of 40 years earlier. Meeting in the last week of 1969, the historians reeked and reeled with discussions about the alleged Song My and My Lai massacres and the police murders of Black Panthers in Chicago and elsewhere around the country.*

During a speech to the some 2,000 historians by Walt Rostow, former foreign policy adviser to President Johnson, several dozen radical historians marched down the center aisle of the meeting hall carrying signs that read: "Rostow Accomplice of War," "Historians say Nixon's a racist at home and abroad," "Historians for peace," "Historians protest the Repression of Black Panthers," and "Stop U.S. Genocide at home and abroad." A group of about 300 of the historians, led by Arthur Waskow of the Institute for Policy Studies and Howard Zinn of Boston University, followed the demonstration with a march to the Justice Department.

"Genocide will come to America," Richard Drinnon of Bucknell said, "as Huey P. Long put it, as a kind of 'hyper-Americanism.' "

"Most of the killers in the twentieth century are usually well-dressed people."

Drinnon's comments were fairly typical of the few hundred historians who regarded themselves as radicals. But perhaps of greater significance were the similar views expressed also by the hierarchy, or establishment, of the AHA. C. Vann Woodward, Sterling Professor of History at Yale University and outgoing president of the AHA, stated:

"The integrity of the academic community and the university and intellectual community is being challenged now for political purposes in some ways comparable to the dictator's assault on those two communities in Germany in the early '30's. I want

---

* Quotes relating to the meeting of the American Historical Association are taken from the author's reportorial notes and from printed tracts officially distributed at the AHA meeting in Washington, D.C. during the last week of December, 1969.

to qualify that by saying that many of the purposes of the attack in America are often nobler than those in Germany in the '30's. The results are, nevertheless, very similar."

Specifically on the black-white situation, Woodward continued: "Blacks are upward bound and on a collision course with white reaction. I think that white reaction is ominous, massive and dangerous, and I think some of the forces that have resisted it during this period of a Second Reconstruction have been depleted, and are apathetic."

In a similar vein, John K. Fairbank, head of Far Eastern Studies at Harvard, said that if he were black, "undoubtedly, I would be apprehensive about my safety in America. Any minority group will have its fears, and there have been examples to justify them."

The clearest incident and warning of the threat the historians saw for America, however, came in the form of a resolution put forward by the "Radical Historians Caucus," although the resolution was rejected by the convention. Many historians, such as Woodward and Fairbank, said they agreed with the sentiment or purposes of the resolution but voted against it rather than politicize the organization. The caucus called it a "Resolution on the War and Repression":

Resolved, that as citizens and historians, we recognize and find intolerable the present direction of the American government. In order to extend the modern American Empire by waging war against the people of Vietnam, the government has increasingly moved to repress political opposition at home. Moreover, the physical and cultural destruction of the Vietnamese people reflects a much older and deeper policy of physical and cultural destruction of the Black community at home, and is now being carried into new versions of racism by the Administration in its betrayal of civil rights and its aid to counter-insurgent police forces in the great cities. The political assassination of the Black Panther Party is the most blatant example. The Justice Department is acting as the domestic Pentagon in this repression.

These murderous policies and the repression which enforces them are increasingly restricting our freedom as historians, have turned

even our classrooms and gradebooks into channels of conscription
and death, have affected the life of our campuses, and have deeply
disturbed relations between teachers and students of history. Even
more important than the damage they have done to our profession,
they are undermining the possibility of self determination and
democracy in the American and world society whose history we
study.

We cannot stand by in silence. To do so is to condone the abuses to
which history has been subjected in the service of power, to condone
a kind of intellectual pacification program. To say nothing at this
point in our own history is to express our indifference to what is
happening around us. The business of this convention is history.
We must renew our commitment to one of the great historic tasks of
independent historians in time of crisis. We must expose to critical
analysis and public attack the disastrous direction in which our
government is taking us.

We therefore demand the immediate withdrawal of all American
troops from Vietnam, the immediate end of all harassment of the
Black Panther Party, and the release of all political prisoners such
as the Chicago 8.

Similarly, Whitney M. Young, Jr., director of the National
Urban League, drew fearful conclusions from his assessment of
the first Nixon year. So moderate have been Young's views that
more aggressive civil rights activists have been known to refer
derogatorily to him as "Whitey" Young. Nonetheless, his conclusions about the threat to all black Americans coincides with
those of his most cynical critics:

This has been a year of broad retreat from the social reformism
that has marked the decade of the sixties. . . . The year has been
marked by a growing and dangerous mood of repression that
threatens the civil liberties of all of us.

The undeclared war on radical groups like the Black Panthers
by the police has left many dead, and a feeling of bitterness in the
ghetto. Shrill calls for law and order have resulted in greater
oppression and denial of justice.

The national mood seems to be one of drifting toward a harsh, repressive society rather than the open, democratic one that has always been the American ideal.

The recent report of the Eisenhower Commission, like the reports of the many commissions that preceded it, gave fresh warning of the self-defeating and frightening course this nation is on.*

The choice the nation had made by the end of the Decisive Decade clearly was a serious threat to the survival of black people in America.

"America has not failed because her professions were wrong," Dr. Samuel DeWitt Proctor rightly told the students at Hampton Institute. "Go anywhere in the world, and nowhere is the promise of human dignity so clearly spelled out, so carefully defined, so neatly described."

Yet, another kind of truth was crudely vented to a session of the black power conference in fire-swept Newark in the summer of 1967. In a session where well-dressed, well-mannered, mostly academic types discussed educational problems and how education might be used to help solve "the problem," a petite brown-skinned lady from Chicago rose and began to give a polite and learned dissertation on how whites had used the school system, in fact, to further the enslavement of Blacks. Others joined in, all citing instances of the same predicament. But most thought that an emerging Black sophistication would ultimately enable Blacks to turn the corner educationally and win the day for black people. Suddenly, a medium-to-smallish black youth, about 19 or 20, shot onto the floor from his chair, one of several dozen staggered in a kind of circle.

"This is bullshit!" he shouted. "Pure damned bullshit!"

The roomful of academicians gasped, then fell into a stony silence.

"What the fuck are we doing sitting here talking all this education jazz?" exclaimed the youth, in a green T-shirt fitting tightly around his muscular shoulders and forearms. "The action is downtown at that damned jailhouse!"

* "To Be Equal," a column by Whitney M. Young, Jr., Washington *Afro-American*, December 30, 1969.

During the uprisings of the recent days, many Blacks had been arrested, some of them persons who would have otherwise been active in the conference. This green-T-shirted youth was one of many who felt that the conference should not adjourn—indeed would fail—without getting those arrested out of jail.

"Young man," the lady from Chicago interrupted, "there are ways to do things. The way *not* to do them is the way you're behaving. If getting them out of jail is the thing to do, then we should get a lawyer and assign him to get a writ and get them out."

"Shiiiit!" pounded the young black man, his massive fist slapping his palm. "You niggers are always talking about how you're going to outfox Whitey. When? That's what I'd like to know—when? Well, goddammit I been looking all my damned life, and I ain't seen you outsmart Whitey yet.

"Now, look, don't get me wrong." He began to rock a bit from the heels to the balls of his feet. "I ain't trying to turn nobody off, see, nobody that wants to help black people get out of this shit. What I'm telling you, though, is that you cats that's supposed to be so fucking smart ain't showing me nothing. Whitey's beating your ass every turn.

"Look," he said, beginning to shake with emotion. "I don't know shit about books. Okay? Okay? I'll give you that. So, I'd be willing to let you do your shit, but you ain't *doing* it. You dig? And you ain't *never* gonna beat Whitey 'cause he got you following some fucking book. Shiit! When Whitey gets ready to off one of us, he lets *you* follow that damned book, while *he* goes and gets his knife and cuts our balls out while you smart niggers are still reading.

"Look," he said, fumbling in his pockets and coming out with a pack of paper matches, "look, like I said, I don't know books, but that don't matter, 'cause that ain't where Whitey's at."

He began poking the air with his match pack.

"Whitey's just like me. When he means business he says to hell with them books. I can't outsmart Whitey and I know it. But, goddammit, I sure can light a fire to his ass, and that's what the fuck I'm gonna do!! Can't *nobody* beat me doing that. I'm going out there and do what I *know* I can do!"

With that, the rugged little black man in the green T-shirt stomped out of the room. Silence rushed in. For the next hour, the "educators" at the Newark black power conference pondered a special kind of truth: For ideology, Whitey uses books; for results, he uses tactics.

And yet Proctor's truth is wholly relevant to the question of black survival in America. The basic threats to that survival can obtain only outside the protections guaranteed to every United States citizen by the Constitution—the warnings of "cracker gas, cracker law, and cracker jury" notwithstanding. Centrally focused, then, must be those guarantees and their erosion, particularly during the last half of the Decisive Decade.

Columnist Carl Rowan, who once served as ambassador to Sweden and later as director of the United States Information Agency (USIA), saw the dangers of such erosion during the 1968 Presidential campaign, which included the candidacy of former Alabama Governor George Wallace:

"The single most important reason why fascism is possible in America is not Wallace, a very insignificant man in his own right," Rowan wrote, "but the fact that the people are today so preoccupied with their fears, frustrations, and prejudices that they seem ready to abdicate from a solemn responsibility to protect our Constitutional safe-guards."

Then, Rowan continued:

There are two ways to circumvent, or trample over, a constitution, however ingeniously contrived may be its democratic precepts.

One way is to arouse public fear and hatred to a point where all concepts of minority protection, or right of dissent, get swept away in a tide of emotion.

It is not mere coincidence that the current spate of fear and hatred over crime in the streets and Negro aggressiveness is accompanied by an attack on the U.S. Supreme Court. . . . But the would-be fascists prepare for every eventuality. In case they can't turn the public completely against the Court, they want to alter its membership—and in that way alter the zeal with which it would apply the safeguards against fascism that are built into the Constitution. . . .

The second way to abrogate a Constitution is to amass enough police or military power to force your will upon a society.*

During the five-year period from the Watts rebellion in August, 1965, through the first year of the Nixon administration, the nation experienced genuinely traumatic and potentially disastrous erosions of constitutional guarantees. Civil upheavals sprang from unlivable and unjust conditions, but troops and Nazi police tactics—not amelioration of conditions—followed. A Nixon administration Southern Strategy was seen by many as feeding distrust and division, and critics saw proof of President Nixon's willingness to create a police state in his quick call in of troops to deliver the mail during the mail strike in March, 1970.

In the meantime, mass exterminations—ruled "justifiable homicides"†—of Black Panthers and other discontented Blacks continued. Data banks were expanded to control those who sought to exercise their constitutional rights to associate freely, with even the crossing of state lines becoming a suspect matter and "inciting to riot" a frequent charge. Civil libertarians who might oppose such methods were similarly intimidated.

In the first month of the Nixon administration, *Jet* magazine's managing editor, John H. Britton, cited numerous aggressive black leaders who had escaped death in the violence that encompasses them but who were, nonetheless, candidates to be either jailed or forced to flee the country—while they live:

The more outspoken black radicals, who two years ago collected as high as $1,500 a speech for their verbal flagellations on the lecture circuit, are more likely now to collect prison denims and are less likely to be free to move about the United States. Criminal indictments, arrests, maximum jail terms for alleged petty offenses, and other forms of legal straitjacketing are slowly and surely

* Carl T. Rowan, "Constitution No Guarantee Against Fascism," *Sunday Star,* October 20, 1968, p. C-4.

† *Jet,* February 5, 1970, p. 28.

putting in a bind most of the visible leaders of radical causes. . . .
In 1968, the roll call of radical black defendants is long, and
growing longer.
    . . . Start with Rap Brown himself. Atty. William Kunstler of
New York told *Jet* his celebrated client is up against 14 criminal
counts in four states and the District of Columbia. Brown is now
appealing a five-year sentence imposed following conviction on a
federal gun charge in New Orleans. And he is due to go on trial
soon in Maryland on a charge of arson that carries a maximum
penalty of 10 years.
    Stokely Carmichael, the firebrand former chairman of SNCC, is
facing riot charges in Atlanta that could bring a maximum of 10
years. . . . Phil Hutchings [current SNCC chairman] faces trial in
St. Louis, as does John Wilson, a Chicago SNCC-man who heads the
Black Anti-Draft, Anti-War Union. In Texas, SNCC-men Lee Otis
Johnson of Houston, Matthew Johnson of Austin, and Ernie Mc-
Millan of Dallas face jail terms. Kunstler said Lee Otis Johnson
drew 30 years for the alleged sale of one marijuana cigarette.
    SNCC's Cleveland Sellers is appealing a five-year sentence on
conviction of draft evasion, and faces inciting to riot charges in
Orangeburg, S.C. In Houston, five Texas Southern University students face murder trials in connection with the death of a policeman during a campus uprising, even though prosecutors admit most
of the youngsters were nowhere near the scene when the officer was
slain.
    . . . Black Panthers from coast to coast are feeling the heat.
Eldridge Cleaver is hunted by the FBI as a parole violator. Huey
Newton is already in a California prison. Panther Capt. John Ford
of New York faces trial on misdemeanor charges. Panther Chairman
Bobby Seale is under restrictive probation in Oakland. Panther
headquarters in Newark, Denver and San Francisco have been
attacked by bombs and bullets. Policemen were suspended in
connection with the San Francisco incident.*
    Indeed, in the last half of the Decisive Decade, unconstitu-
tional tactics ushered in a substantial police state—potentially a
prelude to the broader consequences feared by many. Some of
the police action, of course, is in response to violence and

---

* John H. Britton, "Black Militants Face Showdown in Struggle to Avoid
Prison," *Jet*, January 16, 1969, pp. 14–16.

disruption on the part of the Blackpoor and others. There is the question, however, as to what extent these disruptions are mandated by conditions deliberately imposed by the controllers in the society and enforced by the police.

The centuries of white racism, dutifully reported by the Kerner Commission in 1968, sprouted its inevitable fruit in Watts, Newark, Detroit, Chicago, and scores of other cities throughout the nation. These "riots," as a Kerner Commission study revealed, were not really riots at all. Rather, they were the reactions of "a small but significant minority of the Negro population, fairly representative of the ghetto residents" who were engaging in "a protest against the essential conditions of life there, and an indicator of the necessity for fundamental changes in American society."*

The society did so little to ameliorate the conditions that the Kerner Commission released a second report a year later pointing out that in many places, such as Newark, the situation had deteriorated further and the likelihood for violence had increased. So clear were this failure and the negative responses that some observers, such as Columbia University sociologist Amitai Etzioni, saw them as a tactic of "making riots mandatory." Explained Etzioni:

> Despite repeated assertions [by President Johnson] that the United States is rich enough to have both guns and butter, the country spent more in Saigon alone than in all American cities combined. The war costs now per annum total $24.5 billion by government estimates, $32 billion by U.S. Senate sources. The war on poverty is funded at approximately $2 billion a year.
>
> This was the background for the severest riots the U.S. has known in decades, riots which erupted in Detroit and in Newark in the summer of 1967. The Congress has since cut back those domestic programs which benefit the under-class, including bills aimed at control of rats in slums, welfare for mothers and children, and the Job Corps. Meanwhile, the National Guards have purchased more and heavier arms. The White House responded to the riots by calling for a national day of prayer—and by appointing the Com-

* *City,* September–October, 1968, p. 13.

mission on Civil Disorders. As James Reston pointed out at the time, this was an attempt to handle the politics of the situation rather than the situation itself.*

As Etzioni points out, the Kerner Commission predicted that "to pursue our present course will involve the continuing polarization of the American community and, ultimately, the destruction of basic democratic values."†

This predictability of violence as a reaction mandated by society was put just as accurately, if in less scholarly fashion, by white writer Jimmy Breslin: "If I were black and lived in Newark I'd riot."**

The degree to which black people, even nonradical Blacks, see their people forced into potentially riotous incidents to gain constitutional rights manifests itself in the pronouncements of several distinguished black public servants. On the narrowest possible vote, 7 to 6, the National Commission on Crime and Violence (the Eisenhower Commission) decided in its 1969 report that massive civil disobedience was not an acceptable tactic to be used to counter the unconstitutional tactics employed by the government, its officials, and others in the society. *But,* two black members of the commission—Mrs. Patricia Roberts Harris, a law professor at Howard University, and Judge A. Leon Higginbotham, Jr., of Philadelphia—both dissented. They disagreed with the commission's view that aggrieved persons should "abide by the law involved until it is declared unconstitutional" under the test of a single individual. Disputing that argument, Judge Higginbotham said:

"If the majority's doctrine of 'everyone wait until the outcome of the one individual test case' had been applied by Black Americans in the 1960's, probably not one present major civil rights statute would have been enacted. I fear that the majority's

---

* Amitai Etzioni, "Making Riots Mandatory," *Psychiatry and Social Science Review,* May 1968, p. 4.
† *Ibid.,* p. 2.
** Pete Hamill, "Beyond All Prayer," New York *Post,* July 31, 1967, p. 29.

position ignores the sad actual history of Negroes in this country."*

The inevitability of riots as a concomitant to white racism and benign neglect becomes clear, and preachments against unacceptable methods to redress grievances become academic. This fact was underscored by the Chicago *Daily Defender* editorial agreement with black Nobel Peace Prize winner Dr. Ralph Bunche that such tactics as those employed by the Nixon administration actually *cause* black crime and disorder. Under an editorial entitled "Nixon and Racism," the *Defender* indicates the tactic of requiring violent behavior which, in turn, would require police action:

Dr. Ralph Bunche, the distinguished Under Secretary of the United Nations, expressed the view that he, like other Negro leaders, had little confidence that the Nixon Administration would move forward on the crucial problem of racism.

"Black leaders in the United States do not have great confidence in the Nixon Administration to advance." He said he shared the conviction that there is little black confidence in Nixon, in Attorney General Mitchell or in Vice President Agnew. . . .

Though he is opposed to violence as being an impractical way to redress the wrongs done to American blacks, Dr. Bunche warned that there would be more race riots unless action was taken in earnest to remedy the insufferable conditions of the poor blacks.

The Nixon Administration is not heeding . . . the warnings that both conservative and militant Negro leaders have sounded. So engrossed is Mr. Nixon in devising a political scheme by which to give gratification to the implacable racists below the Mason and Dixon Line that he has neither the time nor the inclination to correct the injustices that give rise to frustrations and turmoil in the black slums. . . .

Eisenhower never once backed up the Supreme Court's school desegregation decision. Negro publishers pleaded with him to put the Presidential prestige behind the court's mandate, but to no avail. Mr. Eisenhower had no use for the court after its May 17, 1954 decision. It was too liberal for him. President Nixon was just as critical of the Warren Court as was Ike.

* Associated Press wire #48, December 8, 1969.

Eisenhower thought the court had gone too far in outlawing racial imbalance in the nation's public schools. Nixon is in demonstrable sympathy with the South's refusal to comply with that mandate. He has been in power a year. So far, he has done little to show that he is concerned about the full constitutional guarantees of civil rights for the black citizenry.

Yes, we agree with Dr. Bunche as to the character and depth of existing racial dissatisfaction and the riots that may ensue. Riots there will be, for the President is doing nothing to douse the fire of racial unrest.*

Thus, as the Kerner Commission indicated, pursuing the same courses of white racism and what Moynihan calls benign neglect could have only the easily predictable result—riots—and police oppression as a justifiable response. This the green-shirted youth in Newark would call "Whitey tactics," resulting, at best, in nondeliberate genocide.

This level of tactics eventually bypasses the lofty alternatives Proctor held up to the Hampton students. The failure to ameliorate the conditions of white racism requires troops and extreme police tactics to suppress the natural growth of resentment fertilized for generations in Newark and elsewhere. These police tactics were not curative but catalytic. A firmer resolve to deal with the increased resentment resulted in the Nixon-Agnew election. In the first Nixon-Agnew-Mitchell year, U.S. constitutional guarantees slipped disastrously.

For example, the federal concern for such rudimentary guarantees as voting rights and an equal chance for a job for black citizens deteriorated quickly. Established civil rights policies regarding school desegregation were abandoned. Even more critically, a national police practice of political extermination resulted in widespread "justifiable homicides" against Blacks who were victims of predawn raids around the country. Even before the Nixon administration pressed such laws through Congress, police officials in various cities began to implement no-knock search and seizure policies and preventive detention. Press intimidation was designed to insure a minimum of dis-

* Chicago *Daily Defender*, January 8, 1970, page 19.

closure of the most odious excesses. While authoritarians prefer the blessing of law to support their acts, they are generally prepared to proceed without them. And, thus, legal sanction lagged behind the actual police state tactics and genocidal conduct of the period.

By the close of 1969, however, elected public officials were beginning to tackle the police state tactics in public forums. One of the first was Senator George McGovern, the South Dakota Democrat who chaired the hunger committee and belatedly sought the nomination at the 1968 Democratic convention in Chicago.

It was a relatively early warning, sounded on the sixth anniversary of the death of President Kennedy. But that McGovern speech on November 22, 1969, at the Brooke County Democratic Dinner in Bethany, West Virginia, was a consummate indictment of the Nixon administration, which McGovern said relied on fear in a "crude campaign to stifle dissent" through confusion, polarization, and intimidation.

McGovern said further:

Hopefully, we have learned from [history] and are a better country, a wiser people, for having suffered from these periods of repression. I think we are; I fear we will need to be in the days immediately ahead. . . .

The President may be keeping secret his plan for ending the war in Vietnam. But he has unveiled his plan for ending dissent in the United States. . . . I sincerely believe that it is not possible to overestimate the sinister effects of the Administration's campaign against the people's freedom of speech, assembly and press. The effects of this campaign are a far greater threat to liberty in this nation than any result, no matter how unfortunate, from the war in Vietnam could ever be. If the President and the Vice-President and the members of his cabinet and his staff do not turn away from this misconceived campaign, they will raise forces of repression that they will not be able to contain and that will ultimately earn for them a place in the dark shadows of American history. . . .

The pattern is becoming familiar. First administration officials add to public confusion by uttering conflicting statements on issues.

Vice-President Agnew, for example, calls the organizers of a recent peace demonstration impudent snobs; Secretary of State Rogers terms them patriotic, if misguided, Americans. After the gathering, Attorney General Mitchell denounces them as violent, while communications director Klein praises their peacefulness. And this official confusion and contradiction has been the pattern on event after event.

The second phase is equally predictable. It involves Administration efforts to polarize public opinion on a given public question. The idea seems to be to isolate each group that holds a position in opposition to the Administration. Those who disagree with the President are characterized as "rotten apples," or an "effete corps." A portrait is painted of a dangerous, radical minority. Each group that opposes the President also, somehow, opposes a vast "silent majority." This "majority" apparently agrees with the President on all issues. It's homogeneous; it has no complaints. But the Administration is fond of reminding us that its silent legions can be dangerous. And that brings us to the third phase of the strategy. The intimidation stage.

Having confused the American people through official contradiction about the right and wrong of an issue; having polarized and divided the American people and made citizens suspicious of one another, then the Administration moves in to try to frighten and intimidate those opponents it feels it has isolated.

The police powers of the State, the Attorney General, the FCC all are brought in play in threats, real and implied, on groups which are believed to be isolated and therefore vulnerable.

There are many examples of this strategy in action, but none is more blatant and offensive than the recent speech by the Vice-President of the United States in which he assaulted Averell Harriman and the television networks. I feel that the speech was perhaps the most frightening single statement ever to come from a high government official in my public career. During the McCarthy period, I always believed that he did not speak for President Eisenhower. But it is impossible to believe that Mr. Agnew, as Vice-President, does not speak for the President. The Agnew speech was carefully thought through and executed. . . . This attack is led by the Vice-President but it is abetted by Federal Agencies ranging from the Federal Communications Commission to the Subversive Activities Control Board. They seek to intimidate the nation's free press into blind approval of the President's policy. They wish to make the press an arm of the administration akin to the United States Information Agency which just released a misleading film designed to show that the nation is not really divided on the war. . . .

Some have said that the Vice-President made some valid points about the concentration of power in television and newspapers. Perhaps. But the President's motive for prompting him to make the speech had nothing to do with such legitimate criticism. That motive, pure and simple, was to intimidate the news media of the nation.

In ancient times, the threat of a messenger who brought bad news was the loss of his head. In these more sophisticated times, the Administration is invoking the threat of the loss of the license to broadcast.

If the President should succeed in intimidating the men who comprise the eyes and ears of the American people into the workings of their government—and I am afraid the President has had some success already—then the nation is truly in for some hard times. For without their eyes and ears, the people will be blind and dumb and at the mercy of any administration which wants to lead them around on a leash.*

McGovern's concern with the Nixon administration's intimidation of the press was, of course, well founded. It is axiomatic in the history of power seized by totalitarians that they must first bind to their will the media of expression between themselves and the people to be controlled. No tactic is more essential to despots than this.

Perhaps the most obvious measure of the Nixon success at press intimidation during his first year in the White House was the result of Vice President Spiro T. Agnew's first of several speeches attacking the press. That first attack came, significantly, on November 13, 1969—just two days before the massive Vietnam Moratorium in which some 400,000 citizens came, in the First Amendment tradition, to petition their government.

On November 15, as the masses—unbelievable masses—

* From the text of the speech distributed to the press by McGovern, November 22, 1969.

swirled about the public grounds and federal edifices between the Capitol and the Washington Monument, the national television network cameras ground incessantly, as always—with two urgent exceptions:

—There was absolutely no live television coverage, such as was given the 1963 march "For Jobs and Freedom," the funerals of JFK, MLK, RFK, and former President Dwight D. Eisenhower, President Nixon's inaugural, nor even such as was given Agnew's speech attacking the press. Thus, the momentousness of the occasion was irrevocably lost.

—Coverage given on the evening television news programs was brief, and it concentrated, not on the great mass of petitioners, but on several inconsequential skirmishes some demonstrators had with police. Thus, even the historical significance of the protest was perverted.

In the meantime, the President let it be known that the dissenters—no matter how many, how disciplined, no matter their message—would have no effect on him whatever: he spent the afternoon watching football on television.

The networks, despite their lukewarm protests from their official caverns on Madison Avenue, simply had not made up their minds to oppose the Agnew message. They chose, instead, discretion as the better part of their valor.

Senator McGovern is further correct in pointing out that the timing and such regulatory agencies as the Federal Communications Commission (FCC) all play their part in the thinly veiled intimidation. The attack was keenly coordinated.

In its persecution of the Black Panther Party, the Justice Department, in the fall of 1969, subpoenaed the unpublished notes of reporters of *Newsweek,* the New York *Times,* CBS, and *Time-Life* who had covered Panther activities. *Newsweek* was most resistant to the requests, but subpoenas were eventually issued, for example to Mike Wallace of CBS and Earl Caldwell of the New York *Times.*

The negotiations went on for several months, but finally the peak in pressure on *Newsweek* came, and the story of the pressure broke in the news media precisely on February 1,

1970—the same day the license expired for the Post-Newsweek television station in Miami. It cannot be immaterial that (a) the Washington Post Company owns both *Newsweek,* whose notes were demanded, and the Miami station WLBW-TV,* whose license was expiring; (b) Dean Burch, Republican Senator Barry Goldwater's campaign manager in the 1964 Presidential campaign, had just been named chairman of the FCC; and (c) the group *seeking* the license in Miami happened to be headed by W. Sloan McCrea, a Miami banker and partner of C. G. (Bebe) Rebozo, a close friend of President Nixon's.†

All of this is not to say, of course, that the Washington Post Company was actually intimidated by these pressures, but there can be no doubt about the complicity within the Nixon administration to exert those pressures of intimidation. Five months after the WLBW-TV license had expired, the FCC was still weighing the political ramifications of either renewing the license for the Washington Post Company or awarding the license to personal friends of the President of the United States. On June 24, 1970, the FCC finally decided (with chairman Burch and commissioner Nicholas Johnson dissenting) to set the case for a hearing which purportedly would form the basis for an eventual FCC decision. However, a spokesman at the FCC indicated that bureaucratic maneuvering could easily delay the hearing for as much as a year. In the meantime, there would be ample opportunity to test how much cooperation with the administration a television license in jeopardy and worth millions of dollars might buy.**

During its first two years, the Nixon administration clearly exerted pressures in an attempt to commandeer and throttle news gathering and dissemination for and by the public. But it also moved with equal alacrity to increase its own storehouse of information on the private and personal lives of individual

---

* The call letters were changed to WPLG-TV on March 16, 1970.
† *Advertising Age,* January 12, 1960, p. 83.
** In mid-August, 1970, the Rebozo group, Greater Miami Television, abandoned its challenge in exchange for the licensee's agreement to reimburse GMT the $60,000 already spent in efforts to acquire the license.

citizens. These moves occurred while the administration further tried to exercise control over the formal educational and intellectual machinery of the country. These were hallmarks of a burgeoning police state.

At Indiana University, for example, activist students feel the weight of government-financed spying on campus by fellow students paid to do so under the guise of scholarship aid. Under the heading " 'Big Brother' is Looking, Students Claim at IU," Patrick Siddons reported for the Louisville *Courier-Journal & Times:*

One of the students who has seen student-activities people at the meetings he had conducted is Rob Saunders, chairman of the campus chapter of the Committee to End the War in Vietnam, a group now reorganized under new leadership with a new name.

"You become aware of surveillance," said Saunders, "when you talk to Schreck (Thomas Schreck, dean of students). He will tell you, 'No, we're not policing you, but we can't be at all meetings at the same time, so we send others.' "

"That sounds polite," Saunders said. "But it's surveillance. And then paranoia becomes truth and realism: We are being watched."

. . . To Saunders, there are two types of college students—the uninvolved student who does little except attend class, and the student activist.

The former, he said, "have an unawareness of what they are supposed to do as citizens. They have not been exposed to varied and widespread opinions about anything."

He said such a student "comes to school for two things—to get an education and to go with girls. He blissfully follows the American dream of being a student."

Such a student, said Saunders, is not paranoid. "He believes the officer is his friend. It doesn't occur to him that an officer might enter his room, secretly drop a bag of marijuana on the floor, and then bust him for possession."*

In addition to the Big Brother pressure felt on the campuses, the so-called youth cultures—black and white—are convinced that the police establishment's heralded concern for drugs is

* *Courier-Journal & Times,* February 8, 1970, pp. 1, 12.

strictly a tactic designed to make the country "legally" into a police state. This view was rather poignantly, if basely, put by a writer in one of a plethora of underground newspapers which have sprung up with the rationale that the regular media are establishment-oriented.

Reported the Washington *Free Press:*

Junk is the pig in our community. It is the Man's weapon against us, disguised as a part of the underground. The biggest lie going about heroin is that it will kill you, that it will do you harm as an individual, that it is a risk. That's crap. It will kill our community, our life style, our revolution long before it will kill many single people.

The police, the city and federal governments, and Richard Nixon (the great priest-pig) are all doing their damndest to encourage the spread of heroin amongst us. If this seems fantastic, remember that it is common knowledge that the shit the cops confiscate in busts finds its way back onto the streets. There are lawyers with proof of this in their hands right now. The detectives and other pigs do not and could not sell dope so consistently without the knowledge of the chief of Police. The little pigs do it for bread, the chief allows it for other reasons entirely. He acts under the orders of the federal government, and is supposed to be implementing Nixon's push against "Drug Abuse."

But if Nixon is trying to end the smack traffic, then why do the pigs only bust kids? Every time I'm arrested for one diddly-shit thing or another the cops who interrogate me brag that no major shipment of any dope comes in without their knowing it. Of course they are far too stupid for that to be true, but the syndicate and the cops are so chummy (one hand buys the other) that at least some of the big shipments must be common knowledge on the force. Yet they seldom hit the big men—and we know that they know who "Mr. Big" is, but they aren't about to bust him.

This all means that Nixon and lesser officials are either bought off or have political reasons for wanting smack in our community. Probably both are true. The potential revolutionaries in the black community, the street people, have been completely torn apart from within by heroin. Those who would have been the heaviest mother-fuckers in town, instead of fighting cops or creating unrest, have been desperately killing and stealing from each other in order to feed their habits. This is how Harlem in New York City is controlled. This is how Watts and Philadelphia's black areas are kept impotent. And this is part of the way that the Haight-Ashbury was changed from one of the finest places in the country to go and free yourself into a ghetto where, in the first months of this year there were 24 murders, many more deaths from disease, girls raped, and freaks beaten. The Haight presented a real threat and was dealt with.

Besides destroying a society from within, smack also provides the police with the best of special informants and agents, people from the community itself. A narcotics detective catches some strung-out cat with dope on him, takes him to an office, gets all the names he can squeeze out of him, scares him to death, then lets him go, giving him a bag of scag for the road. The cat's had it. If he won't come across, he's busted. So he keeps giving names of people he doesn't like much. The cop has him set up deals, giving the kid on a string most of the dope from all the new busts. How many people have been busted with hundreds of dollars worth of dope on them, only to come into court and hear the cops say they found just enough for scientific analysis and conviction? . . .

This is not the first time in history that heroin or other opiates have been brought into a moving society in order to destroy it. The British did it to the Chinese during the last century. It is a myth that opium comes from China. England imported it from India and Turkey in order to string out the Chinese and bring them under the control of the Empire. The People there rebelled with the support of their Empress and were defeated in the "Opium Wars." The Chinese peoples' resentment culminated in the Boxer Rebellion which was crushed by nine imperial powers, including the U.S. It wasn't until the early 1950's that the drug traffic was finally driven out of China by Mao-tse Tung.

Recently the C.I.A. has been pushing grass in Cuba, hoping to open up new markets for Smack by turning the people on first to the good shit, then to heroin.

. . . Nixon and his little old ladies . . . are intentionally clouding the issue by acting "holy," since they are helping the syndicate to push it. They want to misdirect us into thinking the danger is only to our bodies, when, in fact, heroin destroys the spiritual vitality that exists between us.

There is no reason to try Smack, and less reason to get strung out on it. People who try to get you to do it once are pigs—worse than the uniformed kind—in our community. They will keep us from freeing ourselves, and we do have to be together in order to do it.

We can beat the scag dealers by not only refusing to score junk from them but also by not scoring our grass, acid, or mescaline from them. Don't buy anything from the cat who sells junk! Call him a pig. He's earned it and more. Freaks in Ann Arbor are already stomping their asses.

Right on!*

During the last five years of the decade, the gruesome fears of students and others in the intellectual community became widespread. Stated briefly, these fears reflected a rapidly declining confidence in the government to deal honestly, and in the political system to provide remedies for societal ills. Moreover, many activist students, in particular, tended to fear and mistrust governmental motives.

The distrust among white students was compounded among their black counterparts. Together, black and white students early in 1970 exhibited, among others, two basic pervasive fears: (1) The projected near-total exclusion of black students from traditional colleges and universities, accompanied by a white establishment take-over of the traditionally black colleges; and (2) the projected nazification of all campuses, including the tactic of declaring "emotionally ill" any and all students and teachers who dare demonstrate in protest of such national policies as pursuing the wars in Southeast Asia and the repression of black citizens.

In the three and a half centuries of black oppression in America, education and training have been essential to the oppressor's ability to control, and the denial of them has been necessary to black people's inability to defend themselves even in nonviolent struggles. Thus, the black campus and black students play a unique role in the current effort for survival. Those elements in the society still committed to black enslavement, illiteracy, or death are employing massive energy, plan-

* Washingon *Free Press,* Late August, 1969.

ning, and political acumen toward pacification, neutralization, or destruction of the black colleges. The rationale is simple: Black colleges and black students of white colleges have become an effective instrument for the development of black liberation personnel and strategies. The black campuses, in particular, have become "sanctuaries" of black liberation. Thus, they had to be invaded just as the "sanctuaries" in Cambodia required what President Nixon termed a cleaning out.

Those who tried to prevent the true education of black people during the century after the Civil War sought to make black schools inadequate and irrelevant by requiring that black schools be separate from white schools. Booker T. Washington, founder of Tuskegee Institute in 1881 and surely a widely misunderstood man, tried to warn America against that course, but whites in control assumed either that Dr. Washington was stupid or that, if he happened to be right, they could prevent the failure he indicated.

In one of his many epigrams, Dr. Washington warned: "You can't keep a man in a ditch without staying down there with him." Interpreted, this meant that whites could not keep black schools from teaching and liberating black children—could not deny them sanctuary—unless whites were willing to stay in a black school to guarantee its deprivation. This was much of the issue in the debates leading up to the Supreme Court's establishment of the "separate but equal" doctrine in the 1896 case of *Plessy v. Ferguson*. The "separate but equal" doctrine was acceptable to controlling whites because they felt that they could defeat the truism of Dr. Washington with one of two strategies:

—First, instead of staying at the ditch—that is, the black school—whites would go off to run great universities and eventually to the moon and appoint, instead, a black man to guard the ditch for them. This substitute guardian system worked effectively in many instances and over long periods of time, but it also failed just often enough for black campus sanctuaries to develop.

—The second scheme was simply to starve the black schools

financially and in all ways related to resources; then, even if the substitute guardian fell asleep, turned his head, or attempted to help his black brothers, he would lack the resources necessary to give that help. This scheme of denial also failed in ways imperceptible to the white controllers.

Both schemes failed often enough to produce, for example, Thurgood Marshall and his colleagues who revived the constitutional fights which culminated in the *Brown* decision of May 17, 1954—a reversal of the *Plessy* decision of 1896. In the meantime, black schools also produced the Freedom Riders, the Sit-Inners, Martin Luther King, Stokely Carmichael, and thousands of other bright and courageous young black men and women who are determined to see that black people are not illiterate, enslaved, or prematurely dead—except in the cause of freedom and justice for themselves and their people.

What, then, became the new scheme of those still committed to black disadvantage and oppression? Their new scheme basically involved a reevaluation of Dr. Washington's truism; they decided that the black educator had been right all along: to maintain control, the oppressor would have to return to the ditch, as it were. The new plan is either to extinguish or control black institutions which have become so instrumental in the black liberation struggle. The new schemes included:

—Wiping out of funds for compensatory education which have been helpful in establishing the Upward Bound programs under OEO and similar incentives for black students. This was largely achieved in President Nixon's veto of the fiscal 1971 HEW appropriation knocking out funds formerly used to bring black students to the universities under special enrichment programs that assisted their academic success. The propaganda for these cutbacks was Vice President Agnew's attacks during 1970 on the evils of open enrollments and his extolling some rights to education which he said belonged to the "natural aristocracy."

—Stringent new admissions requirements, such as those affirmed for the University of Maryland by the Maryland state legislature in 1968: a "C" average or better, *plus* a ranking in the upper half of the high school class for in-state (*i.e.*, Baltimore) students; for out-of-state students—*i.e.*, black students who commute from nearby Washington, D.C.—a "B" average or better, plus ranking in the upper half of the high school class. Such scores and rankings, of course, fall well within the influence of establishmentarians who historically have discouraged black academic achievement.

—Requirements secretly set in 1969–70 by HEW that would force black schools, even those maintained until recent years entirely without public support, to enroll white students up to 50 percent in order to get badly needed federal aid. Such a requirement automatically cuts by 50 percent the number of black students normally served by those black colleges. The HEW scheme was revealed by several dozen black college presidents who attended a communications seminar in Atlanta, February 16, 1970. By early 1970, ten state governors, all of them in states* with outstanding black colleges, had received letters from HEW signifying that desegregation of black colleges must proceed more rapidly. Although the letters also called for desegregation of white colleges, black college presidents at the Atlanta seminar said the desegregation pressure was being applied more strongly against them and that HEW officials, in their personal visits, set 50 percent as the desegregation goal of the black colleges. On August 6, 1969, HEW's civil rights director, Leon A. Panetta, explained to a group of returning Vietnam veterans: "To date, we have requested desegregation plans from five states—Louisiana, Arkansas, Pennsylvania, Maryland, and Mississippi—which will entail cooperative action between predominantly black and predominantly white colleges to eliminate the racial identifiability of these institutions."

—The drastic raising of fees, such as was done at Indiana University in 1969. This is coupled with the projected raising of entrance scores at both white and black colleges—a statistical reduction of black students.

* The states: Louisiana, Arkansas, Pennsylvania, Maryland, Mississippi, Virginia, North Carolina, Oklahoma, Florida, and Georgia.

—HEW's further requirement that black colleges hire white administrators to aid in the recruitment of white students. As one of the black presidents at the Atlanta seminar stated, "The white administrator would have to be of a caliber to replace the black president when the time comes." This, they said, was a requirement verbally passed on to them by HEW civil rights representatives.

—Grand merging schemes which place black schools under the domination of so-called "university systems"—a simple conversion to white control of what had been black institutions—if, indeed, the black schools remain open at all. On August 15, 1970, in a breakfast meeting with about 50 black citizens of Montgomery County, Maryland, incumbent Governor Marvin Mandel and Secretary of State Blair Lee, III, explained how HEW had given them orders, as Lee put it, "to eliminate the racial identifiability of the colleges" in Maryland.* So ordered in January, 1970, no compliance had been achieved because, since whites make up about 80 percent of the state's population, "if we made the college population conform with the population in the state, all of the colleges would be white," declared Lee, a Democratic candidate to become lieutenant governor. Lee further explained the danger by indicating what would happen to mainly black Morgan State College in Baltimore, which reverted from private to state control in 1939: "Morgan is a very good college, a monument to what the black academic community can do. I question whether we are doing any favors by making Morgan absolutely white." Governor Mandel, a Democratic candidate for reelection, after succeeding Vice President Agnew as Maryland governor, added that HEW officials had urged that all-black Coppin Teachers College in Baltimore either be "closed or merged with other schools." Little wonder, then, that on the day before—August 14— Howard University president, Dr. James Cheek, had said in an interview: "The black institutions are literally fighting for survival. The national policy is integration. The people under-

* Quotes from Mandel and Lee are taken from the author's notes of the meeting.

stand integration and execute integration by closing black institutions. That is a prime example of white racism."*

—The move, in 1970, by the Nixon administration to clear the way in court for the federal government to give tax exemptions to white private and parochial schools, with a corresponding drop in public support for public schools where black students are enrolled. These hastily drawn private schools came to be known in the South as "segregation academies," a clear indication of their purpose.

—Such plans as that revealed in President Nixon's 1970 Higher Education Message to Congress, plans which would begin to reduce black aspiration to the junior college or vocational school level. Reported *Newsweek:* "In a message to President Nixon last month, a group of black junior-college presidents expressed this anxiety: 'The "natural aristocracy" pronouncements of Vice President Agnew, together with your own emphasis . . . on vocational training, strongly indicates that your Administration views the community college as a ceiling for black educational achievement.' "†

Within a span of two weeks in the spring of 1970 after President Nixon announced the expansion of the Indochina war with a U.S. invasion of Cambodia, scores of campuses flared up in protest, with National Guardsmen fatally shooting four white students at Kent State University in Ohio and Mississippi policemen fatally shooting two black students in front of a girls' dormitory at Jackson State College. These actions had been punctuated by invectives against student demonstrators by President Nixon and Vice President Agnew, with the President himself calling student protestors "bums" in off-the-cuff remarks at the Pentagon. With the campuses virtually in open rebellion against the government, President Nixon called in a group of eight white university presidents for advice on May 7 and, following the meeting, appointed one of them, Dr. Alexander Heard, chancellor of Vanderbilt University in Nashville,

---

* Dr. Cheek's statement was made in an exclusive interview with the author.
† *Newsweek,* June 15, 1970, p. 70.

to become a special emissary between the White House and the college campuses.

Less than a week later, on the morning of May 13, the Washington *Post*'s Marquis Childs wrote a column headlined: "Young Anarchists Increase Risk of Nazi-Style Reaction in U.S." In it Childs drew the following parallel between the ascendency of Nazism in Germany and the current unrest in the United States:

In the early '30s the weak Weimar Republic in post-World War I Germany was beset by a variety of ills. The Communists were out to destroy this feeble government that had seen the middle class wiped out by ruinous inflation. They were aided and abetted by wild-eyed young revolutionaries who in manner and dress seem to have been definitely hippie types before hippie and Yippie came into vocabulary.

You could hear them in their cellar rendezvous predicting the revolution they were about to bring on. But, while they were boasting of what they would do on the barricades, the real revolution was being highly organize [*sic*] with the help of big money from German industrialists. Hitler and the Nazis were ready to take over. The young revolutionaries who did not flee the country were shortly in concentration camps or were tortured to death in Nazi prisons.

No one would for a moment suggest that this is where we are today. Yet ominous signs make plain the polarization that is taking place and the deep currents of prejudice and hatred below the surface.

Asked to comment on that portion of the Childs column and whether, in fact, he saw parallels, Chancellor Heard, a former political science professor, said: "I believe that there is obvious danger in the present situation, with deepening and hardening disunity in the society, and in some instances, among students themselves. The threats to intellectual freedom on campuses and in recent years come significantly from extremists who are unwilling to listen to points of view with which they disagree. That is a serious condition present on some campuses now, and in times of turmoil, there is always the danger of an extreme reaction in authoritarian terms."

But did he envision repressive laws being enacted against the campuses? "I'm hoping not," Heard said cautiously. "I'm hoping not."

Meanwhile, on May 14—immediately following the fatal shootings in the back of six youthful Blacks by police in Augusta, Georgia—an urgent letter was sent to President Nixon from the head of a year-old coalition of presidents of the 110 black colleges, Dr. Herman Branson, then president of Central State University in Wilberforce, Ohio. Branson wrote the President: "The National Association for Equal Opportunity in Higher Education is much concerned over the recent happenings in some American colleges and universities and in Augusta as they affect Negro young people: their prospects, their attitudes, their safety, and their continued dedication to the ideals of our society. The Association respectfully requests, therefore, an opportunity to present our concerns to you as soon as possible."*

At the same time, two other black college presidents—Dr. Cheek of Howard, the largest black university, and Dr. Hugh Gloster, head of Morehouse, whose alumni include the late Dr. King—were planning special all-campus programs devoted to the crisis of repression facing black students. Dr. Cheek also sent a letter to President Nixon supporting Dr. Branson's request for a meeting. These were the beginnings of historic pronouncements to President Nixon and to the nation from black colleges on the status of what they regarded as repression and genocide against black Americans.

On May 20, President Nixon received 15 representatives of the black college group in a meeting originally scheduled for forty-five minutes. It lasted two hours and ten minutes. Branson read to the President a statement protesting such "long-standing conditions" as "manifestations of racism in all areas of American life; inadequate educational opportunities . . . widespread

---

* Copies of this and related correspondence were obtained by the author in the course of personal interviews.

poverty and hunger . . . high unemployment rates among the
blacks and racial discrimination in employment; racial differen-
tials in law enforcement procedures; and deplorable housing
conditions."* The statement directly criticized "the policies and
practices of your own administration," and they told President
Nixon that his "Southern Strategy . . . leads to the conclusion
that blacks are dispensable," and that "your own failure to use
your great moral influence to bring the people of this great
nation together" had contributed to unrest and "repression."†

What the black educators told President Nixon had been a
long time coming, but their views were not at all new to persons
attuned to the campuses in general and to the black campuses in
particular. For the most part, President Nixon sat and listened
impassively to the black educators, but at one point, when it
seemed that the President should have shown some sympathy
for their concerns, Dr. Heard, who had helped arrange the
meeting, broke in and said to President Nixon: "What these
colleges want is for the government to say, 'We are with you.' If
this group cannot prevail and succeed then we are lost."**

Dr. Heard was not alone among white men who empathized
with the black educational problem. Months earlier, Dr. John
Munro, who left the Harvard faculty in 1967 to become director of freshman studies at all-black, private Miles College in
Birmingham, had said in an interview: "A college is more than
a college if it is a Black college. . . . People who are interested
in racial order must support Black institutions."‡ But in his
meeting with the black educators, President Nixon struck quite
a different note. He inquired about the "future"§ of black
colleges and universities and asked whether they should not be

---

* From a copy of the statement the black college presidents released to the
press after delivering it to President Nixon in the White House meeting.
   † *Ibid.*
   ** *Newsweek,* June 1, 1970, p. 25.
   ‡ Chicago *Daily Defender,* March 18, 1970, p. 10.
   § Except where otherwise indicated, quotes relating to the meeting of the
black college presidents with President Nixon are based on the author's coverage
of related press conferences and personal interviews with persons present in
the meeting.

"absorbed" by white universities. This infuriated the black educators and further convinced them of governmental schemes to take over the black schools.

At a press conference following the meeting, Dr. Branson was asked to summarize President Nixon's reaction to their pleas. Branson did so by repeating the statement Attorney General John Mitchell had given a group of civil rights leaders at the beginning of the Nixon administration: "Judge me by my deeds, and not by my words." This summarization of the President's attitude received an unusual chorus of taunts from the 50 news men and women jammed tightly into an improvised press room at the Washington Hilton hotel. "But haven't you already seen his deeds?" yelled reporters. "Isn't this where you came in?" "What's new about that?"

"You seem a lot less angry than black students," a white reporter challenged Branson.

"I've had a longer period of not *showing* my anger," Branson shot back unsmilingly. "I'm as angry as anyone."*

If the anger—and fear—of top-level black educators had ever been in doubt, it had come to full evidence by the end of their meeting with President Nixon. Asked for his reaction to the meeting, Howard president Cheek said: "The President heard from Black presidents on how we feel. It is important that it be known that we did not pull any punches." Cheek said they had told the President "about the direction in which the country is going . . . repression. . . . We were respectful, but we were quite firm." Asked whether he thought there were deliberate designs against Blacks, Cheek responded: "I do not think there is any deliberate, sinister plan *yet* devised to repress or liquidate any segment of the population. . . . But we are going into a period in which law and order are given priority at any price. I do not say that this is the policy of the President, but I do say that in the absence of vigorous advocacy to the contrary, this is the climate created."†

Although Dr. Cheek stopped just short of accusing the white

* *Ibid.*
† Washington *Post*, May 21, 1970, p. 1.

establishment of systematic, deliberate repression and genocide, the charge was made directly only one week later in the joint statement of four black private colleges in Atlanta. The four colleges—Morehouse, Clark, Morris Brown, and Spelman—which make up the Atlanta University Center, issued what they called a "considered response to the continuing theme of violence and terror directed against black people in the United States." Presented at a news conference by Atlanta University president Dr. Thomas D. Jarrett, the statement charged public comments, particularly by Vice President Agnew, with aiding and abetting the situation: "In the current era of systematic repression of black people, police authorities are wantonly shooting down black men, women, and children while elected officials, both national and local, by their outrageously false and inflammatory public utterances, fan the fires of hatred and bigotry."

As the *Christian Science Monitor* observed in reporting the Atlanta statement, "For a 'considered' statement from an institution which is notable for the decorum of its staff and students in the midst of racial turmoil, the May 27 document contains quite bitter charges." The statement said, in part:

Events of recent months suggest that a rapid intensification of the violence and terror directed against black people is occurring. Governmental authorities, nationally and locally, are using their powers to thwart the legitimate aspirations of black people, and this, in turn, precipitates greater violence directed against them [Blacks] by individuals and groups. . . .

In the face of an apparent incompatibility of black aspirations for political and economic liberation and the maintenance of a capitalistic system grounded in the doctrine of white supremacy, white governments and individuals have resorted to organized coercion to suppress the black community. *This is genocide.* [Emphasis added.] Victims of this oppression, wherever they may be, along with other men of goodwill must join together to halt this brutal assault.*

Morehouse president Gloster, whose students and faculty joined in the Atlanta statement, said that "after the incidents at

* *Christian Science Monitor,* June 4, 1970, p. 5.

Augusta and Jackson, students on our campus were angry, bitter and frustrated, and they looked for ways to protect themselves." He took bitter exception to the idea of black schools being absorbed by white ones. "If they aren't integrated," he said of the black schools, "the fault is with white students and the white establishment. Custom and prejudice keep whites out—not we."*

But Gloster, whose college is one of only four Phi Beta Kappa colleges in Georgia, regardless of race, is aware of a strong, new sentiment among black students regarding their schools. "Black students would not now welcome white students," he said, despite that fact that 20 of Morehouse's 1,000 students then were white. "I think it would be foolish for us to recruit white students now. Black students say they want these schools for themselves, to make them an instrument for the development of Black people."†

And yet that is a point of great fear on the part of many black students who have made a mission of keeping their schools black. "I came here," said Fisk University student body president William Owens, "because all my life I had heard that this was a great college. The best. I figured that if it was the best, it would be doing something for black people. It isn't. It's still trying to teach them to be white. All of its emphasis is on job security, with none of the black man's need for power."** It was that concern which drove Owens, the son of a North Carolina tobacco farmer, to lead a significant portion of the Fisk student body in revolt in the winter of 1969 to purge that sophisticated university in Nashville, rid it of whites, and make it a bastion of the black liberation struggle.

Founded in 1866 by the American Missionary Association and named for Union Army General Clifton B. Fisk, Fisk University is internationally famous and counts among its alumni some of the nation's most celebrated black scholars, including the late Dr. W. E. B. DuBois, historian John Hope

---

* Quotes are from author's personal interview with Dr. Gloster, May 20, 1970.
† *Ibid.*
** New York *Times Magazine,* June 7, 1970, p. 97.

Franklin, and novelist Frank Yerby. C. Eric Lincoln, '54, and
Cecil Eric Lincoln, '69, are father-and-son alumni who, writing
in the June 7, 1970, New York *Times Magazine,* described the
aborted attempt to make Fisk a black university:

> In what the students called a "Week of Reckoning" that began
> on Dec. 8, 1969, Owens, who was president of the student govern-
> ment, led a demonstration to have Fisk converted into a "black
> university"—which was defined as "an institution structured, con-
> trolled, and administered by black people . . . devoting itself to
> the cultural needs of the black community . . . identifying all
> black people as Africans . . . and that addresses itself completely
> to black liberation." The demands made on the Fisk administration
> included "the removal of all white departmental and administra-
> tive heads," and the severance of ties with "white institutions and
> foundations" not in sympathy with the notion of a black university.

The lack of success of the venture was no measure of the
sincerity of the mission. Seeing the establishment and preservation of black universities as related to black survival, Owens and
others continued the effort: "He subsequently became president of 'the student government in exile,' carrying on his efforts
from an off-campus apartment."

Such behavior and determination by Owens at Fisk and by
his white allies around the country were closely studied in
Washington by both the lawmaking and law enforcement establishments. During 1969, the shouts for "law and order" on the
nation's campuses came largely in response to the white student
rebellion against the country's two ongoing wars, the war against
Browns in Asia and against Blacks in America. White students
raised disturbances on virtually every sizable campus, pitting
their bodies against police lines set up to protect Dow Chemical
and CIA recruiters and against compulsory and academically
credited ROTC programs. They also protested the draft and
provided the bulk of the war protesters at the Democratic
National Convention in Chicago in the summer of 1968 and at
the massive Vietnam moratorium march in Washington in mid-
November, 1969.

Although there were hurried bills thrown into the hoppers both in the state legislatures across the country and in the Congress,* white college administrators did not crack down on the students hard enough and took umbrage at the police helicopter raids over Berkeley, for example. The feeling against "our own children," as Congressmen and columnists began lamenting, was running so high that some members of Congress who were self-proclaimed friends of students and education began to respond with bids for repressive measures.

Most notable in this latter group was the former Oregon school marm, Mrs. Edith Green, a spirited Democratic member of the House Education and Labor Committee, which has legislative jurisdiction over HEW's Office of Education. Mrs. Green, during the Ninetieth Congress, proposed several measures aimed essentially at cutting off scholarship aid to students who demonstrated illegally and, eventually, the cutting off of aid to the college itself if it failed to deal promptly and harshly with such students. She let it be known to her education constituents, some of her colleagues, and some reporters that she regarded her proposed measures mere pablum compared to the measures the Congress was likely to enact if the campus disrup-

* Reported the Associated Press in the Washington *Post,* June 2, 1969:

"State legislatures across the country are enacting laws to curb campus protests and punish the protesters.

"Laws already enacted and others under discussion carry such penalties as jail terms, fines or mandatory expulsion for students involved in campus disorders. Others ban loudspeakers and controversial visitors from campuses.

"Eight states have new laws designed to curb campus demonstrations, according to an Associated Press survey. They are Ohio, Maryland, Colorado, Idaho, Indiana, Minnesota, Oregon and North Dakota. Numerous others are considering measures of varying toughness to deal with the problem.

"Ohio led the pack, having passed in its last General Assembly a bill empowering boards of trustees to expel campus rioters.

"The Maryland Legislature voted to give college officials power to ban from campus anyone who isn't a student or has 'no apparent lawful business to pursue.' The Legislature also approved a bill—later vetoed by Gov. Marvin Mandel —allowing state Senators to cut off state scholarship money to campus rioters. Similar proposals are under consideration in Wisconsin, Connecticut, Michigan and Illinois.

"The Connecticut Legislature also will consider a measure requiring public universities and colleges to dismiss students who participate in violent or disruptive demonstration. . . ."

tions continued. She said, in fact, that her measures, if enacted, stood a chance of staving off the more repressive measures while helping restore order on campus. Through weeks of these debates it seemed impossible that measures more repressive than those already introduced might, in fact, be in the offing. However, on February 3, 1969, an ominous picture began to take shape with the testimony of Dr. S. I. Hayakawa, the semanticist of San Francisco State College, before Mrs. Green's Special Subcommittee on Education. Dr. Hayakawa, who had just been appointed acting president of the college, was one of a parade of witnesses called before the subcommittee, but it was his appearance that first attracted standing-room-only crowds of students and initiated new fears of repression. The new view began to fall into focus in this exchange between Hayakawa and Representative Roman Pucinski, a Chicago Democrat and member of the subcommittee:

Pucinski: I want to congratulate you, Doctor, for your excellent testimony this morning. Over the weekend, one of your former colleagues, Dr. Bruno Bettelheim, who is recognized all over the world as an outstanding educator and psychologist, said that "Student demonstrators are sick and in need of psychiatric treatment." I am reading from *The Chicago Tribune* [Feb. 2, 1969]: "Prof. Bettelheim, who was in Germany during the 1930's and the rise of Adolf Hitler and fascism, said the demonstrations at the U. of C. [University of Chicago] remind him of the student unrests in that country. 'I saw the same thing in German universities which spearheaded the fascist government which led to the rule of Hitler,' he said. 'More disturbing than the minorities who are trying to take over the universities is the attitude of the nation which promotes it.' " Would you agree with Dr. Bettelheim that a lot of these young people are sick and in need of psychiatric attention?

Hayakawa: Dr. Bettelheim is a psychiatrist and he is better able than I am to diagnose actual illness. If I were to say they are sick it would simply be calling them names. I haven't got the scientific background to say that. . . .

Pucinski: Dr. Bettelheim also said that some of the demonstrators are paranoics but he said that there are no more paranoics around than before but now the mass media gives them more attention. Have you had any experience with that sort of a phenomenon?

Hayakawa: Well, perhaps this is right. I keep maintaining that the mass media, especially television, is a branch of show business and one of the functions of their news programs, in addition to informing, is to entertain and attract attention. Maybe paranoics are more interesting as television material than the rest of us.

Pucinski: I have a high regard for Dr. Bettelheim, and I think we can all agree he is a world renowned expert. [Reading again from the *Tribune*] "He said the leaders of the demonstrators are 'very rational people who are trying to foment a revolution. They use the mass of irrational students to gain this end,' he said. 'What they want is Maoism, nihilism, and anarchy.' He said he hoped that the university administration will not try to use force to clear the six-story administration building of the protesters who have taken it over and held it since Thursday noon. 'I don't believe in violence and I don't want to make martyrs out of anyone,' he said." This, of course, raises some serious questions. If, indeed, we had been treating those demonstrations as an act of a group of young people who are practicing dissent and ignoring the fact that they are probably, or do have in their midst, people that need some psychiatric attention, perhaps we ought to start giving some thought to providing either funds for behavior clinics or some way of getting at this whole picture of mental health. I have often felt that this is a problem. Now, what do you think?

Hayakawa: I don't know to what degree colleges should be responsible for the mental health of their students. We obviously have student health clinics and counsellor services which have something to do with mental health problems, but how can you, in a situation like this, diagnose individuals out of a picket line and say, "You need mental therapy, but this one doesn't?" How do you do this?

Pucinski: Years ago it was a common practice for judges, when somebody came before them for violation of the law, and if there was some reason to believe that this person was suffering from some form of emotional disturbance, the judge, before imposing sentence, would first assign the defendant to a behavioral clinic and a report would be made to the judge who then could very intelligently approach the subject. Obviously if the person was emotionally disturbed you are not going to treat him as a criminal. You are going to treat him as a sick person and try to provide some help for him. Now, I am wondering how many of these young students who participate in these riots have ever been subjected to a behavioral clinic study?

Hayakawa: I don't know, but an awful lot of them look as if they needed it.*

Whereas Dr. Hayakawa, the semanticist, was willing but short on credentials for building a case of emotional sickness among the student protesters, Dr. Bettelheim's enthusiasm and psychiatric credentials were made to order. Pucinski asked for and received unanimous consent of the subcommittee to hear the testimony of Dr. Bettelheim, who appeared before the subcommittee on March 20, 1969. In a brilliantly designed paper, Dr. Bettelheim told an impressed subcommittee:

Now of course, history does not repeat itself. There are vast differences, but nevertheless, some of the similarities between the two situations are very striking.

The German student rebels were of the extreme right, where ours presently are of the extreme left but, what is parallel is the determination to bring down the establishment.

In Germany, the philosophy which gained a mass following was racist, and directed against a discriminated minority, the Jews, while here the radical students intend to help a discriminated minority, which is an important difference, but it does not change the parallels that universities were forced to make decisions in respect to the race of students and professors rather than the basis of a disregard of any racial origin.

For example, the German universities began to cave in when students coerced the faculties to appoint professorships in race sciences; that is, professorships teaching the special aspects, merits, achievements of one race versus another, rather than concentrating in their teaching on contributions to knowledge, whatever the origin, of the person who made the contribution. . . .

In my opinion there are today far too many students in the

* *Campus Unrest.* Hearings Before the Special Subcommittee on Education of the Committee on Education and Labor, House of Representatives, Ninety-first Congress, First Session, February 3, 1969, pp. 81–82.

colleges who essentially have no business to be there. Some are there to evade the draft, many others out of a vague idea that it will help them to find better paying jobs, though they do not know what jobs they really want.

And again, all too many go to college because they do not know what better to do and because society and the schools expect it of them.

Their deep dissatisfaction with themselves and their inner confusion is projected against the institution of the college first, and against all institutions of society secondarily which are blamed for their own inner weaknesses. . . .

I think many of the rebellious students are essentially guilt-ridden individuals, too. They feel terribly guilty about all the advantages they have. And there is also the guilt of their exemption from the draft, which I believe is a serious guilt. They cannot bear to live with this guilt, so they try to destroy society, or certain of its institutions, rather than to live with their own inner guilt, because they have it so good. . . .

It is their hatred of society that makes it so easy for the small group of militant leaders to make common cause with another small group that provides temporary leadership for some of the rebellions. These latter are outright paranoid individuals. I do not believe the number of paranoids among students is greater than their number would be in any comparable group of the population.

They become dangerous again because of their high intelligence which permits them to hide more successfully the degree of their disturbance from the nonexperts.

Having worked professionally with some of them for years, I know that student revolt permits them to act out their paranoia to a degree that no other position in society would permit them.

How understandable, then, that all paranoids who can, do flock into the ranks of these militants. Unfortunately most nonexperts do not know how persuasive paranoics can be, at least for a time, until they are recognized as such.

The persuasiveness of a Hitler and a Stalin is now recognized as the consequence of their own paranoia, and their unconscious appeal to the vague paranoid tendencies that can be found among the immature and disgruntled.

I have no doubt that the ranks of the militants contain some would-be Hitlers and Stalins, hence again their dangerousness. . . .

Thus, being one of the faculty, I believe efforts should be concentrated on strengthening the will of the colleges and universities to resist disruption and coercion. If we succeed in doing so I believe we shall have little need to take recourse to punitive measures; beyond setting into practice that those who do wish to have no part of our universities should have their will: they should not be permitted to be, live, and work at a place they hate. Not as a punishment, I believe, but because to remain at a place they hate and despise serves no purpose and is detrimental to their emotional well-being.*

The sum total of Dr. Bettelheim's contribution was to show student dissenters as the real molders of nazification of America, as being emotionally sick in a way that requires their being put away to protect society and the student dissenters. And, finally, he lectured Congress on its responsibility to deal with these young neo-Nazis, as it were.

When Dr. Bettelheim had finished, Pucinski was exultant. He sat back in his chair and savored the moment while Dr. Bettelheim treated reporters and others swarming about him to some additional comments. Pucinski let the other admirers have at the guest for a time, then he came down and rescued the clean-headed psychiatrist and escorted him to an elevator, literally massaging him in praise and thanks.

Back in his office, Pucinski, a former news reporter in Chicago, was delighted that a working newsman (the author) wanted a copy of the *Tribune* article and had shown a genuine interest in Dr. Bettelheim. Asked what he *really* had in mind and why it was so important to him to have Dr. Bettelheim's testimony, Pucinski was glad to respond.

"You know," he said, with an appreciative gleam in his eyes, "you're the first reporter to ask me that, so come on in and I'll tell you." Entering his inner sanctum and having instructed his secretary for a few undisturbed minutes, he closed the door and sploshed down in a big, soft, high-backed chair behind his desk.

"You see," he explained, "this is very serious, and that's why

* *Ibid.*, March 20, 1969, pp. 258–69.

I'm glad you asked me about this. I'm not against the students, you understand. I'm for them and the rest of the people, too. I just think many of them are sick and need help.

"You know," he went on, holding up his hand to stop a question, "I actually sympathize with the young people today. I *do*. They are under an awful lot of pressure. More pressure than we ever faced. Look at it, they are concerned with the draft, but also with the pressures of education in a highly competitive society. Making the grades alone is a tough deal for a kid in these good schools today. They've just got all kinds of pressures of today's society, and I'm not really surprised that some of them crack up. A lot of them really are cracked, you know!"

"Perhaps," the reporter granted. "But these hearings are supposed to result in some kind of legislation. What have you got in mind?"

He held up his hand again, this time to delay that question for a moment more. "Now just think about it," he said. "You take just the other day I saw where some of those kids were going around on the street buck naked. Now"—he gave an exasperated laugh—"you know that they've *got* to be sick, and they need help—for their own good as well as for the good of others."

"So, what do you plan to do?" he was asked.

"Well, I'll tell you," he said in a newly confidential tone. "I'm going to introduce a bill that will put this in the hands of the proper people—the courts and the mental institutions." Pucinski went on to explain that his bill would provide new funds to pay for a psychiatrist on each campus, a person competent to judge on the sanity of protesters and, upon the concurrence of a court judge, such persons would be put away "until they can think straight."

Before the reporter could phrase another question, Pucinski rose from his chair and walked from behind the desk, giving additional emphasis to his next point. "Now, I don't blame these poor kids for all their trouble," he said. "You see, as witnesses have told the subcommittee, a lot of this wouldn't go on if the kids weren't encouraged by their teachers. Their own teachers. So, my bill would not cover just the illness of the kids; it would also cover any teachers who either encouraged them, or who didn't exercise reasonable authority in *dis*couraging them."

When would his bill be introduced, and how much support did he expect to get for it?

Pucinski held back on this piece of strategy, but hinted that he would first give the subcommittee chairman, Mrs. Green, a chance to have her bill passed and that its passage might even make his bill's chances better. As for support, he smiled and with a wink indicated that he would have the votes when the time came. Mrs. Green's bill was staunchly opposed in the full Education and Labor Committee and was beaten back in a tricky maneuver that sought passage on the floor of the House without committee approval. Pucinski's bill was not introduced at all during the Ninety-first Congress, 1969–70.

President Nixon vetoed the $20-billion HEW appropriation in January, 1970. The official reason was that the President opposed the $4-billion portion designated for impacted aid— money paid to communities (many of them rich, such as Montgomery County, Maryland, and Fairfax County, Virginia) where federal employees live and/or work. With considerable merit, the White House argued that a cutback in such funds would end an inequity against poorer communities. But some critics of the veto saw it as a move by the President to put his "stamp" on the nation's education system. One disgruntled but well-informed source high in the Office of Education explained that the administration's withholding of funds from the schools would bring state and local education officers and college administrators begging at the door of the administration, asking what they could do to get their funds restored.

"At that point," the source said, "the administration will state its price, and the price will be steep." The price, he said, would include lobbying support for passage for such bills as college officials had opposed but which Pucinski and others favored. Added the source: caught in a serious financial dilemma, the educational bureaucracy would be forced to give at least tacit approval. "One final point," the source said,

"[Education commissioner] Jim Allen is not the kind of guy to want to do this, so he won't be around when things start getting rough."

As the source predicted, by mid-year 1970, things had begun to get rough, and liberal education commissioner James E. Allen, Jr., was fired on June 10 for his outspoken opposition to Nixon administration policies on the war in Indochina and education back home. In mid-August, President Nixon vetoed the $4.4-billion appropriation for the U.S. Office of Education,* and although Congress later overrode the veto, such policies were already being felt down in the education bureaucracy. On the day following the veto, presidents Lloyd H. Elliott and Robert J. Henle of George Washington and Georgetown universities, respectively, told the House District Committee that their medical schools would either have to close or be offered to the federal government unless they received emergency financial support.†

During the 1969 hearings before the Special Subcommittee on Education, Robert S. Powell, Jr., president of the U.S. National Student Association, had tried to dissuade Congress and the federal government generally from giving in to fear legislation and repression and further pointed to the basis for the white student fears and defense of their black counterparts:

Let me begin by saying that I am acutely aware of the position that I am in, and of the repressive sentiment that you and other Congressmen and Senators receive daily in your mail. I can appreciate the pressures that your representative position puts you in as you attempt to respond to strong constituent pressures to crack down on student dissent.

Understandably, public officials, young Members of Congress, have frequently reacted to recent events on campus out of fear. I hope this morning to put your fear in perspective so that this and other public bodies might respond constructively to the very serious problems higher education is confronting today. . . .

If you will learn from the turmoil on the campus, you should

* New York *Times*, August 12, 1970, p. 1.
† Washington *Post*, August 13, 1970, p. 1.

understand that millions of middle-class youths who have shared rather richly in our touted affluence not only do not prize it, but in fact consider it a positive handicap in the search for personal development and national integrity.

And you should understand that the black and brown population of this generation of American youth who, because of the operational racism of our economic, political, and educational institutions, have been systemically denied any of the benefits of our higher education, are angry because they have been frauded, cheated, and ignored by those who make higher education policy. The only doors that are open to even a small percentage of black and brown students lead them to grossly inadequate white-dominated segregated educational facilities, such as the black college system in the South, and they are now saying in long overdue tones of anger, that we must do better. . . .

The war in Vietnam goes on, and the universities continue to comply mindlessly with it in every possible aspect—research, recruitment, training, and cooperation with the draft. The black man in America still struggles to be free, yet the university still chooses to be part of the problem, with its indifference and lack of commitment, rather than choosing to be part of the solution, which it could so courageously choose to be. . . .

Let me say frankly that this challenge will not be diminished by attempts to suppress us with punitive measures. Pleas for law and order serve only to deepen the growing divisions that immobilize us, and can never replace a working commitment for change on the silence those who are bringing it to your attention.

As I emphasized at the outset, the student revolt now sweeping our campuses is an indication of a deep and severe crisis in American higher education, bound to so many of the tragic injustices and inequities in our national life. That crisis will not go away even if you manage to silence those who are bringing it to your attention.*

In the spring of 1969, a number of students at Missouri's mainly black Lincoln University at Jefferson City presented a list of demands to the university administration: "We demand that all dormitories be exterminated more frequently . . . more

* *Campus Unrest*, Hearings before the Special Subcommittee on Education of the Committee on Education and Labor, House of Representatives, Ninety-first Congress, First Session, March 26, 1969, pp. 500–5.

frequent checks and repairs of washrooms and related facilities
. . . No intimidation of athletes for chosen hair styles . . . an
extension of practice hours for music students in the Fine Arts
Building . . ."*

Almost instantly, dozens of armed and helmeted guards descended on the Union Building. Students not involved in the sit-
in became frightened and angered at the storming by police.
Interference ensued. Students were beaten. Fires broke out.
Reported sniping followed. Arrests were made.

In a front-page editorial, "Madness in Missouri," the St.
Louis *Sentinel* warned:

> We see America today in the same posture as Germany stood in
> the early thirties. Its social ills at that time gave impetus to extreme
> dissenters. This resulted in a counter mood of middle class resis-
> tance and the ultimate development of a repressive society—a
> society, under Hitler, stifled all dissent and contained in a vise-like
> grip the revolutionaries as well as the comfortable middle classers
> who suffered it to happen. It is because we drift toward this
> dreadful possibility that it behooves these idealistic young minds in
> their Quixotic quest for a Utopian world to ponder as they reach a
> point of tolerance.†

The American people were already gripped in a police vise
far tighter than most would believe. For example, barring
some rare snafu back at the Pentagon in Washington, D.C., a
dossier was promptly filed on every Lincoln student identified
in any way with the sit-in. These dossiers became a part of a
massive computerized file—a pickup list—covering individuals
in 150 cities throughout the nation. In the event of a general
"domestic crisis," giant computers would spit out the names of
such persons to be picked up and detained or otherwise handled
in a manner that is among the best-kept secrets of the Pentagon.

This new Pentagon facility was ordered set up within a
month after President Nixon's inauguration. At a cost of $2.7
million, it has as its closest parallel the logistical arrangement

* St. Louis *Sentinel,* May 24, 1969, p. 1.
† *Ibid.*

for the Strategic Air Command (SAC), whose responsibility it is to retaliate—destroy a foreign enemy—should the United States ever be attacked from the outside. It is both shocking and significant that, with rarest exception, the establishment of this "domestic crisis" facility raised few eyebrows and there was no public protest, no outcry whatever when it was routinely reported in 1969. One of the more complete reports was this one in the July 9, 1969, issue of the New York *Times:*

The United States Army opened to newsmen today a $2.7-million operations center built beneath a Pentagon parking lot.

The center contains 40,000 square feet of space and is topped by five feet of earth fill, concrete and asphalt. It is directly under the Pentagon mall entrance, where 100,000 peace marchers demonstrated in 1967.

The structure was converted from a storage area to provide greater space for the soldiers and civilians who work in the crisis management headquarters. Work has been under way since February, Army spokesmen said, and is still not complete.

During the transition stage, the old operations center on the Pentagon's second level will continue to carry out some functions. Three other military services maintain facilities that are alike in purpose. In addition, the Pentagon houses a joint operations center for all military services.

The new Army facility consists of two rooms for computers and computer processors, a high-ceilinged situation room whose walls are lined with maps and screens, and a control room that is the heart of the Army's worldwide communications network. A telephone booth that provides a "safe" link to the White House stands in one corner.

A glass-enclosed "command balcony" has been set up for military commanders. From this second-level area, they can watch the development of a crisis as it unfolds on the maps across the room. The balcony is designed to monitor the center's activities.

Computer data can be fed into the four screens in the situation room, and they can be used to brief military commanders in the viewing balcony.

The computers are fed from a mass storage drum that contains 130 million characters, or bits of information. The ability to gather and transmit all this information rapidly is a key to the successful function of the center.

If computer operations are overloaded, a back-up system is used for partial secondary support. An Army spokesman called this a "fail-soft" system, because "it means we don't fail completely."

The facility includes the Pentagon's civil disturbance directorate, which is the command center of Federal involvement in the monitoring or control of riots.

An Army spokesman said "information packets" were available on 150 cities across the country that may have disorders. The directorate is prepared, he said, to monitor up to 25 such disorders simultaneously and to direct Federal support to local law enforcement agencies if ordered by the President.

The packets contain vital information on the cities. They were selected because they have "a history of possible disturbances occurring in them," according to the Army.

No police state would be complete without surveillance, tenacious surveillance to the point of prying into the far recesses of the personal lives of its subjects. Technology and intensity are the ingredients added to the U.S. police establishment's domestic spying which hastened the imminence of a police state by 1970.

On June 28, 1970, the New York *Times* carried a lengthy page-one story out of Washington by Ben A. Franklin detailing some of the ways in which this computer technology was already being used and what little was being done to counter it:

The police, security and military intelligence agencies of the Federal Government are quietly compiling a mass of computerized and microfilmed files here on hundreds of thousands of law abiding yet suspect Americans. . . .

The leader of a Negro protest against welfare regulations in St. Louis, for example, is the subject of a teletyped "spot report" to Washington shared by as many as half a dozen Government intelligence gathering groups.

The name of a college professor who finds himself unwittingly, even innocently, arrested for disorderly conduct in a police roundup at a peace rally in San Francisco goes into the data file.

A student fight in an Alabama high school is recorded—if it is interracial.

Government officials insist that the information is needed and is handled discreetly to protect the innocent, the minor offender and the repentant.

The critics—including the Washington chapter of the American Civil Liberties Union and Representative Cornelius E. Gallagher, Democrat of New Jersey—charge that the system is an invasion of privacy and a potential infringement of First Amendment rights to free speech and assembly.

Senator Ervin, a conservative, a student of the Constitution, a former judge of the North Carolina Superior Court, and the chairman of the Senate Subcommittee on Constitutional Rights, says that the advent of computer technology in Government file keeping is pushing the country toward "a mass surveillance system unprecedented in American history."

In a recent series of Senate speeches, Mr. Ervin said that the danger was being masked by a failure of Americans to understand "the computer mystique" and by the undoubted sincerity and desire for "efficiency" of the data bank operators and planners.

The Government is gathering information on its citizens at the following places:

¶A Secret Service computer, one of the newest and most sophisticated in Government. In its memory the names and dossiers of activists, "malcontents," persistent seekers of redress, and those who would "embarrass" the President or other Government leaders are filed with those of potential assassins and persons convicted of "threats against the President."

¶A data bank compiled by the Justice Department's civil disturbance group. It produces a weekly printout of national tension points on racial, class and political issues and the individuals and groups involved in them. Intelligence on peace rallies, welfare protests and the like provide the "data base" against which the computer measures the mood of the nation and the militancy of its citizens. Judgments are made; subjects are listed as "radical" or "moderate."

¶A huge file of microfilmed intelligence reports, clippings and other materials on civilian activity maintained by the Army's Counterintelligence Analysis Division in Alexandria, Va. Its purpose is to help prepare deployment estimates for troop commands on alert to respond to civil disturbances in 25 American cities. Army intelligence was ordered earlier this year to destroy a larger data bank and to stop assigning agents to "penetrate" peace groups and civil rights organizations. But complaints persist that both are being continued. Civilian officials of the Army say they "assume" they are not. . . .

"The Warren Commission and the riots legitimatized procedures which, I grant you, would have been unthinkable and, frankly, unattainable from Congress in a different climate," one official said. "There are obvious questions and dangers in what we are doing but I think events have shown it is legitimate." The official declined to be quoted by name.

Senator Ervin contends that in the "total recall," the permanence, the speed and the interconnection of Government data files there "rests a potential for control and intimidation that is alien to our form of Government and foreign to a society of free men." The integration of data banks, mixing criminal with noncriminal files, is already underway, according to his subcommittee.

Although he was generally ignored, both by the press and individual citizens, Senator Ervin has repeatedly protested the nation's abdication of individual rights to privacy. His was a rare outcry. In a speech before the Senate on November 10, 1969, Senator Ervin listed a number of what he regarded as unconstitutional abuses of computer invasion of individual privacy, with the entire federal establishment becoming infested with spying responsibilities.

At one point, Senator Ervin told his colleagues:

The social security number once was treated as a private matter, sacred to the individual. That was in the 1930's before the computer age. Now, with this number on almost every Government form, and every private questionnaire, no man can be lost. And this is reassuring. But, similarly, no man can ever again be alone. And this is despairing.

The new plan of the Health, Education, and Welfare Department to tie in a national welfare program to the social security system raises specters of surveillance and privacy invasion on a scale never before experienced. Only time will tell what the bureaucrats will do with this. Sadly enough, it will be the poor, the sick, the unsophisticated, the inexperienced, who will have to fight the computers in this program.

It is not just the chance of wrong or one-sided information being fed into vast Government and private computer systems that should give us cause to worry.

The increased use of computers makes it cheaper and vastly more simple for Government as well as private businesses to collect and store information about people for reasons that would give us serious pause.

There is, for instance, the Secret Service's well-meaning program to keep track of people who might harm the President or other public officials. But consider this Secret Service memorandum telling employees of Federal agencies to supply—

Information about individuals who "make oral or written statements about high Government officials in the following categories": Threatening statements; irrational statements; and abusive statements.

Information on professional gate crashers.

Information on persons who insist upon personally contacting high Government officials for the purpose of redress of imaginary grievances, and so forth.

Information pertaining to a threat, plan, or attempt by an individual, a group, or an organization to physically harm or embarrass the persons protected by the U.S. Secret Service, or any other high U.S. Government official at home or abroad.

Many people, with complete faith in their Government, believe that the place to start with a complaint is with the President or Vice President. Yet some of these people who write a strong letter will never know they have been fed into yet another Government data system. Are these records now to be part of standard employment checks for suitability and security clearances?*

Senator Ervin's further concerns about the 1970 census, while phrased more gently, were supportive of the concerns of the black militant at Indiana University who saw the most ominous motives in this police state prying. The suspicious militant felt sure that the excessive and otherwise extraneous data collected

* *Congressional Record,* November 10, 1969, p. S-13981.

would be used to guide police in their predawn raids and guerrilla wars against the black ghetto.

On the floor of the Senate, Senator Ervin continued:

It has been estimated that by 1970 the total statistical budget of the Federal Government will probably exceed $200 million. If complaints to Congress are any indication, the impact on individual rights of these programs is proving devastating.

The decennial census questionnaire, with civil and criminal penalties, is one example of this, with such questions as:

How much rent do you pay?

Do you live in a one-family house?

Do you use gas?

If a woman, how many babies have you had? Not counting still births.

How much did you earn in 1967?

If married more than once, how did your first marriage end?

Do you have a clothes dryer?

Do you have a telephone, if so, what is the number?

Do you have a home food freezer?

Do you own a second home?

Does your TV set have UHF?

Do you have a flush toilet?

Do you have a bathtub or shower?

Another example of this computer prying occurred last spring when the Constitutional Rights Subcommittee began receiving complaints from elderly, disabled, or retired people in all walks of life about a 15-page form sent out by the Census Bureau. It asked questions such as:

What have you been doing in the last 4 weeks to find work?

Taking things all together, would you say you are very happy, pretty happy, or not too happy these days?

Do you have any artificial dentures?

Do you—or your spouse—see or telephone your parents as often as once a week?

What is the total number of gifts that you give to individuals per year?

How many different newspapers do you receive and buy regularly?

About how often do you go to a barber shop or beauty salon?
What were you doing most of last week?*

Why does a federal computer need to know whether you live
in a single-family dwelling or an apartment? And what difference does it make whether you would get cold by turning off
the gas or the electricity?

Plenty.

Census officials explained a few months before the 1970 forms
went out that there would be three different forms to be filled
out by different groups of citizens. A so-called "random sample"
of 20 percent sought the most complete data of all—such as
whether you normally entered your dwelling by the front, side,
or rear door. This "random" percentage also happened to be
approximately the percentage of collective nonwhite minorities
in the nation. The 80 percent form contained only 28 questions, while the "random" form, sent heavily to ghettos and to
Blacks wherever they lived, contained roughly 80 questions.

Even without the 1970 data, the nation's omnipresent police
web already had established the penultimate in surveillance
even on the private and *legal* activities of individual Americans.
Writing in the January, 1970, issue of the Washington
*Monthly,* Christopher Pyle, a former captain in Army Intelligence, reported copiously on the Army's establishment of a
national computerized data bank:

> For the past four years, the U.S. Army has been closely watching
> civilian political activity within the United States. Nearly 1,000
> plainclothes investigators, working out of some 300 offices from coast
> to coast, keep track of political protests of all kinds—from Klan
> rallies in North Carolina to anti-war speeches at Harvard. This
> aspect of their duties is unknown to most Americans. They know
> these soldier-agents, if at all, only as personable young men whose
> principal function is to conduct background investigations of per-
> sons being considered for security clearances.
>
> When this program began in the summer of 1965, its purpose was
> to provide early warning of civil disorders which the Army might be

* *Ibid.*

called upon to quell. In the summer of 1967, however, its scope widened to include the political beliefs and actions of individuals and organizations active in the civil rights, white supremacy, black power, and anti-war movements. Today, the Army maintains files on the membership, ideology, programs, and practices of virtually every activist political group in the country. These include not only such violence-prone organizations as the Minutemen and the Revolutionary Action Movement (RAM), but such nonviolent groups as the Southern Christian Leadership Conference, Clergy and Laymen United Against the War in Vietnam, the American Civil Liberties Union, Women Strike for Peace, and the National Association for the Advancement of Colored People.

The Army obtains most of its information about protest politics from the files of municipal and state police departments and of the FBI. In addition, its agents subscribe to hundreds of local and campus newspapers, monitor police and FBI radio broadcasts, and, on occasion, conduct their own undercover operations. Military undercover agents have posed as press photographers covering anti-war demonstrations, as students on college campuses, and as "residents" of Resurrection City. They have even recruited civilians into their service—sometimes for pay but more often through appeals to patriotism. For example, when Columbia University gave its students the option of closing their academic records to routine inspection by government investigators, the 108th Military Intelligence Group in Manhattan quietly persuaded an employee of the Registrar's Office to disclose information from the closed files on the sly. . . .

To assure prompt communication of these reports, the Army distributes them over a nationwide wire service. Completed in the fall of 1967, this teletype network gives every major troop command in the United States daily and weekly reports on virtually all political protests occurring anywhere in the nation. . . .

Because the Investigative Records Repository is one of the federal government's main libraries for security clearance information, access to its personality files is not limited to Army officials. Other federal agencies now drawing on its memory banks include the FBI, the Secret Service, the Passport Office, the Central Intelligence Agency, the National Security Agency, the Civil Service Commission, the Atomic Energy Commission, the Defense Intelligence Agency, the Navy, and the Air Force. In short, the personality files are likely to be made available to any federal agency that issues security clearances, conducts investigations, or enforces laws. . . .

Daily recipients of this raw intelligence include all of the Army's military intelligence groups within the United States, riot-control units on stand-by alert, and the Army Operations Center at the Pentagon. The Operations Center, sometimes called the "domestic war room," is a green-carpeted suite of connecting offices, conference rooms, and cubicles from which Army and Defense Department officials dispatch and coordinate troops that deal with riots, earthquakes, and other disasters. . . .

There is no question that the Army must have domestic intelligence. In order to assist civilian authorities, it needs maps and descriptions of potential riot or disaster areas, as well as early warning of incidents likely to provoke mass violence. . . .

The Army needs this kind of information so that it can fulfill long-established, legitimate responsibilities. But must it also distribute and store detailed reports on the political beliefs and actions of individuals and groups?

Officials of the Intelligence Command believe that they must. Without detailed knowledge of community "infrastructure," they argue, riot-control troops would not be able to enforce curfews or quell violence. To support this contention, they cite the usefulness of personality files and blacklists in breaking up guerrilla organizations in Malaya and South Vietnam. One early proponent of this view was the Army's Assistant Chief of Staff for Intelligence during 1967–1968, Major General William P. Yarborough. At the height of the Detroit riots of 1967 he instructed his staff in the domestic war room: "Men, get out your counterinsurgency manuals. We have an insurgency on our hands."

Of course, they did not. As one war-room officer who attempted to carry out the General's order later observed: "There we were, plotting power plants, radio stations, and armories on the situation maps when we should have been locating the liquor and color-television stores instead." A year later the National Advisory Commission on Civil Disorders reached a similar conclusion about the motives of ghetto rioters. "The urban disorders of the summer of 1967," it declared unequivocally, "were not caused by, nor were they the consequence of, any organized plan or 'conspiracy.'" After reviewing all of the federal government's intelligence reports on 23 riots, it found "no evidence that all or any of the disorders or the incidents that led to them were planned or directed by any organizations or groups, international, national, or local."*

The Pyle report was especially disturbing to Congressman Cornelius E. Gallagher, a New Jersey Democrat, who is chairman of the House Special Inquiry on Invasion of Privacy. Although Congressional use of the right of inquiry into such security-related aspects of running the government has been meager at best, Congressman Gallagher quickly and sternly tackled the issues raised by Pyle. On January 6, 1970, Gallagher wrote Army Secretary Stanley Resor that he was particularly concerned at Pyle's report that the plethora of data collected on civilians by the Army was to be "stored in, and disseminated from, a computerized data bank at Ft. Holabird, Baltimore, Maryland," and pointed out that such a data center would be in violation of agreements established in 1968. Gallagher wrote further that if Pyle had accurately described the activity, "it would represent an unconscionable and unconstitutional threat to the privacy and spontaneity of Americans."†

A month later, in lieu of a reply to *specific* assurances sought by Gallagher, the Army's general counsel, Robert Jordan, wrote a letter conceding that "the collection of civil disturbance-related information by the Army increased after the disturbance in Detroit in 1967." The two men met personally two days later, and Gallagher reported to the press on February 27, 1970, that Jordan had given further assurances that:

—"Mr. Jordan further emphasized that the lists of identifiable individuals had been withdrawn, including all black lists."

—Jordan would further "recommend" to Secretary Resor that "should the Army feel that increased surveillance over domestic activities was called for, such as the erection of a data bank, the Congress will be consulted."

Despite the Army's assurances, more credible sources believed

* *Washington Monthly*, January, 1970, pp. 4–8.
† Revealed by Gallagher in a press statement, January 26, 1970.

that the Army likely had already microfilmed and stored in the Pentagon all data it said had been destroyed at Ft. Holabird.

During the Decisive Decade, individual Congressmen who opposed the nation's police and war machines have not scored very highly. Even in this instance, Gallagher's courage was more evident than his success. But an indication of the extent to which Gallagher had become aroused was revealed in his remarks a week later, on March 1, 1970, to the New Jersey American Civil Liberties Union, one of the organizations Pyle had listed as being under Army intelligence surveillance.

"My friends," he told the New Jersey group, "never before in our history has the group of basic concepts embodied in the first Ten Amendments to our Constitution been under such constant and concerted attack as now. . . . Mere necessity would not be sufficient, according to our founders, in order to justify a violation of that [right of privacy] security; something more would be required: *probable* cause. [Emphasis original.] The steady erosion of that founding conception has proceeded apace during the latter portion of the sixties and the opening months of this new decade. . . . In a nation as large and complex as the United States, a nation which contains so many different cultural and ethnic heritages, no single class of men can be permitted to impose the standards of their group on the remainder of American society. Yet, in a very real sense, that is exactly what is happening today."*

What had been happening, of course, was the tightening of a police state web which was part of the total choice the country was making about its life style and the valuelessness of certain ideals—and certain kinds and classes of people. To that particular moment and issue, Congressman Gallagher spoke superbly:

My friends, I must be candid with you and reveal to you my firm belief that we are in the process of losing our form of government and our way of life as it has developed since the founding of our Republic. We are replacing democracy with something else, with something we have rejected throughout our history.

* From the text of the speech Congressman Gallagher released to the press, March 1, 1970.

Perhaps an illustration of what I mean may be found in the fact that a change from democracy to totalitarianism in those European states where such a change occurred was always preceded by stripping away of the same concepts as those guaranteed by our Fourth Amendment.

The ruination of individual privacy has always heralded the destruction of human freedom.

Indeed, the greatest privacy invader, dossier collector and information keeper known to this century was Adolf Hitler.

And Hitler carried forth his privacy invasion, his destruction of the human personality without the benefit of computers—though I should tell you, in all seriousness, that one of the first orders for the new IBM punch cards was placed by the government of Nazi Germany. . . .

Total information about individuals means total control over those individuals. . . .

There are those in the government who are trying to use the opportunities for control created by this technology precisely for that purpose. As I stated when I began this afternoon, these men may be, and no doubt are, motivated by sincere intentions; but the effect of their actions is astounding.

They have created an atmosphere of terror in this society, a terror which is being utilized to justify taking a torch to the Bill of Rights. Their attack on the Fourth Amendment is no less than an attack on all of our freedoms for, as we have seen, privacy is indispensable to an exercise of those freedoms. . . .

It is time to make the American experiment a continuing, everyday reality. I believe that the ACLU's goals have always been in this direction and perhaps if we are both effective and fortunate, others will see events in this same light. This may come in time; but my whole point is that there is not much time left.*

Few tactics of colonization or genocidal control are better established and understood than police brutality. Another tactic increasingly well established, but far less understood, is that of "health brutality." Although the parallels between health brutality and police brutality are overwhelming, there are many reasons why the fact of health brutality as a tactic is difficult for American masses to perceive.

One reason for this difficulty is the sacrosanct status—the

* *Ibid.*

godlike awe—which has traditionally been attributed to the family physician, his professional heirs, and the institutions associated with them. To a lesser degree, the same halo was given to farmers—those who produced food, and willingly, even prayerfully, made things grow.

A concomitant view of this hallowed status was that whatever was done by the medical practitioners (and farmers) was done to create, preserve, and improve on the quantity and quality of life. There were times, of course, when this actually was more true than it became in the throes of twentieth-century American politics. What American health systems became, however, is much akin to what Congressmen from the Rice Cup practice when they deny Asian rice to Asians and hand millions to rich U.S. farmers who farm little and earn much.

Similarly, rich physicians of the American Medical Association fought hard to defeat Medicaid and Medicare, preferring— not all, but many of them—to serve a rich, psychosomatic-prone, white clientele, but then unconscionably raked off padded Medicaid-Medicare payments once federal law and taxes provided the money.

These tactics of selfish medicalists and legislators are similar to those of bigoted Rice Cup farmers and their legislators, for the simple reason that they respond to common motives and directions: the Blackpoor, whether they be in Asia or Alabama, are granted access to life systems—food and medical care—only to the extent that they serve colonial purposes.

This fact was outlined on November 3, 1969, in a paper delivered before the Senate Select Committee on Nutrition and Human Needs by two public health physicians who dared to state the facts. They were Dr. Lester Breslow, president of the American Public Health Association, and a black physician, Dr. Paul Cornely of Howard University, the new president-elect of the APHA. With Senator George McGovern chairing the committee, Dr. Breslow described the conditions the two physicians saw on a cross-country inspection of medical and health systems:

As public health physicians, Dr. Cornely and I thought we knew pretty well the nature and extent of those conditions. But frankly,

Mr. Chairman, we were shocked and we are still reeling. Circumstances that can only be called health brutality pervade the lives of millions of American people who live in communities that seem designed to break the human spirit.

The national and State programs which purport to deal with these conditions, when viewed closely, appear to represent a policy of domestic brinkmanship. These programs simply skirt disaster and do little to alleviate underlying problems.

President Nixon recently spoke about a "massive crisis" in health care, and warned that "we will have a breakdown in our medical system which could have consequences affecting millions of people throughout the country." In fact, the breakdown has already occurred, and the consequences are already affecting our people.

The consequences of the "massive crisis" are reflected in such facts as these:

The infant mortality rate of the United States in 1950 was higher than that of 14 other countries. Today it is higher than that of 13 other countries.

The nonwhite infant mortality rate is almost twice that for whites.

Children in families with incomes under $3,000 per year see physicians 2.6 times per year as compared to 4.4 times per year in the case of children in families with incomes over $10,000 per year.

Forty-five percent of all women who have babies in public hospitals are delivered without prenatal care.

Poor families have three times more disabling heart disease, seven times more visual impairment and five times more mental illness than the more fortunate of us.

More than 20 percent of all persons in families with incomes under $3,000 a year have never seen a dentist.

This partial recitation of indices reflects the failure of "the system" in meeting human health needs in our country. Although these statistical facts were well known to us, we were not prepared for the awful conditions we observed on the tour.

We recall with pain:

The approximately 50,000 persons who reside in the Kenwood-Oakland area of Chicago, in rodent- and insect-infested housing, with burst plumbing and broken stairs and windows, for which the residents pay one-third to two-thirds of their incomes as rent; 50,000 persons who are served by a total of five physicians in their community—a physician-to-population ratio less than one-tenth that of the country as a whole—with the county hospital and clinics 8 miles away.

The 53-year old American Indian in Great Falls, Mont., veteran of the South Pacific in World War II, raising a family of six children (and one grandchild, whose father is now in Vietnam) on a pension and what he can scrounge by salvage in a junkyard, so poor that he cannot buy food stamps and cannot return to the hospital for postcancer treatment—closure of his bowel, which now opens on his abdomen—because his family would not have food while he is gone.

The farmworker in Tulare County, Calif., who said that exposure to pesticides from airplane spraying of fields, contrary to regulations and often leading to illness, was frequently not reported because "What's the use? We lose wages going to the doctor, get better in a week usually, and get no compensation, and they don't stop spraying."

The woman in Tulare County, 8 months pregnant, whose Medi-Cal (Medicaid) eligibility has been canceled last month because her husband had just found a temporary job, thus forcing her to seek care in the county hospital which previous experience had taught her to hate, and to break off care provided by her own choice of physician.

The young woman in Houston, whose welfare check for a family of eight children had been cut from $123 to $23 per month. . . .

Everywhere we encountered the lamentable excuses offered by local health and welfare officials, who seemed as trapped by "the rules" as the people they were supposed to serve.

While there has been considerable improvement in the quality of life for most Americans, the fact still remains that a large proportion of the 22 million blacks, the 5 million Mexican Americans, the 500,000 American Indians and millions of others live day in and day out in conditions we would not let our animals endure; and the "system" of care for people with diseases associated with such conditions seems designed to obstruct their receiving the care that is needed.*

In addition to Drs. Breslow and Cornely, many other physicians who became aware of the life-denial health systems operat-

* *Hearings Before the Select Committee on Nutrition and Human Needs of the United States Senate,* part 15, November 3, 1969, pp. 5536–38.

ing against the Blackpoor became vocal in their protests and opposition to them. Such was the spirit of the disruption that struck the AMA convention in mid-July, 1969.

Meeting in the Imperial Ballroom of the New York Americana hotel, the 244 members of the AMA's ruling House of Delegates had been treated to an opening patriotic ceremony, featuring a bewigged Marine Corps drum and bugle corps, when, as the New York *Times*' Sandra Blakeslee reported: ". . . The meeting was thrown into pandemonium as a group of about 75 doctors, nurses, medical students and their supporters took over the podium to assail the organization's 'conservative' leadership."*

As the *Times* reported, the medical demonstrators "were protesting against what they say is the reactionary attitude of the American Medical Association to the total health needs of the country."

The demonstrators swept down the aisle vacated by the Marines, and AMA president Dr. Dwight L. Wilbur decided to yield the microphone for two minutes to a spokesman for the demonstrators. Reported the *Times:*

The speaker, Dr. Richard Kunnes, represented a coalition of the Student Health Organization, the Medical Committee for Human Rights, the Movement for a Democratic Society, the Health Police Advisory Center and other liberal organizations of health professionals. Dr. Kunnes, who is 27 years old, is a senior resident in psychiatry at Albert Einstein Hospital.

"Let's get one thing straight," Dr. Kunnes said, straining to be heard above the boos of the doctors still in the audience, "The American Medical Association is really the American Murder Association."

"You're the criminals, who rather than developing a preventative health program have prevented health programs. You're the criminals, who through your monopolistic, exclusionary and racist practices have created a vast shortage of health manpower, resulting in the needless death of countless millions."†

---

* New York *Times,* July 14, 1969, p. 1.
† *Ibid.,* p. 20.

Those medical protesters have their counterparts in other direct-action groups who during the Decisive Decade took some measures into their own hands. But—just as their raucous methods were greeted in the Imperial Ballroom of the Americana with equally raucous shouts of "Shut up!" "Get out of here!" and "Go to hell!"—the more sedate, establishmentarian methods of Dr. Breslow and Cornely drew an equivalent negative response from the Rice Cup Senator present at the committee hearing.

After Dr. Breslow completed his statement detailing health brutality against the Blackpoor, Louisiana's Senator Allen J. Ellender asked him: "You have given us all the bad. Have you found any good at all?"—a kind of "shut up, get out, go to hell" response.

Dr. Breslow cited some instances of local groups organizing to remedy the situation, but Ellender proceeded to make his point:

Don't you think that this matter should be looked into and treated by the local people? I have been in many cities where a lot of filth exists, and unless the people themselves insist upon it, it is never changed. Would you agree to that? . . . What effort has your health association made to correct the conditions of which you are complaining?*

Dr. Cornely insisted on responding:

May I make a comment on the question that Senator Ellender made that this has to be a local effort at all times? First of all, let me say this: I think that the insensitivity and apathy shown by the agencies for human services which we find in many cities and many areas throughout the United States, have brutalized people. They have been brutalized by the welfare department, the department of sanitation, the department of recreation. These individuals have become what I would like to call "battered adults," just as we talk about battered children.†

---

* *Hearings before the Select Committee on Nutrition and Human Needs of the United States Senate,* Part 15, November 3, 1969, p. 5550.
  † *Ibid.,* p. 5551.

Senator Ellender continued to insist that he "always felt that there should be local cooperation [in health programs]. You wouldn't expect the Federal Government to do all of it, would you?"

Even as Senator Ellender was critical of reliance on government and insisted that the job of health and medicine should be done by the needy people themselves, the Black Panther Party in Chicago was trying to do just that—against governmental opposition. In fact, a Panther-sponsored community health facility was a major project of the Chicago Panther group when their leader, Fred Hampton, was slain by police in a predawn raid, December 4, 1969.

Writing in the Chicago *Daily Defender,* Toni Anthony reported on the official government opposition the Chicago Panthers met in trying to provide the kind of medical self-help Senator Ellender demanded:

The Black Panther Medical Center, 3850–52 W. 16th St., remains open to serve the people despite efforts last week by the City Health Department to close the new facility.

Officially named the Spurgeon Jake Winters People's Medical Care Center, in memory of Jake Winters, the . . . Panther party member killed in the Nov. 13, 1969 shoot-out with Chicago police at 58th and Calumet, the medical center is the realization of slain Illinois Black Panther Party Chairman Fred Hampton's dream—free medical service to the poor.

The Panther Medical Center opened its doors to the public on Jan. 5. It is staffed by volunteer professional nurses and doctors, who are specialists in their respective fields.

The young men and women at 3850–52 W. 16th St. are dedicated—to the forgotten Americans, the unhealthy and infirm, and to the prevention and eradication of disease in the ghetto.

The government says it can't be done. These youthful volunteers, doctors and nurses say it can, and are proving it, in what is one of the most unique medical centers in the nation—The Spurgeon Jake Winters People's Medical Center, staffed and directed by the Black Panther Party of Illinois. . . .

Death and devastating disease are stark realities for most Lawn-

dale residents, many of whom have never seen a physician in their
adult lives. The Panther Medical Center, located in the heart of
this impoverished area, represents a ray of hope for these abandoned and hopeless citizens—a chance for some sickly child to grow
into manhood, and the opportunity for some young man to realize
the promise of maturity as a result of the dedication of these young
men "to the people," the manifestation of Fred Hampton's dream.*

Predictably, just as Asians are prevented from consuming
their own rice—and being accused of venality and lack of initia-
tive in the meantime—Black Panthers establishing a health
center or Muslims forming dairies would inevitably meet official governmental opposition. That health systems have become
a part of the colonial control or genocidal capability was put
succinctly by Dr. Breslow in his testimony before Senator Mc-
Govern's committee investigating hunger and health: "We tend
to resist the community takeover of health programs by people
in impoverished neighborhoods, who have found that they must
participate in setting the rules as a means, literally, of survival."

The extent of that resistance is almost total, indicative of the
strategic importance of the health systems. So urgent are they
that when the political-medical establishment must fight openly
to keep health systems under the control of a carefully hand-
picked few, they give up niceties, fight as openly as necessary—
and for keeps.

This fact was demonstrated in a crucial end-of-the-decade
appointment in New York City. On November 29, 1969, New
York Mayor John Lindsay quietly asked for the resignation of
Dr. Bernard Bucove, who had won the confidence of many
neighborhood groups as director of the city's Health Services
Administration. On the next day, the job was handed to
Gordon Chase—a move which, for starters, prompted the
aborted resignation of one of Mayor Lindsay's closest advisers,
Werner H. Kramarsky. Kramarsky, a special assistant, was persuaded by the Mayor to stay, but the oddly loud protest from a
confidant of the Mayor set off a round of searching questions
and criticisms.

* Chicago *Daily Defender,* January 26, 1970, p. 5.

"The abrupt resignation of Dr. Bernard Bucove and your subsequent appointment of Mr. Gordon Chase as Health Services Administrator has caused grave concern in the community," came one wire to the Mayor from George W. Goodman, chairman of the Committee on Health Priorities for Harlem, and otherwise a potent political force in local politics. A measure of Goodman's political importance to Mayor Lindsay is the fact that Goodman's committee represents some 40 organizations and community leaders, and Lindsay himself had appointed Goodman to a legislatively mandated task force to study the city's health needs.

There was other considerable pressure—political and professional—against Lindsay's appointment of Chase. The prestigious New York Academy of Medicine, for example, bluntly told the Mayor that Chase was "professionally unqualified."* Even that was not sufficient discouragement: a decision had been made beyond the reach of concerned, prestigious, and otherwise influential groups and individuals.

As the New York *Times* reported, "One of Mr. Chase's principal advocates was the city's budget director, Frederick O'R. Hayes."† Hayes' best-known identification with medical matters prior to the Chase appointment was as deputy director of OEO's Community Action Program, where he exerted considerable influence toward OEO birth control programs for the poor. This, of course, is not a criticism of either Hayes or birth control, *per se*. However, given priority in cost and availability over the care and feeding of the poor already born, birth control, as practiced by OEO and advocated by others, does become suspect in the context of health brutality against the Blackpoor. Journalist Carl Rowan makes the point in a question put to Senator Robert Packwood (Republican of Oregon) in the May 17, 1970, program of *Meet the Press:*

Rowan: Senator, you have said that any woman who asks for an abortion ought to be able to get one. This was proposed recently at D.C. General Hospital here. Patrick Cardinal O'Boyle called that

* New York *Times,* December 16, 1969.
† *Ibid.*

exterminative medicine designed to eliminate the poor. How do you answer that criticism?

Packwood: Mr. Rowan, that just isn't true. If we are talking about the voluntary right of a woman from her own personal conscience standpoint to make a decision as to whether or not she wants an abortion, that doesn't apply to just the poor and it doesn't apply to just the rich. It means that those who want it can have one and I don't see how anybody can say that is a compulsory method to eliminate the poor.

Despite denials such as the one offered by birth control advocate Senator Packwood, there are the strongest indications that, as the black nationalist at Indiana University charged, aspirin costs money but abortions can be had free of charge. One might have hoped that OEO's greatest contributions would have been feeding the hungry, housing the unsheltered, and generally giving hope and health to the oppressed and downtrodden. But this was not so. Texas Congressman George Bush, chairman of the House Republican Task Force on Earth Resources and Population, enthusiastically placed into the *Congressional Record* a series of articles from the San Antonio *Evening News* which told of OEO's (and Hayes') biggest success: "A top OEO research official, Joseph A. Kershaw, has reported: 'We looked into the family planning with some care and were amazed to discover that here is probably the single most cost-effective antipoverty measure.' "[*]

As budget director, Fred Hayes, the big booster of Gordon Chase, could be expected to exert some influence on Mayor Lindsay in the direction of such cost-effectiveness as birth control had achieved at OEO. But, who is Gordon Chase? What qualified him so preeminently for the job as chief of medical programs for the nation's biggest city? Why was he a must?

Reported the New York *Times:*

The appointee, who is scheduled to take over at the end of the year, is currently winding up his internal management functions in the Human Resources Administration, which include budgeting, auditing, accounting, personnel and office services.

[*] *Congressional Record,* January 27, 1970, p. E-369.

Mr. Chase came to New York a year ago, after serving in a series of Federal positions in the Kennedy and Johnson Administrations. . . .

One of yesterday's protests came from the East Harlem Health Council, where a spokesman called Mr. Chase's managerial talents excellent, but added: "It's been our experience that whenever someone's primary interest is good administration and a balancing of the books, the interests of the people are forgotten."

That commentator, Mrs. Letitia Diaz, called the Chase appointment "a blow to community participation in health planning and the setting of health priorities."

Mr. Chase has refused to comment publicly on the controversy over his appointment.*

Back in Washington, some experienced federal bureaucrats gasped at the Chase appointment; they knew something Chase's New York critics might only have felt intuitively: Chase was listed as a solid member of the Central Intelligence Agency (CIA) .† To some, such qualifications eminently qualified him to run the health programs for the nation's biggest city.

On May 30, 1970, a page-one report in the New York *Times,* headlined "City Is Planning for Abortions At the Rate of 25,000 a Year," presaged events that would affect the concepts of life and death. Implementation of these new concepts would require a new kind of health administrator, one carefully chosen. Reported by Jane E. Brody, the *Times* story stated:

"The municipal hospital system here has committed itself to full implementation of New York's liberalized abortion law, to take effect July 1, and funds were earmarked this week to make possible 25,000 to 30,000 abortions a year on city residents."

By July 1, however, an updated *Times* story had more than doubled the estimates for abortions.

The nation's most liberal abortion law goes into effect in New York State today amid controversy and confusion over how many women will seek abortions, how an abortion can be obtained, how

---

much it will cost and whether the hospitals will be able and willing to meet the demand. . . .

For the last two months, hospitals in New York City have been preparing to meet the demand for abortions under the new law, which leaves the decision to have an abortion up to the woman and her doctor. The law permits most abortions to be performed within the first 24 weeks of pregnancy. . . .

More than 700 women have already been scheduled to receive abortions in municipal hospitals, beginning today, and abortion services in a number of hospitals—both municipal and voluntary— are already fully booked through July. . . .

Estimates of the demand for abortions among city women have ranged from 50,000—representing one abortion for every three live births—to 100,000 a year. A Health Department survey has indicated that hospitals in the city could handle the lower figure and perhaps as many as 75,000.*

While some detractors of new liberal abortion laws might oppose them solely on moral or religious grounds, the implications are more basic for large segments—though not all—of the Blackpoor. Some, like spokesmen for the Black Panthers, fear that voluntary abortions will quickly gravitate to *in*voluntary abortions, then to "compulsory sterilization."† Others, like the black psychiatrists and other delegates who vigorously dissented from prevailing views of *a mid*-1970 convention on population growth, see such schemes as blatantly genocidal.

"I think that whites are into a psychological state of denial of their own fears and anxieties about their annihilation," reasoned Dr. Alyce Gullattee, staff psychiatrist at St. Elizabeth's Hospital in Washington, D.C. "Therefore," she continued, after walking out of the first National Congress on Optimum Population and Environment in Chicago, "what they are talking about represents the survival of all peoples but at the expense of certain peoples, and those certain peoples just happen to be black people. So we perceive it as a genocidal attempt."**

* New York *Times,* July 1, 1970, p. 36.
† *Black Panther,* July 4, 1970, p. 2.
** Valerie Jo Bradley, "Black Caucus Raps About Planned Genocide of Blacks," *Jet,* August 6, 1970, p. 14.

On June 24, 1970, six black medical students called a press conference in Washington to protest what they called the "racist and repressive" policies of the nation's medical schools which systematically pass over, exclude, and flunk out potential black physicians and dentists. "The health care delivery system of this country is in a real crisis," said their spokesman, Therman Eugene Evans, a fourth-year student at the Howard University Medical School and executive secretary of the Student National Medical Association. "One of the most serious aspects of this crisis," Evans continued, "is the health manpower shortage. This problem, this crisis situation, is greatly magnified in regard to Black people. When we consider the health statistics of this country: infant mortality, maternal mortality, infectious diseases, heart disease, mental illness, and others, *we are constantly reminded of black genocide in ways that are not as blatant as a shot in the back or a lynching, but just as deadly as both.*"

The shot in the back and lynchings are, of course, direct forms of genocide. So is the denial of food and health services to a needy individual or group, as the black medical students and others pointed out. But health brutality is also used as an exterminative tactic by indirection. The indirect forms—instead of attacking an individual or group on a personal level—attack more at the *deservedness* of the individual or group. These forms search for fault and in that way are akin to the psychic preparation discussed in Chapter 3.

Health brutality as an indirect tactic enjoyed a revival that grew rapidly as the Decisive Decade drew to a close and the new decade began. Packaged in an aura of impersonality, it takes on the trappings of scholarly research. It has respectability. Its practitioners purport to be frontline helpers of educators, social workers, even the police, and all those who work toward the betterment of the society. In the 1969–70 transition, these researchers turned up several "discoveries"—either commissioned by or received in the highest councils of government. They earned hearings and gathered followers much as the earlier sellers of snake oil did: by promising quick, facile, and permanent cures for complex, age-old miseries. Some of these "discoveries" would virtually eliminate the need for hospitals or jails. Such institutions are for misfits, but under these impersonal tactics, all misfits could easily be identified at birth or earlier and destroyed.

*Newsweek* described the "discovery" of an identification process:

The blood samples, the fingerprints and the other tests run on the prison inmates revealed a curious pattern: the sex chromosomes—those genes that determine a human's sex at the time of conception—were consistently abnormal in a small but significant percentage of the convicts. Furthermore, this genetic fluke was reflected quite plainly in the fingerprints of the men; they differed noticeably from the prints of average men in their lack of distinctive marks.

This was the report of two investigators, Drs. Frank R. Ervin of Harvard University and Massachusetts General Hospital and Lawrence Razavi of Stanford Medical School, to the 136th meeting of the American Association for the Advancement of Science in Boston last week. What made their findings significant was that the abnormal convicts were all dangerously violent men—murderers or rapists. . . .

Most normal fingerprints are characterized by whorls and loops and by the number of ridges that can be counted according to a formula. The average male has 148 ridges on all ten fingers, while the typical woman has 127 ridges. The Bridgewater inmates, carrying an extra sex chromosome, had an average of 118 ridges on their fingers. In these cases, the fingerprints showed small arches rather than loops or whorls.*

The two researchers offered tepid denials that their discoveries might eventually become a substitute for judicial due process. But, in a repressive and technocratic climate, the implications of their findings, however tentative, were clear and present dangers, as *Newsweek* pointed out:

The results of their research, both physicians agreed, could not be used to stamp a person with extra chromosomes or low ridge-count

* *Newsweek,* January 12, 1970, pp. 60–61.

fingerprints as potential criminals. "I don't want to alarm people," Razavi said, "and have them look at their own prints with dread." But such tests might serve as a rough screen for men either at the time of their induction into military service or at the time of their first run-in with the law. Anyone showing such indications of sexual maldevelopment could then be referred for deeper testing and treatment.*

But these whorl vs. loop discoveries of Ervin and Razavi were a second phase of the series. The first phase ostensibly established a neat genetic connection between race and intelligence—a not unexpected complement to the discovery that such scant physical differences as fingerprints might identify the criminals or potential criminals in society. But, perhaps the least surprising aspect of the earlier discovery is that any differences found in intelligence will clearly show that black individuals are genetically inferior to white ones.

The author of this "discovery" is educational psychologist Dr. Arthur R. Jensen of the University of California at Berkeley. The *U.S. News & World Report* summarized Jensen's findings:

Shock waves are rolling through the U.S. educational community over a frank and startling reappraisal of differences in classroom performance between whites and Negroes.

In a lengthy article, taking up most of the winter issue of the "Harvard Educational Review," one of the nation's leading educational psychologists, Dr. Arthur R. Jensen of the University of California at Berkeley, presents these major findings:

—Negro scores averaging about 15 points below the white average on I.Q. tests must be taken seriously as evidence of genetic differences between the two races in learning patterns.

—Research suggests that such a difference would tend to work against Negroes and against the "disadvantaged" generally when it comes to "cognitive" learning—abstract reasoning—which forms the basis for intelligence measurements and for the higher mental skills.

—Conversely, Negroes and other "disadvantaged" children tend to do well in tasks involving rote learning—memorizing mainly

* *Ibid.*

through repetition—and some other skills, and these aptitudes can be used to help raise their scholastic achievement and job potential.

—Unfortunately, big programs of "compensatory" education, now costing taxpayers hundreds of millions of dollars a year, are doomed to failure as long as they pursue old approaches stressing "cognitive" learning.*

One of several of the new medical Moynihans, Jensen further explains his fault psychology by explaining that "brain mechanisms which are involved in learning are genetically conditioned just as are other structures and functions of the organism."† Summarized U.S. News: "Altogether, his summation of studies on individual differences in I.Q. concluded that heredity accounts on the average for about 80 per cent of those individual variations, as against only 20 per cent resulting from environmental influences."**

Like the others, Jensen, of course, had his critics, and occasionally found cogent answers difficult to come by when facing a barrage of questions. On April 29, 1970, Jensen spent the day expounding his theories before a convention of scientists at the National Academy of Sciences in Washington, then appeared that night before the Washington chapter of Sigma Delta Chi, the national journalistic society. At the Sigma Delta Chi meeting, he debated with linguist Dr. William Labov of Columbia University on the question: "Are Whites Smarter Than Blacks? Labov answered "No" and said much of what is regarded as innate ability is mere acculturation, with language a significant factor. Jensen, of course, argued that whites are innately 15 points superior to blacks, and to "prove" this he presented numerous charts and sample tests designed to show questions black children could not answer.

In the question-and-answer period, a black reporter asked to raise a "slightly unorthodox question, but one not nearly so difficult as those Stanford-Binet questions you have been put-

---

* U.S. News & World Report, March 10, 1969, p. 48.
† Ibid., p. 49.
** Ibid.

ting to the black children." Jensen, somewhat patronizingly, assured the black reporter that any question would be welcomed.

"Who discovered America?" the black reporter asked.

After a long, silent pause, Jensen began by saying: "I know that the answer I'm going to give is not the answer you're looking for." But the reporter assured him that such was the nature of test questions. Then Jensen offered his answer: "Christopher Columbus discovered America."

Someone in the audience suggested that it might have been Leif Ericson. The reporter asked if all of them wouldn't agree that it was "some European" who discovered America.

"Definitely," Jensen and the others agreed.

"What did they find here?" the black reporter pressed.

There was another long pause, and Jensen finally said: "Aboriginal tribes . . . Indians, I guess."

"People?" the reporter asked.

Reluctantly, Jensen said, "Yes, people."

"Then, who discovered America?" the question came again.

Jensen indicated that the point of the question was not clear, so the black reporter elaborated: "Suppose, just suppose for a moment that I came to your home tonight and 'discovered' it, killed off your family and beat you, then restricted you to some reserved area of the house. And in another section of the house, I beat and chained some men, women, and children I kidnapped in the park on my way to your house. Then, under penalty of death, I denied all of you hostages the knowledge of the house and how to run it; and, then, if I devised a test over the things I had denied you to learn, and if you failed that test—just as I had intended—would I be fair or correct to call you stupid? And if I did call you stupid, for what purpose would I do it?"

Jensen then rose, and for some ten minutes he attempted to explain how what he was doing—although quite similar to what Hitler was doing 40 years earlier—was being done for quite different reasons. He was forced to agree, however, regardless of the motives, that what he was then doing in the United States

his counterparts in Nazi Germany were doing a few years before
six million Jews died in gas chambers.

In a discussion following the meeting, Jensen said the questions raised were valid, and added that the best critique of his
theories had been a current article in *Ebony* magazine. This was
a significant comment from Jensen about the work of a black
man, but the comment is all the more remarkable in view of
Rowan's scathing criticism:

> Other critics have expressed fear that Jensen's article and the
> furor around it would strengthen conservatives in the White House
> who already were arguing that 1) blacks are congenitally un-
> educable, or 2) no school can do much for the poor, especially the
> black poor, until their home life is altered radically, so it is useless
> for federal agencies to waste billions on educational efforts to give
> blacks "an even chance."

Was Jensen sure enough of his "findings" to justify either his
assertion that IQ is controlled 80 per cent by genetic factors and
only 20 per cent by environment? Or his equally controversial
declaration that there is a significant difference in the intellectual
capacity of various racial groups and that an inferior gene pool is
what causes blacks to score on the average of 15 points lower than
whites on IQ tests? The challenges of other scholars have shown
Jensen to be far from sure of himself.

When psychologist Benjamin Bloom pointed out that the IQs of
Oriental Jewish children were being raised from 85 to 115 by the
manipulation of environmental factors, Jensen admitted that
"there can be no doubt that moving children from an extremely
deprived environment to good average environmental circumstances can boost the IQ some 20 to 30 points, and in certain
extremely rare cases as much as 60 or 70 points." But Jensen clung
to his doubts that the large gains would be permanent.

He hedged even more when asked how he could deny the effect of
environment when educators see poor black children start off
showing high intelligence and performance, only to have both
decline progressively. Is this not clearly an erosion attributable to
the harsh home-school-neighborhood environment of these
children?

Jensen concedes only that "We do not know how much of this

decline is related to environment or to hereditary factors." A remarkable admission for a man who earlier professed to a degree of certainty that IQ is four parts genetic and one part environment!

As the debate wore on, the professor seemed to become more and more aware that somewhat irresponsibly he had tossed forth hypotheses that would be used even more irresponsibly by the most benighted elements in society. He said in an interview at the Center for the Study of Democratic Institutions:

"I think that the degree of probability with which racial genetic differences can be stated today is not adequate as a basis for policies to deal with racial issues."

But it was too late. The damnable hypothesis was halfway 'round the world before the truth could saddle up.*

Jensen is only one of the merchants of black inferiority criticized by Rowan in the *Ebony* article. His critique of a fellow journalist, Carleton Putnam, goes to the heart of this tactic of indirect health brutality:

Why do Putnam and his kind harp incessantly on this thesis that the black man is "200,000 years" behind the white man in evolution? Some say it is just a search for scientific truth, with no malice toward black people intended. But Putnam reveals a lot when he says that "the American people are entitled to know what the available evidence discloses so that it may be considered in the forming of public policy. Changes in laws and customs which have as their purpose, or will produce as a result, the infusion into our white gene pool of perceptible amounts of Negro genes, or the alteration of white standards and traditions to accommodate those of Negroes, will in all probability in the long run have a profound and adverse effect upon our society."

Putnam contends, for example, that crime among black people is rampant because Negroes have a false sense of being abused; that whites have a false sense of guilt, and thus whites follow a policy of "permissiveness and appeasement."

Notice Putnam speaks of blacks in terms adults usually use in speaking of children. Everything would be lovely in this society, he holds, if the white majority would just face up to the fact that black

* Carl T. Rowan, "How Racists Use 'Science' to Degrade Black People," *Ebony*, May, 1970, p. 40.

people are intellectual children and take whatever stern measures
are required to make them behave. So here we see claims of black
inferiority being used as justification for policies of oppression that
could lead to the genocidal tactics black militants fear.

Yet Attorney General John Mitchell and others in Washington
profess to wonder why black people are so suspicious of and hostile
toward whites who go around talking incessantly about get-tough
campaigns to produce "law and order!"*

The indirection of such theories as those expounded by
Jensen rests largely on the fact that they were not specified for
action, although they provided the bases upon which others
might take action. Whatever of this was lacking in Jensen and
Putnam was clear and abundant in the tactics of another "dis-
coverer" with unique White House connections. This "dis-
coverer" described his relationship with President Nixon seven
months after the President was inaugurated. Writing on "The
Mental Health of Our Leaders," in the July 15, 1969, issue of
*Look* (p. 54), psychotherapist Dr. Arnold A. Hutschnecker
said:

The race between Kennedy and Nixon in 1960 needs to be
mentioned here because the question of the health of the two
candidates almost became an election issue. On the Saturday before
Election Day, the networks had announced that a statement on the
health of the candidates was due on Monday. On Saturday night, the
Associated Press tracked me down at my country home in Connecticut, asking for a statement on Mr. Nixon, since it had become
known by then that I had treated the Vice President. The discovery
of this fact had been a comparatively easy matter because, on
several of his visits to me, the Secret Service men accompanying
the then Vice President were in evidence in front of my Manhattan
office. Avoiding the ambiguous "no comment," I made it clear to
the press that while it was true that I had treated the Vice President, it was at a time when I was still engaged in the practice of
internal medicine. Naturally, no specific diagnosis can be given
even now. What I as a physician am allowed to say is that Mr.
Nixon came for physical checkups, none of which showed evidence
of any illness. Because of rumors that the Vice President was seeing

* *Ibid.,* p. 34.

a New York psychiatrist, we had come to an understanding, years before the 1960 elections, that we should discontinue our doctor-patient relationship.

Hutschnecker's connections alone identified him as a man of special influence, a relationship which took on frightful significance when his "discovery" was made public in the spring of 1970, reported by Robert C. Maynard of the Washington *Post:*

President Nixon has asked the Department of Health, Education and Welfare to study the proposals of a New York psychiatrist that psychological tests be administered to all the six-year-olds in the United States to determine their future potential for criminal behavior.

Dr. Arnold Hutschnecker further proposed massive psychological and psychiatric treatment for those children found to be criminally inclined. He said such a program is a better short-term solution to the crime problem than urban reconstruction.

Teen-age boys later found to be persisting in incorrigible behavior would be remanded to camps under the proposals submitted to the President last December.

The determination of criminal tendencies of children 6 to 8 years old would be made by psychologists using such tests as the Rorschach, which depends for its predictive insights on the reactions of the person being tested to a series of ink blot images.

. . . Dr. Hutschnecker, formerly an internist, treated Mr. Nixon in that capacity when the President was Vice President in the 1950's. . . .

"No doubt," Dr. Hutschnecker told the President, "there is a desperate need for urban reconstruction but I would suggest another, direct, immediate and I believe effective way of attacking the problem at its very origin, by focusing on the criminal mind of the child.

"The aim is to prevent a child with a delinquent character structure from being allowed to grow into a full-fledged teen-age delinquent or adult criminal," Dr. Hutschnecker said.

"The sooner this destructive trend is recognized and reversed, the better the chances for the prevention of crime and the cure of the individual," he wrote.*

* Washington *Post,* April 5, 1970, p. 1.

According to the *Post* article, Dr. Hutschnecker's memorandum to President Nixon continued with a rather clear over-concern for the constabulary needs of the society:

The government should have mass testing on all 6 to 8 year old children. . . . These tests could help detect the children who have violent and homicidal tendencies. Corrective treatment could begin at that time.

The more disturbed, the more angry, rebellious, undisciplined and disruptive boys, especially those who show criminal tendencies, should be given aptitude tests to determine areas of interest which should be carefully encouraged. There are Pavlovian methods which I have seen effectively used in the Soviet Union.

. . . For the severely disturbed, the young hard-core criminal, there may be a need to establish camps with group activities under the guidance of counselors, under the supervision of psychologists, who have empathy (most important) but also firmness and who can earn the respect of difficult adolescents.*

Other psychiatrists and sociologists decried this incredible "discovery" and action proposal from Dr. Hutschnecker,† but the first high-level denunciation came from the alert libertarian, Congressman Gallagher of New Jersey. Congressman Gallagher referred to the *Post* article, then told his Congressional colleagues:

Mr. Speaker, in 1965 my Special Subcommittee on Invasion of Privacy conducted hearings into the use of psychological tests by Federal agencies. At that time, we discovered that psychological tests were not a reliable way to predict individual human behavior, that they could work on isolating a large group of individuals who might possibly behave in one way, but they could not strictly focus on one person in that group.

Yet, here we have one of the most influential psychiatrists in the Nation proposing that a child's future should be dictated by what kind of a score he makes on a psychological test when he is 6 years old. And from the test result possibly torn from his mother's arms by Federal agents taking him to an American Dachau. . . .

* *Ibid.*, p. A-16.
† Washington *Post*, April 11, 1970, p. 1.

Congressman Gallagher was particularly struck with Dr. Hutschnecker's fascination with how Russia handles such problems:

. . . And so, Mr. Speaker, as the ultimate means to deal with crime in the United States, we are offered schemes which are alleged to be successful in the Soviet Union.

I would ask why we should stop with "Pavlovian methods?" Why do we not just go ahead and use the Russian's extremely successful totalitarian methods: Perhaps this is what was meant by those "rehabilitation camps." Perhaps banishment to Siberia is the ultimate domestic weapon to deal with those who deviate from the norm.*

But even as Congressman Gallagher spoke, government-financed investigation had already gone beyond mere "Pavlovian methods." A study financed by the U.S. Navy and delivered in January, 1970, had already explored the public's attitude toward mass murder—genocide. This crucially significant study, performed by Purdue University psychology researchers Siegfried Streufert and Glenda Y. Nogami, seems to culminate the essential meaning of the several other medico-legal "discoveries."

Entitled "The Value of Human Life: An Initial Analysis," the Streufert-Nogami study relied largely on the reactions of individuals to a questionnaire "developed to measure the components of persons' attitude toward human life." The responses of fifty-six university students and forty-one other subjects showed a strong national tendency toward "aggressive punishment" of nonconformists and disrupters in the society. The researchers concluded that the study "demonstrated that value of life consists of several dimensional components which are similar in size (factor loadings) and remain relatively stable over several administrations of the questionnaire (both across and within samples) ."

But the most revealing part of the study—aside from the *fact* of such a study—was the discussion of the authors in providing a rationale for the study and a background for the conclusions.

---

* *Congressional Record*, April 8, 1970, p. E-2916.

The authors acknowledge that while the study was ordered by a military organization—the U.S. Navy—its applications were clearly broader than *traditional* military needs and carried broadest implications for the society in general. This is how the researchers explained it to the Navy:

The research reported in this paper is an initial attempt to isolate the components of the "value of life" concept. If such a concept can be identified, and if the components of the concept appear to be stable, then one might expect some important interpersonal differences in decision making by military personnel under constraints of complex situational requirements.

However, value of life is not only relevant to military settings. Several writers have in the last months and years been concerned with life and death, particularly with the future life of the human species on this planet. Probably the most vocal has been [Paul] Ehrlich (1968, 1969), who proposes that life as we know it might be destroyed by the "population bomb," by overcrowding, and the polluting and destructive side effects of overcrowding. Others have made similar predictions based on related evidence. *For instance, [J.] Bonner (1967) has suggested that if current trends are continued, the "haves" will eventually exterminate the "have nots" so that the "haves" can benefit even more. [H. J.] Muller (1970) points out a number of effects of "overdevelopment" in the nations of the "haves" that will destroy the "good life," acceptable human values, and human nature as we now know it. Konrad Lorenz (personal communication) is even more pessimistic; he suggests the respect for others' life will cease as overcrowding reaches levels that are not yet themselves destructive.* [Emphasis added.] A slightly less pessimistic view is expressed by [J.] Weir (1967). He proposes that the more people become the way they want to be, the more excited with life they would become. This would turn them away from aggression and destruction. However, it appears that the views of Weir are—to say the least—reflecting a minority position.

*Whether or not any of these theorists will have an impact on the behavior of individuals or groups—or for that matter societies— should in part depend on the value placed on human life. Events in recent history (destruction of Jews in Germany during the Hitler regime, the wholesale killing of Indians in Brazil, incidents reported from Vietnam, and now more recently from Cambodia) suggest* *that not all persons hold similar values about life and death.\** [Emphasis added.]

Similarly, research conducted in October, 1968 (consisting of 1,176 interviews with a representative national sample of adult Americans) revealed that only 18 percent of the American public would protest—even nonviolently—mass repression of American Blacks. An even smaller number—only 9 percent— would resist with necessary violence the official mass repression of black Americans. These findings were made in a study for the National Commission on the Causes and Prevention of Violence and were reported in the November, 1970, issue of *Psychology Today* by California sociologists Dr. James McEvoy III and Dr. Rodney Stark.

The sociologists asked those interviewed to "Imagine that the government has just arrested and imprisoned many of the Negroes in your community even though there had been no trouble." Characterizing their responses, McEvoy and Stark wrote:

The over-whelming majority of white Americans would apparently be "good Germans" if the government turned to massive racial repression; only 18 percent would protest nonviolently and nine percent would turn to violence. Blacks, understandably, would be more willing to act; but even so, activists are a minority: 43 percent would use civil disobedience and one fourth would attempt counterviolence. This may reflect a pragmatic judgment that if such things came to pass, Blacks would be wiped out if they rebelled.†

Thus, as the new decade began, an ominous interchangeability of roles and views had taken place between high echelons of the medical and police establishments. Not surprisingly,

---

\* Siegfried Streufert and Glenda Y. Nogami, for the Office of Naval Research Group Psychology Programs, "The Value of Human Life: An Initial Analysis," Technical Report No. 27, January, 1970, an unclassified document, pp. 1–2.

† Rodney Stark and James McEvoy III, "Middle-Class Violence," *Psychology Today*, November, 1970, p. 111.

Daniel P. Moynihan began to call for tougher measures against crime as his medical counterparts increasingly picked up the chant.

The end-of-decade "discoveries" amount to a tactic of nudging ever closer to reestablishing in the public mind the inferiority of black people, on the one hand and, on the other, elimination of the need for such lengthy processes and extraneous measures as judicial due process to determine guilt or innocence or medical due process to determine life or death.

For two weeks, White House press aides had been tipping off reporters that President Nixon would have something important to say to national law officers at the Denver meeting of the Law Enforcement Assistance Administration (LEAA). Indeed, he did. On August 3, 1970, flanked by his Attorney General, John Mitchell, and other high officials, the President chastised the press for giving undue attention to undeserving matters, and gave a startling example:

This is not done intentionally by the press. It is not done intentionally by radio and television, I know. It is done perhaps because people want to read or see that kind of story. I noted, for example, the coverage of the Charles Manson case when I was in Los Angeles, front page every day in the papers. It usually got a couple of minutes in the evening news. *Here is a man who was guilty, directly or indirectly, of eight murders without reason.* Here is a man, yet, who, as far as the coverage was concerned, appeared to be rather a glamorous figure to the young people whom he had brought into his operation. . . .*

Final arguments in the trial of Charles Manson on charges of murder would not be made for months. Press secretary Ronald Ziegler offered "clarifications" of the President's summary, declaratory finding of guilt, but the people of the nation had gained two impressions they could not easily dismiss:

—Judicial due process is a waste in cases of "obvious" guilt, and

—The press should spend less time covering court trials:

Arrests have already been made, and the government has stated its case.

If the public accepted these impressions about the fate of a white man—Manson—how less valid could these impressions be regarding the fates of black men?

* New York *Times*, August 4, 1970, pp. 1, 16.

# Chapter 6

# The Laws: A Legal Police State

An obvious function of a constitution in a free society is to preserve those guarantees that keep it free. This fact makes the erosion of those guarantees and the establishment of a police state prerequisite to possible genocide. In the Decisive Decade, the police state tactics preceded new legal sanctions, but sanctions, too, would come.

On May 11, 1969, Michael Klonsky, national secretary of the Students for a Democratic Society, appeared on one of the Sunday afternoon interview programs, *Face the Nation* on CBS. He talked of increasing lawlessness on the part of the police establishment and, as an example, predicted that police would soon begin storming the headquarters of such groups as the SDS.

To most Americans, it must have sounded ludicrous, and to many, a case of simple paranoia.

However, on the very next morning, Monday, May 12, firemen banged on the doors of Klonsky's headquarters office in Chicago, claiming that there was a fire inside. Klonsky and others insisted that there was no fire. The firemen persisted.

A contingent of Chicago policemen just "happened" to be at the corner, and "hearing the commotion," came to investigate— or so first reports stated. Later in the day, the Associated Press reported:

A scuffle broke out early today after police and firemen were summoned to the national headquarters of Students for a Democratic Society and five leaders of the radical organization were arrested.

Among those arrested was Michael Klonsky, 26, the SDS national secretary who charged in a television interview yesterday the U.S. Justice Department had plans to make "sweeping arrests" of leftists within 10 days.

The five were charged with battery and interfering with police and firemen.

Firemen said they responded to a fire reported in the West Madison Street headquarters which proved to be a false alarm. Police said they received a report of a man shot in the hallway at the headquarters address, which also proved false. *

Before the year was out, Chicago police would make a similar raid on the Chicago headquarters of the Black Panther Party, leaving two of the party members dead, others wounded and jailed. A similar raid on the Black Panther headquarters in Oakland rendered no party members dead—but only because they were able to hold off police with gunfire until daylight. The mayor of Seattle rejected the pleas of his police hierarchy who wanted to conduct such raids in Seattle.

In a television interview early in 1970, Congressman John Conyers, Jr., of Detroit, one of the nine black Congressmen who investigated the police raid of Panther headquarters in Chicago, said, on WTOP-TV in Washington, that a high Justice Department official had admitted to him that their intention was to "exterminate" the Black Panther Party "by whatever means necessary."

Activists in the SDS and Black Panther Party, because of their public image, had become fair game in the minds of many citizens who rationalized that both groups were trouble-makers and exceptions—that such atrocities would be visited only upon extreme groups who threaten society and bring such action upon themselves.

However, the routineness of such police persecution against

* *Evening Star*, May 12, 1969, p. 1.

people conveniently restricted in areas called ghettos is indicated in a series written as far back as 1966 by Jerrold K. Footlick in the *National Observer:*

Life as it is lived in the ghetto was illustrated by a recent event in Oakland that could have set the city on fire. In a rundown house lives a Negro family named Smith. One son, who had been in trouble with the law, decided he would try to keep his brothers and their friends out of trouble by setting up a recreation room in the basement, complete with weights, barbells, and a pool table.

Negro youths and white youths too from the slums would frequent the room; regular police in the neighborhood knew about it. One night, however, two plainclothes policemen, who suspected that the house next door was a house of prostitution, saw two white boys emerge from the Smith home, then return.

Apparently suspecting the worst, they pounded on the door. The boys inside asked if they had a search warrant, and getting no answer would not open the door. The officers broke in. The boys resisted and a head-cracking battle ensued. The father, Luther Smith, Sr., came downstairs and tried unsuccessfully to end the fighting. The officers, outnumbered, rushed to their car and radioed for help.

Soon afterward, squad cars roared up, and police broke into the house. In a struggle officers overpowered three Negro men in the family and two white boys, and took them to jail, where they spent the week end until they could get bond.

Whether the building next door was a house of prostitution is disputed, but no one says there was anything illegal taking place in the Smith house. The case against one white boy, a juvenile, has already been dismissed. The others, on charges of resisting arrest and assaulting an officer, are pending.

The Negroes say they were only defending their home against police who had broken in violently without a search warrant. The father is now undergoing psychiatric treatment, which, doctors say, was caused by the beating he took on the head. The father and one son lost their jobs; they are now on welfare. The family has filed a $340,000 civil law suit against the police.*

* *National Observer,* July 11, 1966.

Underlying these incidents pitting police against the SDS, the Black Panthers, and the ordinary existence of black people is the fact that the legality of the police action was obviously in serious question and, therefore, subject to legal redress. The police almost never lose such a case, but the *possibility* of their losing serves as both a modicum of restraint against such abuse and as an encouragement to black people to tolerate the system in some hope of justice.

That possibility and hope were extinguished early in 1970 with the enactment of President Nixon's omnibus crime legislation. Congressman Cornelius Gallagher described part of it in his speech to the New Jersey ACLU on February 28, 1970:

We are facing a new Joe McCarthyism in the United States. Only there is a difference. The current version is worse, since the prototype was never actually given the legitimate substance of legislation.

Let me be specific. In January of this year, the United States Senate passed by a vote of 99 to 1 what is perhaps the most unconstitutional piece of legislation ever conceived in Washington; I refer to the new so-called omnibus anti-crime bill. It may be an omnibus bill, but the only crime involved is that of ever having passed it. . . .

The philosophy behind this bill is that catching the criminal, or the suspected criminal, validates any invasion of rights guaranteed to all of us. . . . The new bill creates a new type of Grand Jury which will do nothing but issue reports on the activities of local citizens whom the Government does not have the necessary evidence to indict, much less convict.*

In other words, in 1970, the police state not only became fact, it became legal.

Before the scaffolding had been hauled away from the site of the Nixon inaugural in January, 1969, Justice Department lawyers, under the command of Attorney General John Mitchell and his deputy, Richard G. Kleindienst, had begun patching together the administration's model police state law,

---

* From a copy of the speech delivered at the Rutgers University Law School by Congressman Gallagher on February 28, 1970, and released to the press, March 1, 1970.

which, in its final form, was titled, "The District of Columbia Court Reform and Criminal Procedure Act of 1970." Aside from its obvious unconstitutionality, the bill ran a conspicuously irregular course through Congress before reaching the desk of President Nixon, who signed it into law on July 29, 1970.

Although the bill was in fact the brainchild of the Republican Nixon administration—with the technical details worked out in the Justice Department and with the reluctant cooperation of the D.C. Corporation Counsel's office—the bill was legislatively sponsored by a reputedly liberal Democrat, Senator Joseph D. Tydings of the neighboring state of Maryland. Yet, even though Tydings was the bill's actual sponsor, it was technically introduced into the Senate on July 11, 1969, by Nebraska's conservative Republican Roman L. Hruska on behalf of Tydings, who found an alibi that enabled him to be absent from the Senate floor at the time his major bill was introduced.

The companion bill was introduced in the House of Representatives on February 26, 1970, by John L. McMillan, a South Carolina Democrat, who, as chairman of the House District Committee, ostensibly was concerned about the welfare of the citizens of the nation's capital who have not the right to elect their own representatives.*

The Senate passed Tydings' bill (S. 2601) with little fanfare on September 18, 1969. The House passed McMillan's version (H.R. 16196) on March 19, 1970. Because of essentially minor differences between the two bills, they were sent before a Senate-House conference committee to bring them into line.

That was in late March, 1970, and only then—ironically, with the exception of North Carolina's Senator Sam Ervin, a constitutionalist—did the reputed liberals on Capitol Hill and elsewhere show any measurable concern for the two major Hitlerian provisions, present in both the House and Senate

---

* Shortly before its adjournment for the fall, 1970, elections, Congress passed legislation permitting the citizens of Washington to elect a single "non-voting Delegate" to the House of Representatives—a weak and obscene effort to disguise the fact of taxation without representation.

versions: no-knock search and seizure and preventive detention. Those two provisions not only legitimatized predawn raids but also took away the right of the victims either to resist physically as the Panthers did in Oakland or protest through the courts as the black Smith family sought to do in Oakland in 1966.

Although proponents of such Nazi-type laws argued that the laws would apply only to the District of Columbia, it was evident *even before the bill had passed* that the District boundaries would not contain official eagerness to tear down doors and brutalize admittedly innocent citizens. Washington *Post* reporter Gerald E. Bunker described one vivid instance of how, in the spring of 1970, police in nearby Prince George's County, Maryland began no-knock raids months ahead of the District law:

A Prince George's County woman was awakened about 1 A.M. yesterday by a crew of armed county deputy sheriffs who had broken into her apartment with a sledge hammer.

Maj. Daniel D. Ballard of the Prince George's County sheriff's office yesterday confirmed the incident but said it was all a mistake.

He said that a squad from the sheriff's office conducting a drug raid had divided into three sections in order to assure surprise and to cover all entrances to a nearby apartment that was the actual target of the raid.

Ballard said that one section blundered into the apartment of Margaret O. Malloy. That section had been assigned to enter through the rear of the apartment that was to be raided and erred because there were no numeral markers there, Ballard said.

Mrs. Malloy, 58, who lives at 7308 Forest Rd. with her son John, 23, came into the living room to find a half-dozen men armed with pistols and with blackjacks protruding from their rear pockets. They were wearing civilian clothes, not uniforms.

As Mrs. Malloy recounted the incident yesterday, she said she found herself staring down the barrel of a rifle held by a crouching man who wore a bandolier across his sports shirt.

"My God, what's happened?" asked Mrs. Malloy, shaking, as she later said, "like a leaf."

"This is a raid. We're Prince George's County sheriffs," a spokesman for the group told her, she said.

"Isn't this 7302 Forest Rd.?" he asked.

"No," answered Mrs. Malloy's son. "This is 7308," she recounted.

"We've got the wrong apartment. I'll be right back and explain," the spokesman told her.

Mrs. Malloy and her thoroughly awakened neighbors then watched the group make its way to the nearby apartment.

They saw the search party go to 7302 Forest Rd. to a third floor apartment similar to Mrs. Malloy's.

Mrs. Malloy and her neighbors said they could hear screams and an unexplained shot as they saw pictures being removed from the walls and vases smashed, she said.

Ballard said that at the second address eight arrests were made and that $2,500 worth of heroin and other illegal drugs were seized.

After the raid, a deputy returned to apologize to Mrs. Malloy, she said.

Mrs. Malloy said she believes in upholding the law but that she hopes the sheriff will be more careful next time.

"I have high blood pressure," she said.*

In addition to no-knock search and seizure and preventive detention, the Nixon administration sought—and got—the legal right to such extensions of the 1967 Omnibus Crime Bill as virtually unlimited wiretapping and such mandatory physical evidence as fingerprinting against persons not even charged with any crime.

Of the no-knock provision, Senator Ervin, fighting virtually alone on the Senate floor, declared during debate: "Under this provision, an officer of the law can come and break into a man's house without ever telling him he's there, without ever telling him he's got a warrant and without ever telling him he's an officer. And under the law of nearly all states, a householder has the right to kill that officer of the law," because he has no way of knowing that the intruder has the legal right to break and enter.†

From the outset, whenever the merits of the bill were debated at all, there was general acclamation of the fact that the

* Washington *Post*, April 30, 1970, p. 1.
† Washington *Post*, January 25, 1970, p. 1.

incredibly repressive provisions of the bill would apply primarily to the District of Columbia, where seven out of every ten residents is black and where none out of ten can vote. Argued Attorney General Mitchell: "This Administration is firmly committed to a vigorous and comprehensive action program to combat crime in America, *particularly street crime.* . . . The amendments we propose will apply to all Federal jurisdictions, but their *primary impact will be in Washington.*"\* [Emphasis added.]

At one point, the voice of Arkansas Senator John L. McClellan was raised in a way that suggested that he might not have favored these unconstitutional measures. A closer examination of his remarks, however, shows that his concern was that the laws be secure from successful challenge in court.

During debate on the crime package, Will R. Wilson, Assistant Attorney General in charge of the Justice Department's Criminal Division, appeared before the Senate Subcommittee on Criminal Laws and Procedures. McClellan, chairman of the subcommittee, lectured Wilson on the necessity to make the crime package impervious to court challenges. The part that most interested McClellan was a provision by which policemen may require anyone suspected of criminal activity to be fingerprinted and give samples of their hair, blood, handwriting, and voiceprints, as well as to stand in police lineups—even when police lacked "probable cause" to make an arrest. McClellan himself had authored a similar fingerprint bill which apparently served as the administration's model.

"We must take care to make this within the framework of the Constitution," McClellan advised Wilson, pointing out that they were treading in "a very sensitive constitutional area." Should the Courts find the new laws unconstitutional, said the Arkansas Senator, then "all of our efforts are in vain."†

The crime package, often referred to as the "D.C. Crime bill," passed the Senate with extraordinary calm and virtually

\* *Wall Street Journal,* October 30, 1969.
† New York *Times,* March 11, 1970, p. 19.

no opposition: No Senator could see selfish political gain in opposing it; it was not (on paper) an issue or threat in his state and, since the people of Washington have no representative in Congress, there would be no one in Congress either to represent the fears of those 900,000 disfranchised persons, or trade votes in a way to rally Congressional opposition.

A letter sent to Congressmen by the National Capital American Civil Liberties Union vainly tried to drum up enough opposition to defeat the measure in the House. "Once again," NCACLU President Allison W. Brown, Jr., said in his letter to Congressmen, "a majority of the members of the House District Committee have shown themselves willing to authorize serious invasions of liberty on the voteless residents of the District of Columbia which they would never tolerate, much less support, against their own constituents."*

The letter continued to comment on various aspects of the bill: "In discussing the disturbing features of this bill, I should like to begin with the most offensive of them—preventive detention, 'no-knock' search warrants, warrants to compel physical evidence, and almost unlimited wiretap authority. It should be noted that this dreadful collection of police-state measures has been hidden by the drafters at the end of Title II in a section innocuously labeled 'Codification of Title 23.' Neither the bill's title nor the table of contents, therefore, gives an inkling to the wide-ranging police powers which this single section of the bill would permit in the District of Columbia. We find it difficult to believe that this at-first-blush invisibility is accidental."†

One of the biggest arguments offered by Senator Joseph Tydings (Democrat of Maryland) and others in favor of preventive detention is that some means had to be found to prevent "potential" criminals from committing or repeating crimes. The obvious fault, however, is in the fact that the accused is detained for at least 60 days *without ever going to trial to determine guilt or innocence.*

---

* The letter was sent to Congressmen the week of March 16, 1970—shortly before the House voted adoption. A copy of the letter went to members of the NCACLU, the author being one of them.
† *Ibid.*

The ACLU condemned these "mere guesses about future behavior" without establishing guilt in the first instance, and warned Congressmen how such a measure could be "easily interpreted as an attack on Washington's black community." Each Congressman was urged to "resist efforts to undermine the Constitution and to avoid these dangers by rejecting preventive detention and concentrating on improving the courts in order to end once and for all the present long delay between arrest and trial."

Senator Ervin had already warned his colleagues that the bill was "unconstitutional and unwise and deceptively appealing legislation." During Senate debate, he said:

I am personally satisfied that preventive detention prostitutes the purpose of bail and runs afoul of the Eighth Amendment. Fundamental to due process of law is the tenet that a man is presumed innocent until proven guilty beyond a reasonable doubt. Under our system of justice the Government cannot deprive a man of his liberty on the basis of a mere accusation or assumption that he has committed a crime or is likely to do so. In practical effect, preventive detention legislation convicts individuals of "probable" guilt and "dangerousness" and sentences them to 60 days' imprisonment without trial and conviction of a crime. Such flagrant violation of due process smacks of a police state rather than a democracy under law. It is reminiscent of similar devices in other countries which have proved all too useful as tools of political repression.

. . . The law will most assuredly result in the imprisonment without trial of many persons who are not dangerous and who are innocent of the charges. If the preventive detention law is judged by its susceptibility to abuse, plainly it is an evil law.*

Preventive detention, as Senator Ervin, the ACLU, and others expert in constitutional law contend, destroys the Eighth Amendment guarantees against excessive bail and "cruel and unusual punishment." The frightful companion of preventive detention—the no-knock search and seizure provision—similarly

* Sam D. Ervin, Jr., "Bail Reform: Two Law-and-Order Views," *Wall Street Journal*, October 30, 1969, p. 18.

destroys the Fourth Amendment guarantees against "unreasonable searches and seizures." While the preventive detention measure permits seizure and detainment of the individual without adequate constitutional recourse, the heinous no-knock provision permits the breaking and entering of private property and the seizure of the individual's personal effects.

As the ACLU letter to Congressmen pointed out, Section 23-591 of the bill authorizes no-knock searches *with or without a warrant* where notice "may" result in evidence being destroyed, disposed of, or concealed.

Adds the ACLU:

Since almost any evidence could fall under this loosely drawn standard the effect will be to permit "no-knock" searches in almost every case. Moreover, the police are not required to give notice where notice would be "a useless gesture." Nothing prevents the police from concluding that the simple fact that the occupants might object to a police visit makes notice "useless" since they will have to use force anyway. . . . Citizens, supposedly protected by the Fourth Amendment, will be forced to accept the "no-knock" entry into their homes as the normal situation. This cannot be so in a democracy under law.

The ACLU letter, in a final vain attempt to persuade Congressmen to oppose the Nixon administration anticrime package summarized its provisions in a true-to-life situation:

As disturbing as each of these provisions is by itself to anyone concerned with the continued existence of civil liberties, even more troublesome to contemplate are the serious inequities and harassment which can and will be inflicted upon District residents as the police begin to realize the uses to which these techniques can be put in combination. Imagine the innocent citizen who, never having even been arrested before, is wrongly suspected of committing a crime. His phone—both home and business—can be tapped. He can be picked up by the police and detained to be fingerprinted and forced to submit to other physical tests even though the police could not arrest him. If the police should wish to search for evidence, they can do so without warning by breaking into his home in the middle of the night. And if the police, knowing full well that they lacked probable cause to arrest, decided to arrest him anyway, this bill would rob him of the right to resist—no matter how illegal or brutal the police's methods. Should he be charged with a so-called "dangerous crime" (which in this bill is defined broadly to include attempted robbery and the sale or even the use of marijuana) and should a judge decide, perhaps because he threatened the officers who broke forcibly into his home, that his release would jeopardize "the safety of any other person," he could be placed in preventive detention.

This sounds disturbingly like a police state, rather than the seat of democratic government—our nation's capital.

Unfortunately, the National Capital ACLU's big effort to defeat the Nixon anticrime package came much too late—after the Senate, the less reactionary of the two houses of Congress, had already passed the measure with a minimum of public discussion, and just before final House action.

But the meaning of such new laws to the fate of black people was recognized—and stated—from the pool halls to the highest counsels of the most establishment-secure black spokesmen.

Urban League director Whitney Young, Jr., put it succinctly:

The Administration's plan for preventive detention of persons accused of some crimes is a threat to the civil liberties of all, and can only be seen as a very dangerous threat to minority groups. . . . Black people, especially, have never really had a fair deal from the courts. Study after study has shown that black people charged with the same crimes as whites are convicted more often and get tougher sentences.

Many people are afraid that this preventive detention plan would just work out to be a way to lock up black people accused of crimes, and that it even might be the first step of a series of repressive measures that could lead to racial concentration camps.

It's easy to say "it can't happen here," but in fact it did. During World War II Japanese Americans who were accused of nothing more than of being of Japanese ancestry were thrown into concentration camps.*

* Whitney Young, Jr., "To Be Equal," Washington *Daily News*, August 11, 1969, p. 21.

The existence or nonexistence of concentration camps was an emotional issue that grew in dread and fervor as the Decisive Decade drew to a close and with ever-increasing evidence that black Americans had great cause for fear. The recurring question was not a matter of mere fascination with horror stories. Even so, any history of U.S. concentration camps was more likely to be denied than conceded, even among well-informed individuals.

Like Young, Dr. King was an exception in that regard. Both knew that the United States had laws providing for concentration camps. Both said so, but Dr. King said so fairly early—shortly before his death, in fact. Even Blacks who did not share his heavenly dreams felt sharply Dr. King's concern for their welfare. So when the shot rang out in Memphis, hell broke loose in Washington.

For days, the burning and looting leveled large sections of black concentrations in Washington. On the Sunday following the death, as black church-goers quietly walked around charred rubble and National Guardsmen, Ramsey Clark, the Attorney General of the United States, was guest on *Meet the Press*. Clark was asked whether he would counsel for or against demonstrations Dr. King had planned and demonstrations likely at the King funeral the following day. Clark answered: ". . . These are turbulent times. We are a disturbed nation, and the risks are great, and violence more than anything else risks further division and we have to maintain our self-discipline. We have to maintain our national discipline. We have to avoid anything that will tend toward violence. We can show reverence, we have to show reverence, but we have to do this within the rule of law."

Further, Clark was asked (by the author) : "Mr. Attorney General, this nation prides itself on being a nation of law. At this time we hear, however, rumors of the possibility of concentration camps for Black people in order to maintain, as you say, 'order and stability.' What are we going to do with respect to concentration camps and that kind of concern?"

Responded Clark: "There are no concentration camps in this

country. There have been no concentration camps in this country. There will be no concentration camps in this country. Rumors and the fear that arises from rumors, are a great threat to us. Fear, itself, is a great threat, and people who spread false rumors about concentration camps are either ignorant of the facts or have a motive of dividing this country."*

In saying that there *were not, had not been,* and *would not be* concentration camps in the United States, the Attorney General was obviously incorrect on the second point and almost as certainly wrong on the other two.

One need not be so well informed in legal history as the Attorney General to know that this country did, indeed, incarcerate more than 109,000 U.S. citizens of Japanese ancestry in concentration camps during World War II. In the 1945 Supreme Court case of *Korematsu v. The United States* the question the court was asked was not whether concentration camps existed, legally or illegally, or even whether Japanese-Americans should be held prisoner in them. These were so indisputable in point of fact that they were not even at issue. The question in the case was whether one such citizen, Korematsu, under his extenuating circumstances, should be included among the many thousands of other citizens who were being held. By a 5 to 3 vote, the Court decided that Korematsu *was* legally imprisoned in a concentration camp—even without being accused, much less being found guilty, of any crime.

Apologists for that bit of American history a quarter of a century later try to erase the facts with semantics, such as arguing that they were "detention" camps, not concentration camps. They should be reminded, however, that in taking positions on the decision, Supreme Court Justices themselves used the term concentration camps.

But the new clear and present danger is not so much what happened 25 years ago as the threat of its repetition. Remaining are the urgent questions of whether in the 1970's such camps exist and the status of legalities permitting their activation and use. This is not to say, however, that they would not be used

* From the official transcript of the program.

without all the legal niceties being met. History here serves to indicate that, given the circumstances, they would be.

Whenever feasible, authoritarians prefer to have the sanction of law. This was precisely the expedient of the Internal Security Act of 1950 (the McCarran Act) which, in effect, attempted to legitimatize, *ex post facto,* the use of concentration camps during World War II. Rewriting history, however, was only one major purpose of the act. Its more major purpose, and one clearly more possible and practicable, was to legitimatize *future* concentration camps. This the McCarran Act did.

The McCarran Act had its beginning in 1948 as the Mundt-Nixon bill, sponsored by Karl Mundt of South Dakota, James O. Eastland of Mississippi, Joseph McCarthy of Wisconsin, and Pat McCarran of Nevada in the Senate and in the House by Richard M. Nixon of California, Harold Himmel Velde of Illinois, and Francis E. Walter of Pennsylvania. The undeclared Korean War and the anticommunist hysteria, promoted mainly by Wisconsin Republican Joe McCarthy, triggered passage of the bill in 1950 and a massive Senate vote that overrode President Harry S. Truman's veto.

Title II is that section of the act which specifically provides for what police state advocates prefer to call detention camps. Specifically, Title II authorizes the President of the United States summarily to declare an "internal security emergency" in such events as declarations of war or "insurrection" at home which is influenced by a "foreign enemy." Included in such insurrections, of course, would be civil rights disturbances, peace demonstrations, or any other disruption which the President alone might interpret as a qualifying emergency.

Under such an emergency, the President may implement the provisions of Title II, which would authorize the Attorney General of the United States, without charges or warrants, to arrest and detain "in such places of detention as may be provided by him . . . all persons as to whom there is a reasonable ground to believe that such person probably will engage in or probably will conspire with others to engage in acts of espionage and sabotage."

Although President Lyndon B. Johnson did not invoke Title II during the 1960's, virtually all such uprisings as those in Los Angeles, Newark, Detroit, and scores of other cities could have been construed as qualifying emergencies.

In 1966, journalist Charles R. Allen, Jr., was commissioned by a group called the Citizens Committee for Constitutional Liberties to investigate the status of camps established immediately following passage of the act.* Allen, who had made a similar inspection in 1952, also had covered the actual passage of the bill through Congress. In his publication, *Concentration Camps USA,* Allen writes:

I could not help but recall the anguish of the late United States Senator, William Langer, the wonderfully non-conforming Republican from North Dakota, one of a handful in Congress who fought a truly principled struggle against the McCarran Act during those stormy days of 1950 when the country was fighting a war 10,000 miles away in Korea and wracked by the hysteria of McCarthyism at home.

"So now it is proposed to have concentration camps in America!" he cried at the end of his long, one-man filibuster against final passage of the McCarran Act.

"We can be absolutely certain that the concentration camps are for only one purpose. Namely, to put in them the kind of people those in authority do not like. So we have come to this!"

He had no sooner uttered the last words when he suddenly crashed forward to the Senate floor.

In the ensuing clamor, the stretcher bearing "Wild Bill" Langer's prostrate form was carried out of the Senate chamber. A reporter covering the tumultuous uproar was heard to remark: "They've just carried out the Bill of Rights—and don't you forget it!"†

---

\* Reveals Allen: "The [AP] report went on to say that the camps were being 'quietly' erected at Wickenburg and Florence, Arizona, and El Reno, Oklahoma, the latter places having served as prisoner-of-war camps during World War II. Other sites were specified as Allenwood, Pennsylvania; Avon Park, Florida; and Tule Lake, California."

† Charles R. Allen, Jr., *Concentration Camps USA* (New York, under commission of the Citizens Committee for Constitutional Liberties, New York, copyright Charles R. Allen, Jr., 1966) pp. 3–5.

It is at least a noteworthy coincidence that the McCarran Act was adopted at the outset of the Korean War—the country's first big undeclared war in violation of the Constitution—and became a pronounced threat during the second such war, the war in Indochina. Both wars were undeclared, and neither was popular, although antiwar sentiment was far sharper over the latter. The act itself and the six camps readied for use in 1952 stood as subtle reminders to those who would oppose either such a war or demonstratively oppose oppression at home.

The fact that the camps were intended for practical use beyond their symbolic effect quickly became a matter of record. Allen's 1966 exposition recalls how Attorney General J. Howard McGrath announced on New Year's Eve, 1952, that the six camps were for occupancy. Then, Allen states:

> Within two weeks, Senator James Eastland, Democrat of Mississippi, the ranking member of the Internal Security Subcommittee charged with overseeing the McCarran Act, placed a bill before the Senate demanding that "a state of internal security emergency be declared immediately by Congress." He insisted he had "reliable information" that 50,000 "Communists" were ready to overthrow the government of the United States.
>
> "If we are to keep faith with those of our own flesh and blood who are facing the bullets of the Communists on the battlefields of Korea, the least we can do is to promptly seize and detain under lock and key, each and everyone of the 50,000 identifiable, trained and hardened traitors," he said.
>
> Against a rising tide of McCarthyism at home and sensational reverse in the Korean war abroad, the United Press reported that J. Howard McGrath had expanded the Justice Department's Internal Security Division and was "quietly pushing a program pinpointing dangerous subversives for immediate arrest" at a time of "emergency." *

The Allen exposition continues:

> Master "pick-up lists" had already been prepared in Washington on the basis of "many thousands of FBI reports," the wire service

* *Ibid.,* p. 7.

stated, and "Operation Dragnet" (code name for the mass arrests) could start a round-up of "tens of thousands of potential spies and saboteurs *within a few hours.*"

"Justice Department officials—including FBI Director J. Edgar Hoover—are understood to feel that the program is necessary to make sure an anti-subversive round-up can be carried out without confusion and as quickly as possible," the UP added.

Even *The Chicago Daily Tribune,* that caricature of Midwest reaction, found all of these developments too much. Denouncing 'Concentration Camps in America,' a long, thoughtfully and well written editorial published a few days after the announcement of the selection of the six camp sites underscored the feelings of many Americans when it pointed out: "The zeal of the attorney general in getting ready to put this section of the internal security act into effect . . . is strange and ominous.

"The constitutional rights of the individual now face dangers without precedent, and the Truman Administration could easily use the Korean war as pretext for the jailing of political opponents or critics of the existing administration.

". . . a man or woman can simply be made to disappear into a federal concentration camp without even anybody knowing of his fate or coming forward to defend him," the newspaper warned.†
[Emphasis original.]

Considering the existence of both an enabling law and camps in readiness, it is remarkable that concentration camps were not, as such, knowingly used during the 1960's. The explanation may be simply that the right combination—the men and the circumstances—had not quite jelled. Ramsey Clark's denial of the existence of the camps probably indicated more of a revulsion from the truth than an ignorance of the facts. *But the same cannot be said of such men as Assistant Attorney General Richard Kleindienst, his boss, Attorney General John Mitchell, or even President Nixon, who, after all, was a cosponsor of the McCarran Act.*

Events during the Johnson administration would have provided opportunities too tempting to believe that under the

† *Ibid.,* pp. 7–8.

Nixon administration they would have been rejected. For example, the aftermath of the assassination of Dr. Martin Luther King, Jr., April 4, 1968, would have been a prime opportunity to invoke Title II of the McCarran Act. Washington burned for several more days before the violence in the aftermath subsided. In the interim, President Johnson had permitted the city of Washington to employ an unusual policy of leniency which kept down the fatalities and injuries from police reaction to the violence and looting. Even so, scores of Blacks arrested were taken to detention facilities in Virginia after those in the District of Columbia were filled to capacity. So ripe was the situation, in fact, that it was only one month later that the House Un-American Activities Committee urged President Johnson to invoke Title II—and more. Chaired by Louisiana Democrat Edwin E. Willis, HUAC called on the President to commit open war against the black population.

Willis, a Representative of a major rice-producing state, released HUAC's report, first imputing to black "revolutionaries" a plan to engage the U.S. government in "guerrilla warfare," then showing how racial identity and the concentration of Blacks in the ghettos would assist in their being "isolated and destroyed in a short period of time."

While President Johnson did not act on the recommendations of HUAC, neither were the recommendations repudiated in any audible way by the White House or either house of the Congress. Implicit in developments of the first two years of the Nixon administration is the conclusion that similar opportunities for military or paramilitary counterforce would not be passed over. On the contrary, during the comparatively uneventful first year of the Nixon administration, it came forward with incredible police state suggestions of its own, ranging from the President's call for no-knock searches and preventive detention, Attorney General Mitchell's call for the wider use of wiretapping, to the call of his deputy, Richard Kleindienst, for the use of detention camps—all accompanied by an unparalleled facilitation of such steps.

In February, 1969, just a month after the Nixon administration took over in Washington, Labor Secretary George P. Shultz was dispatched to the Miami Beach convention of the AFL-CIO executives, where Shultz set out to smooth relations with that giant arm of organized labor. Outstanding was the issue of the administration's announced intention of controlling inflation by—bluntly stated—causing unemployment, thereby lowering the price of labor. Treasury Secretary David Kennedy had said as much in his confirmation hearings, and members of the Federal Reserve Board had loudly intimated the same. In an interview at the convention, Shultz essentially reaffirmed that inflation would be controlled at the expense of the workers rather than at the expense of industry. AFL-CIO president George Meany plainly told a news conference that labor would stoutly resist any administration move toward unilateral price controls against the working man.

Other points of interest and concern included what plans Shultz and the administration had in mind for the Job Corps, which Shultz's Department of Labor had just inherited from OEO. There were quiet stories current in Washington that some members of Shultz's staff were proposing that the Job Corps emphasis be switched from teen-agers to a "family Job Corps." This idea had some appeal to Shriver when he was head of OEO. There were other reports that some members of the Nixon administration were fascinated with the idea of mandatory birth control in connection with family Job Corps programs. All these things Shultz acknowledged* as "possibilities" but insisted that they were just ideas that "might not work . . . we're just thinking about them." He and his advisers had thought that "we could do something especially for unwed mothers," he said.

He did not spell out what he would have done "especially for unwed mothers" beyond what would be done for wed mothers who needed economic help and training. For the unwed mother, he said, the Job Corps was a unique answer in that it could provide for "all a family's needs"—education for the

* Except where otherwise indicated, the Shultz quotes come from author's notes of personal interviews.

children, a job of some type for both the mother and father, food and clothing supplies shipped in to them and, as Shultz put it, "they wouldn't have to leave for anything." Shultz denied, however, that there was any plan to change the Job Corps from a voluntary to a mandatory enrollment program.

Later, back in Washington, it became impossible to find anyone among usually good news sources at OEO and Labor who would commit himself on what really was to become of the 59 massive Job Corps camps the Nixon administration had announced would be closed.

Inflation and labor uncertainties continued to mount. On April 27, 1969, Shultz was guest on *Meet the Press*. During preparation for the interview, news sources would either clam up or hint suspiciously whenever the question of the disposition of the closed centers was introduced. Thus, settling this question became a major effort on *Meet the Press*. As a member of the panel, I asked for a direct reply:

Yette: Mr. Secretary, President Nixon switched the Job Corps from the Office of Economic Opportunity to the Labor Department, and you have recently announced that you will close about 59 of those centers. You, yourself, have said that closing those centers will effect a $100-million budget appreciation, but opening the new centers will cost about $24-million. However, there is no indication just yet as to what is to happen to those centers which you are closing, in which the public has invested about $50 million in terms of physical improvements. What is to become of them?

Shultz: We are working with state government and others in terms of possible usefulness of the physical property involved. Some of it may be useful in new centers that are opened in cities and near cities. In general, we are addressing ourselves to a proper disposition of the property that is present there. I do think that you should remember, just as in a poker game, if you have a bad hand but you have put a lot of money on the table and you find yourself getting called, there is no point in putting good money after bad. I think the same thing holds true here. Just because you have made an investment—if the investment isn't productive, the best thing to do is to withdraw.

Yette: Two of these largest camps, Camp Kilmer in the New York–New Jersey area, and Camp Parks in California, were improved at a combined cost of about $8 million. These are federal properties. What, exactly, is to be done with them?

Shultz: I think the same point holds again, that just because you have made a bad investment doesn't mean you should continue to pour money into something that isn't working. We are working at the problem of the disposition of these assets, as I said, in an orderly way. I can't tell you precisely what will happen to those properties.

Yette: At the labor convention in February in Miami, you indicated to me that you were "favorably disposed"—to use your term—toward a family Job Corps, that is, a Job Corps in which the entire family might be enrolled. Might these centers be used in that way?

Shultz: I think one of the thoughts that we have in mind as we project the Fiscal-1970 picture—and the Labor Department won't be running the Job Corps until the first of July, it is not in the Labor Department right now—but one of the things we have in mind is what we have called in-city or near-city type of centers. We think one possibility to try out is to bring the unwed mother into a center of that kind where there can be a reasonable residential setting, an opportunity for some training and some day care for children. That is an idea and we will try it out. It may not work. We hope it will. We will proceed to examine it as we try it and judge it as we go along.

Secretary Shultz, of course, did not answer the question of what actually would happen at these centers in which the taxpayers had invested so heavily. Shultz was an economist with a national reputation, having been dean of the Graduate School of Business at the University of Chicago. Someone so professionally dollar-conscious could not have overlooked a $50-million detail—like what would be done with 59 closed Job Corps camps.

Too, as journalist Allen pointed out in his report on concentration camps, the six camps set up in 1952 were, from a space standpoint, simply inadequate to handle the masses entailed should Title II of the McCarran Act be implemented. Such implementation would move the federal and local police to apprehend and detain astronomical numbers of antiwar pro-

testers, civil rights demonstrators, "intellectual eunuchs," Black
Panthers, Communists, Panther sympathizers, Communist
sympathizers, and others whom the administration would regard as violence-prone or ideological misfits.

Allen's 1966 investigation of the Title II camps showed a
total known capacity—even counting seven "other sites available" for use as detention centers—of only 26,500. Thus, assum-
ing that a respectable number of the detainees would be kept
alive and require normal space, that 26,500 capacity would not
cover those, say, in the lead flank of the November 15, 1969,
Vietnam Moratorium of some 400,000 persons who marched in
the nation's Capital.

But closed Job Corps camps?—that's another matter.

Thus, a final series of questions to Secretary Shultz:

Yette: Mr. Secretary, I'd like to go back, if I may, to the disposition of these Job Corps centers which are being closed and relate
them to current social problems. The May issue of the *Atlantic
Monthly* magazine quotes Deputy Attorney General Richard Kleindienst as saying, "Protest demonstrators should be rounded up and
put in a detention camp." Both Washington papers this morning,
the *Post* and the *Star,* carry stories in which Mr. Kleindienst denies
he was accurately quoted. However, in view of the enormous
investment that such facilities as Kilmer and Parks have experienced, with no apparent use for them, as you indicated a few
minutes ago, might they, in fact, be used for such purposes?

As he saw the question coming, Secretary Shultz began a kind
of frown and wagging of his head, as if to plead with me not to
complete the question. When the question was through, he sat
for a long, embarrassing pause, and finally responded with a
classic dodge which was, in effect, an admission that even an
obvious dodge would be less incriminating than the truth:

Shultz: I think I will just duck on that one.
Yette: In other words, they might be?
Shultz: No, I am not going to get into the argument between the
Washington *Post* and Mr. Kleindienst.

Yette: It isn't an argument between them, sir. The question is: since you have the authority with respect to these centers, the public has invested at least $50 million in their improvement, they are there now, they are federal properties—some of them—what is to be done with them?

Shultz: This is something that we are studying, and we are going to have some constructive uses, as much as we possibly can.

The interview ended a few minutes later, and the reporters gathered around Shultz to hear his reactions.

"That was unfair for you to ask me that question," he said.

"I don't see why, sir. You're a responsible public official, and the taxpayers have a right to know."

"I know," he said, in words that seem to wink, "but *I* don't want to be the one to say that those kids are going to be locked up in those camps."

He *never* denied that they *would* be.

No alarms (or even well-mannered inquiries) greeted the Nixon administration on the concentration camp question "ducked" on national television by a member of the President's Cabinet. But there was an increase in public awareness and concern, and that concern began to be reflected in the efforts of certain Congressmen. Those of Japanese-American descent felt the experience of the World War II concentration camps, and in 1969 they led the move toward repeal of the McCarran Act, followed closely by black Congressmen.

On April 18, 1969, two weeks before the Shultz *Meet the Press* interview, Senator Daniel K. Inouye of Hawaii, a Japanese-American who lost an arm fighting his racial kinsmen during World War II, introduced a bill seeking to repeal Title II of the McCarran Act. By Senate rules, the bill went to the Senate Judiciary Committee, chaired by Mississippi Senator James O. Eastland.

In the House, companion bills were introduced by Japanese-American Spark Matsunaga of Honolulu, Abner J. Mikva of Chicago, Chet Holifield of Montebello, California, John Conyers, Jr., of Detroit, and others. By House rules, the bills for repeal were referred to the House Internal Security Committee (formerly HUAC), the same group which in 1968 called for the *use* of such camps.

Introducing his repeal bill to Congress, Matsunaga told his House colleagues:

Following the enactment of the Internal Security Act of 1950, six detention camps were prepared and maintained by the Department of Justice from 1952 to 1957—two in Arizona and one each in Pennsylvania, Florida, Oklahoma, and California.

Beginning in 1958, Congress stopped appropriating funds for their continued maintenance, so these camps were either abandoned or converted to other uses. With these camps no longer in existence, and with the unreasoning anti-communism of the early fifties no longer a political fetish, Title II was more or less forgotten.

About two years ago, however, rumors were rampant that the Government was again preparing detention camps, under the authority of the Emergency Detention Act for dissidents, activists, militants, and others with whom those in public office might disagree. . . .

The present national climate shows that it is not enough for Justice Department officials to deny the existence of emergency detention camps, or for the Government to say that it does not intend to build them or that there are no present plans to invoke Title II.

As President Truman stated in his 1950 veto message:

It is not enough to say that this probably would not be done. The mere fact that it could be done shows clearly how the bill would open a Pandora's box of opportunities for official condemnation of organizations and individuals for perfectly honest opinions. The basic error of these sections is that they move in the direction of suppressing opinion and belief.

. . . I strongly urge others who believe in justice and fair play to join in cosponsoring this legislation which would remove the legal sanction for American concentration camps and thereby uphold the constitutional safeguards for individual liberty. A law as repugnant to our American way of life as the Emergency Detention Act should not be permitted to remain in our statute books.*

Holifield also urged his House colleagues to repeal the concentration camp measure, and reminded Americans that use of such camps could happen again:

In the years since this measure was enacted, no Government official has put it to use. The fact that it exists, however, has been the basis for serious anxiety among certain segments of the population. These anxieties generally are brought about because of our memories of the way such camps were used in Nazi Germany. And the fact that U.S. citizens of Japanese extraction were once incarcerated in "protective custody" does little to allay fears that this could happen again—in America. . . . As long as title II is on the books, it could be used, and some American citizens would probably be arrested and detained before its constitutionality could be ruled on by the courts.†

Perhaps the most direct message sent to the black masses about the danger and reality of concentration camps came from Representative Shirley Chisholm of Brooklyn, the first black woman in Congress. *Jet* magazine, perhaps the most thoroughly read publication by the black masses, reported Mrs. Chisholm's testimony before the House Internal Security Committee in an effort to repeal Title II:

Cong. Shirley Chisholm testified in favor of the repeal of the Emergency Detention Act of 1950 before the House Internal Securities Committee in Washington, D.C. The freshman legislator said, "I stand here today looking over events of the past two decades and I am afraid—afraid and angry. I see democracy dying and it is not the 'red menace' that is killing it. I see the roots of fascism . . . in this country. . . . There is a distinct pattern emerging . . . to repress freedom of the press and freedom of the individual." Cong. Chisholm, who says she feels that she and the other eight black members of the House must, because of their small numbers relative

* *Congressional Record,* June 4, 1969, pp. H-4497–H-4498.
† *Ibid.,* pp. H-4498–H-4500.

to the nation's 22,000,000 black Americans, respond to the needs of all minority groups, added: "The majority of black people do not believe that . . . the Emergency Detention Act has been on the books for 20 years. They reason that white supremacist organizations such as the KKK and the Minutemen have armed themselves to the teeth and no attempt such as the 'law and order' events I have mentioned were used to stop them. Why now and why against the Panthers? The history of this country necessitates that people of color regard a bill of this nature with fear of even further oppression. History has recorded the white man's treatment of the American Indian. . . . It has recorded the events of slavery . . . and again the events during World War II when Japanese-Americans were ruthlessly swept into concentration camps." She further noted that despite highly organized and visible activity by the German-American Bund during the Second World War "no German (Americans) were thrown in American concentration camps . . . why? There could be only one reason, because they were white."*

These appeals, plus increasing public concern and awareness of the danger, eventually moved the Nixon administration to pose on the side of those who wanted the McCarran Act repealed. In fact, the public attention given the provision diminished to some degree its impregnability; hence, its tactical value was open to reassessment in view of the growing public awareness and concern.

On October 23, 1969, a group of black persons descended on the office of Attorney General Mitchell for a secret meeting on civil rights. The group included SCLC president Dr. Abernathy; Dr. King's widow, Mrs. Coretta Scott King; Gary, Indiana, Mayor Richard G. Hatcher; and Detroit Congressman John Conyers, Jr. The White House was represented at the meeting by Leonard Garment, one of President Nixon's closest advisers on minority affairs.

Reported columnists Roland Evans and Robert Novak:

After airing grievances against the administration's position to extend the Voting Rights Act beyond the South and deteriorating

* *Jet,* April 9, 1970, p. 4.

relations between big city police departments and black ghettos, Mitchell's visitors pulled no punches in asking administration backing for repeal of Title II.

With congressional liberals pushing hard for the same thing, Mitchell agreed to consider it—but left the final decision up to Deputy Attorney General Richard Kleindienst, who was not present. Kleindienst read the minutes of the October 23 meeting and—six weeks later—rendered his decision. He announced it last Wednesday [Dec. 3, 1969] in a letter to Chairman James O. Eastland (D-Miss.) of the Senate Judiciary Committee (who favors repeal, but as a trade-off to liberals for a new, tough internal security law).*

This Deputy Attorney General Kleindienst, of course, is the same Deputy Attorney General who had been quoted as calling for the use of concentration camps for protest demonstrators just six months earlier. And Senator Eastland is the same Senator Eastland who had called for the use of camps two weeks after Title II was enacted in 1950.

The mystery of this apparent change of heart by these two men is largely solved in the fact that there was no change of heart at all, but rather a change in tactics. Evans and Novak hinted at the tactics in Eastland's willingness to suffer a repeal of Title II in exchange for a "new, tough internal security law," thus publicizing the *possible* surrender of a demonstrably heinous law in exchange for an obscure law that achieves the same thing—with a few new flourishes.

Responding to the Inouye bill for repeal of Title II in the summer of 1969, Senator Eastland said concentration camps could be sacrificed "because I don't think they are necessary."† The Mississippi Senator could say that, secure in the knowledge that repeal of Title II was still in the hands of himself and his counterparts on strategic committees of the House. In short, regardless of what he and others said, Eastland and his rice empire confreres would have the clout to block the repeal if

---

* Roland Evans and Robert Novak, "Concentration Camp Switch," Washington *Post*, December 7, 1969, p. C-7.
† Washington *Daily News*, June 25, 1969.

they chose. Beyond that, Eastland—six months earlier, in January, 1969—had already quietly arranged for any such eventuality as sacrificing Title II of the Internal Security Act of 1950. He had introduced his own new version: the Internal Security Act of 1969.

He and his compatriots could control the repeal of one just as handily as they could control passage of the other. But there was absolutely no likelihood that the old one would disappear without the new one being on the books. Eastland, again, through his power as chairman of the Senate Judiciary Committee, was assured control of either eventuality.

In any event, Eastland's Judiciary Committee approved and reported out to the full Senate the Inouye repeal bill on December 8, 1969—just five days after the Nixon administration publicly agreed to the idea. It was not the kind of action that results from a lack of warm understanding between the White House and a Congressional committee.

Senator Eastland could say the McCarran Act concentration camps are unnecessary also because of the fact that his substitute would literally make every man's home his own detention center. For example, Title IX of the Eastland bill, entitled "Travel Control," empowers the Secretary of State to curtail sharply areas of foreign travel by U.S. citizens. Title V provides penalties up to a $5,000 fine and a year in jail for any citizen outside the United States who fails to respond to a subpoena from any Congressional committee. Title IV would fine any citizen $5,000 and jail him up to five years for failing to surrender his passport upon the request of the State Department. And, under the same title, no person failing to swear allegiance to the United States would be permitted to receive or use any credentials identifying him as a U.S. citizen.

The substance of the provisions mentioned above is to tie every citizen closer to the lines of control held tightly by Senator Eastland and those of like power and sentiments in Congress. Those who remain in the United States will not find the pursuit of happiness an easy venture under the Eastland bill, should it be enacted. There are provisions which would go

even beyond the McCarran Act by making the McCarran wartime prohibitions against sedition apply even when there is no
declaration of war. Title I states:

> Whoever, owing allegiance to the United States knowingly and
> willfully gives aid or comfort to an *adversary* of the United States
> by an overt act, within the United States or elsewhere, shall be fined
> not more than $10,000 or imprisoned not more than ten years, or
> both. . . . As used in this section the term "adversary of the
> United States" means any foreign nation or armed group which is
> engaged in *open hostilities* against the United States or with which
> the Armed Forces of the United States are engaged in *open hostil-
> ities.* [Emphases added.]*

Such a prohibition, of course, would cover all of the peace
demonstrators against the undeclared war in Indochina, since
the Vietcong "engages" U.S. forces.

Similarly, the Eastland bill defines sedition as anyone "advancing the objectives of the world Communist movement."
Indiana University constitutional law professor Patrick Baude
calls such a definition "void for vagueness—clearly unconstitutional." Professor Baude further points out that "one of the
announced objectives of the Communist doctrine is world
peace. Under that you could be jailed for advocating world
peace."†

The Eastland bill provides other measures such as one that
destroys the Fifth Amendment granting immunity against self-
incrimination. A riot under the bill is "an act or acts of violence
by one or more persons part of an assemblage of three or more
persons, which act or acts shall constitute a clear and present
danger of, or shall result in, damage or injury to the property of
any other person or to the person of any other individual" or
even "a threat or threats of the commission of an act or acts of
violence by one or more persons. . . ."

---

* S.12, "A Bill to strengthen the internal security of the United States," introduced by Senator Eastland, January 15, 1969, Title I, Sec. 105, p. 6.

† From an unpublished term paper by Rick Musser, graduate student of
journalism at Indiana University, February, 1970.

Laws, whether they be the McCarran Act, the Eastland Act, or the Civil Rights Act of 1964, are merely the tools which may be used to reach an objective. The McCarran Act and the Eastland bill are as demonstrably oppressive as no-knock search and preventive detention measures. The political machinery which controls the passage or defeat of such legislation rarely favors the less extreme forces in Congress. The machinery is in the hands of men who want bad tools.

For example, in both the Ninetieth and Ninety-first Congresses, Senate Judiciary chairman Eastland introduced his Internal Security Act, whose threat of possible passage he uses to keep in hostage those Congressmen who wish to repeal the McCarran Act. He is aided by his position as committee chairman, which gives him the authority to call a bill up for action or to let it die at the end of each session of Congress. Political pressure on Eastland during the Ninety-first Congress forced him to release Senator Inouye's bill for the repeal of Title II of the McCarran Act, but at the same time, as chairman also of the Senate Internal Security Subcommittee, Eastland achieved favorable subcommittee action on his own bill which he could call up for final action at the strategic moment. That strategy is synchronized with delayed House action on the Senate-passed bill for the repeal of the McCarran Act. The bill for repeal had 133 cosponsors in the House but could not get House action: House Internal Security Committee chairman Ichord opposed the measure and let it die in committee.

With these oppressive measures have come the facilities for carrying them out—such as the McCarran Act concentration camps, closed Job Corps centers, and the "regional detention facilities"* under the new Law Enforcement Assistance Ad-

---

* At a White House press conference, May 27, 1970, Norman A. Carlson, director, Bureau of Prisons, and Richard W. Velde, associate administrator, Law Enforcement Assistance Administration (LEAA), discussed the report of the President's Task Force on Prisoner Rehabilitation: "The Criminal Offender— What Should Be Done?" Ostensibly, it was a report on prisoner rehabilitation, but the most salient aspects of the report—and of the discussions by Carlson and Velde—were a million-dollar "criminal justice information and statistic service," including a $60,000 grant to the Census Bureau "to make a survey of jails," and what Velde described as "roughly $50 million . . . being spent by the States in

ministration. The existence of oppressive legislation alone makes a strong case for the capability of legal genocide; but the existence of both an oppressive climate and detention camps begin to make the minimal case for probability and intent.

---

the form of block grants for improvements in the corrections area . . . particularly in the area of community treatment centers and regional detention facilities." Richard W. Velde is the son of Harold Himmel Velde, an original sponsor of concentration camps under Title II of the McCarran Act of 1950.

# Chapter 7

# The Reality

"So now it is out in the open," began an editorial in the Washington *Afro-American*. "Now the sordid truth has pressed its ugly mien through the bland, respectable-looking cover of the House Un-American Activities Committee report."* This reaction to the HUAC report calling for the "destruction" of black people in ghetto colonies came from a black newspaper whose optimism over a 76-year history had buoyed the spirits of oppressed people newly out of slavery and into what had appeared to be a decade of genuine fulfillment. The Afro-American newspapers had confidence in the ultimate reversal of the 1896 *Plessy v. Ferguson* decision setting up "separate but equal" forces with the strength of constitutional law. Their editors had urged black men to fight in two world wars with the confidence that ultimately their loyalty and sacrifice would be rewarded with "life, liberty and the pursuit of happiness." Their publisher had financed signal court cases leading to the 1954 *Brown* decision against "separate but equal," and had provided the nation and Congress with evidence on which to base the Civil Rights Act of 1964. Through it all, the Afro-American and other major black media had unstintingly counseled nonviolence in seeking redress and patience in the struggle.

But this report from HUAC, quoted in Part I, was different. It did not arrive unrelated to its time and the events around it,

* Washington *Afro-American*, May 7, 1968.

294

and its call to "destroy" black Americans came in a context of reality: *Their destruction was taking place.* Thus, the *Afro-American* editorial continued:

Now it is admitted that if some colored Americans are sufficiently determined to assume by force their rightful place of manhood in this society, some of the white power structure is prepared to set aside Magna Carta, the Constitution, preachments on Due Process and all the rest.

Now an instrumentality of the legislative branch of federal government has admitted that in its sinister mind it has prepared to follow the morally verminous route of Hitler's Germany by using concentration camps in which to detain colored political militants. . . .

Responsible colored leadership has been telling ghetto dwellers that such proposals were only rumors conjured up by political radicals like H. Rap Brown and Stokely Carmichael. . . .

Colored citizens will want to know why in the case of poverty-stricken slum-dwellers in a land that preaches equality before the law the idea of individual guilt and punishment could be so quickly recommended into limbo and replaced by one of mass guilt and mass punishment.

They will want to know why other important structure figures allowed 10 minutes to pass before damning these proposals by racist-minded HUAC members.

They will ask themselves, are Stokely and Rap right? Is the ultimate plan genocide for all non-whites in sight?*

Many black intellectuals and civil rights activists had been answering those questions in the affirmative with increasing fervor during the Decisive Decade. Only six weeks before he died, Dr. Martin Luther King, Jr., foresaw the government's cordoning off the ghetto with barbed wire fences.† But, a year earlier, in 1967, others were beginning to face the reality in general-circulation publications.

---

* *Ibid.*
† William Hedgepeth, "America's Concentration Camps: The Rumors and the Realities," *Look,* May 28, 1968, p. 86.

A new level of danger-consciousness began to emerge during the summer of 1967, underscored by serious uprisings in Newark and other cities and in the mood of the black power conference in Newark. During that period, the New York *Post* ran a series of articles on black power, featuring interviews with key men in the black struggle. The interviewer, Jerry Tallmer, put questions to such men as Lincoln Lynch, then forty-six and associate national director of CORE, and Conrad Lynn, then fifty-eight and a lawyer long active in radical causes.

Said Lynch: "The simple fact is that the vast majority of white America is racist. Now please, Mr. Tallmer, I'm giving you my own experience. That is my experience. So that what is at stake here is not whether I can get a decent apartment in Manhattan or Mississippi, or sit on a beach in California, *but whether I live at all.*" [Emphasis original.]

Lynch tried to explain what some black activists call "black nationalism." "Let me put it another way," Lynch said. "We think of Harlem as a colony, a nation within a nation. Now, our aim is not to establish a separate nation, but I do not see why we could not have an independent city."

Tallmer had Conrad Lynn react to Lynch's "colony" concept of black existence: "In American society," Lynn was quoted, "it is not possible to have a successful revolutionary change with black people alone because they'll [whites will] just isolate the black people and smash them in the end. . . . Imagine talking about Harlem as a nation! How long would Harlem survive as a nation? Six days?"

Then Tallmer put the issue to Lynch again: "Okay," said Tallmer, "an independent Harlem. But let me ask: Where would Harlem get its water? Its gas? Its electricity? Its money? Its food? Its automobiles? Its jobs? I mean, pushed to the last analysis—absolute and complete independence."

Tallmer reports that Lynch's response came in "a fusion of feeling." "Do you know what you're saying?" Lynch asked his interviewer. "You're saying that when it gets right down to it, white people are ready to cut us off. To kill us."

Conceded Tallmer: "If you push it to the last analysis, that's exactly what I'm afraid will happen."*

If this was true when Lynch spoke in 1967, it was more true in 1969.

In 1968, for example, the late Senator Everett McKinley Dirksen (Republican of Illinois), himself no semblance of John Brown and, instead, a supporter of Presidential candidate Nixon, reached a point of disgust in the call for "liquidations" in mail sent to him by people who thought him likely to go along. In his syndicated column, Senator Dirksen discussed "some of the less explosive demands" pressed upon him:

I want to expose to you an example of some of the terrible stuff that comes to us in Congress from little organizations that attempt to chip away at the greatness of our freedom. It is a folder of hate and deceit that comes to Washington out of the west.

The theme of the "message" in the folder is one of hate because it proposes terrible things like concentration camps for militant Americans and work camps for so-called lazy Americans. The theme is also one of deceit because it purports to reflect the mood of the grass roots of our population and because it ties hateful ideas to the most welcome cry of the century—"Reduce taxes!"

. . . Its front-page title—or blurb—screams out: "This is what the people want! Based on a meticulous survey in the grass roots." Inside, it sets forth 49 items of demand that send the chills down your back. The items are listed in highly extreme, very racist and quite illogical language. Here are some of the less explosive demands made by the little organization that pretends to speak for the grass roots. . . .

Now, presuming that the reader of the folder has been won over with the demand for less taxes, the message goes on: "Destroy Castro and liquidate the communist regime in Cuba!"

Cuba is a sovereign country. To destroy Castro would mean a declaration of war upon another nation with all that such a venture implies. And what is that word "liquidate" doing in a communication—however anonymous—to a senator?

. . . This one is frightening in concept: "Enlarge our prison complexes into great outdoor encampments for disciplinary action!"

* New York *Post*, June 21, 1967, p. 41.

Who would want concentration camps in America?

There you have a prime example of racist propaganda that would try to tear us apart even more than we are torn today.

Nobody in his right mind could believe this stuff that comes out of a hole in somebody's head as an expression of the people, the "grass roots." Yet, it is only one small example of the terrible proposals that are made to congressmen, that try to convince us that Americans are not, after all, freedom loving, sane people.*

Almost a year before Senator Dirksen's column and the HUAC report, Floyd B. McKissick, then national director of CORE, was already asking black people to face the reality of their danger. The title and content of his speech, "Genocide U.S.A.—A Blueprint for Black Survival," set the context of the threat of the new decade. McKissick told a starkly attentive crowd:

You ask: Would America intentionally starve Black People in Mississippi, feed Indians only if they agreed to domination by white people? Would America allow thousands of Blacks to be wasted on the streets of Newark or Buffalo, Watts or Atlanta, because they simply said: "Take your foot off our necks?"

Would America destroy the lives of millions of Blacks whose fore-bearers, as slaves, made and developed this economic-political system, by their blood, sweat and free labor? Is there not a word called Respect—another word called Mercy—another, Justice?

Many Jews in Germany thought so. During Hitler's regime, they discovered differently.

Would America systematically destroy 22 million Blacks? My answer is: Look at the record! More specifically, I believe they can. I believe they will.†

No, genocide is not a simple matter. It cannot just happen. One group of people cannot just go ahead and wipe out another group of people. They must first pass through several stages—they must live out a peculiar and deadly pattern.

The first prerequisite for a nation capable of genocide is the belief that they are superior to their victims. They must believe that they are entitled to the control of the life and death of their victims.

* Washington *Daily News*, June 5, 1968, p. 35.

† Floyd B. McKissick, "Genocide U.S.A., A Blueprint for Black Survival," a printed speech delivered in Newark, N.J., July 21, 1967, and distributed by the National Congress of Racial Equality, New York, N.Y., p. 4.

During Hitler's regime, the Germans were supplied with elaborate charts and complicated theses, supposedly proving the superiority of the German people. It is interesting to note that, at the bottom of these charts were the colored people of the world, most conspicuously, the Black people. . . .

Genocide is a political decision. It can be made by a town, city, state, nation or group of nations. It was a political decision, for example, to exterminate the Communists in Indonesia. It was a political decision for the CIA to engineer the coup. . . .*

*It will be interesting to watch what will happen in the near future in such places as Thailand, Cambodia, and Laos.* [Emphasis added.]

We cannot let those patterns which have already been applied so successfully around the world and which are already in motion in this country be carried to their logical, ultimate conclusion. These patterns must be halted now.

And we must be the ones to do it. We cannot expect help from anyone but ourselves. . . .

This is not a problem of Civil Rights—it is a problem of Black Survival. The concept of civil rights is pitifully insignificant when our very lives are at stake.†

Fear, pessimism, even alarm are not new to the postslavery struggles of black Americans. But, always during the Decisive Decade, there were public pronouncements and public stances to counter fears, pessimism, and alarming rhetoric. The new decade is different. Serious reassurances from the Nixon administration are rare. Such rarity caused reporters to press black college presidents as to *why* they would feel hopeful after leaving their more than two hours with President Nixon in the spring of 1970.

"I have hope and confidence," Morgan State College president Martin D. Jenkins explained in plain consternation. "There is little in the historical record which would lead to this conclusion, and yet, as a black and an American, I must believe—if I believe in this nation—I must believe that it will

* *Ibid*, pp. 5, 10.
† *Ibid.*, p. 11.

move forward, and that it will move forward under the President of the United States. I can take no other position than that."*

On this, the Washington *Post* commented:

This constitutes, perhaps, the highest form of loyalty—loyalty not to a particular government or administration but to the ideals and purposes for which that government was established. What Dr. Jenkins was saying was that against admittedly great odds and in the face of the available evidence, he clings nevertheless to a conviction that the American people are still going to make good on the promise of American life.†

The *Post* editorial recited some of the barriers a black American's hope and confidence had to hurdle:

Consider that Dr. Jenkins made his statement only a few days after six black men, all shot in the back by police firearms, were found dead in Augusta, Ga. He made the statement in the immediate aftermath of a grand jury finding that Chicago police, on the pretext of making an arrest, had wantonly fired nearly 100 rifle shots into a Black Panther hangout, killing a Black Panther national leader. He made the statement on the heels of the tragedy in Jackson, Miss., where two college students were killed and nine more were wounded because state highway police poured a fusillade of shots into a dormitory. And he made the statement immediately after talking to a President whose Department of Justice had announced support of tax exemption for private schools set up in the South to circumvent the civil rights laws and the Supreme Court's school desegregation decision.**

Indeed, there was little in the new decade to warrant black hope and confidence based on a protective, rather than a punitive, federal government. Small wonder then that black Georgia state legislator Julian Bond would say, "If you could call Adolf

---

* Washington *Post,* May 20, 1970, p. 1.
† Washingon *Post,* May 23, 1970, p. A-14.
** *Ibid.*

Hitler a friend of the Jews, you could call President Nixon a friend of the blacks,"* or that then Harlem Congressman Adam Clayton Powell would admonish Blacks to "go without food if necessary and buy a gun" to halt such "murders" as those at Jackson State.†

Such dread was not even confined to black politicians who feared for their young. Addressing an Indiana University alumni gathering May 14, 1970, in Roslyn, Virginia, Senator Vance Hartke (Democrat of Indiana) expressed the fear that federal repression against students and the campuses will "take our children and relegate them to the gas chamber, at least in the rhetorical sense, if not in the physical sense."**

The most alarming fears expressed by the Carmichaels, Lynns, McKissicks, and others were being given substance in reality by the Agnews, Moynihans, and Hutschneckers. It was the beginning of a new era, and in a tribute to former Chief Justice Earl Warren, who symbolized a more hopeful period, Senator Edward Kennedy (Democrat of Massachusetts) recited a litany of repressions ushered in by the Nixon administration:

Now I fear that we are entering another era of crisis, an era of inaction and retrogression and repression easily matching that which faced Chief Justice Warren when he arrived in Washington, an era which will demand frequent profiles in courage if we are to survive as a free people. Many of the signs are small, but they are ominous. Taken separately, some may not seem unbearable or worth fighting about. But taken together they suggest a trend and a pattern which could lead to an ever faster circle of repression and reaction with no conceivable end. They are gnawing at the precious foundations of our freedom, chipping away piece by piece the barriers against tyranny and oppression which the framers of the Constitution erected.

Even to recite calmly a list of the symptoms is to give the impression that 1984 may be less than 14 years away, and that "Z" could happen here:

---

* *Jet*, February 19, 1970, p. 34.
† *Jet*, June 11, 1970, p. 14.
** From author's notes on the event.

More wiretapping in more kinds of cases, and assertion of the absolute power to bug dissenters without court orders.

Pressures for no-knock searches and for detention without bail.

The use of scare tactics to discourage attendance at protest gatherings, and the obsessive focus on the few lawbreakers in peaceful crowds of tens of thousands.

Growing use of domestic spys [sic]—in schools, in political groups, at public meetings, of informants who sometimes help to foment the very acts they are supposed to be investigating.

Verbal harassment of dissenters by political leaders, not on the merits of the issues involved, but through guilt by association and exaggerated codewords.

Total lack of sensitivity by those leaders to the issues involved— the Attorney General trying to tell jokes about his wiretapping to an audience that is quite seriously concerned about his wiretapping; the Vice President and the President making light of their affinity to "Dixie" at a time when the nation's stability may depend on whether that affinity outweighs their affinity to justice.

The new application form for Washington demonstration permits with blanks for everything from philosophy to arrest records.

A new attempt to prevent disagreeable protests near the White House altogether.

The installation in the White House of a journalist with carte blanche to fish through federal tax files and other confidential materials.

Executive resistance to a bill to eliminate an anachronistic and frightening provision for federal detention camps, resistance which melted only when it became publically [sic] embarrassing.

Serious consideration being given to a proposal to remove 5 and 6 year old children from their homes into correctional camps on the basis of tests of their potential for later criminality.

Federal stockpiling of huge amounts of teargas, and equipping of federal marshals with shotguns that they do not need or want.

Sharp curtailment of the availability of federal parole, the best incentive known to give prisoners hope and a goal as they are rehabilitated.

Refusal to support extension of the Voting Rights Act of 1965, the most successful contribution to universal suffrage since the 19th Amendment.

Federal encouragement of continued resistance to Constitutionally required school desegregation.

Court nominees chosen for their willingness to resist Constitutional mandates, rather than for eminence or leadership.

Official solicitation of letters of endorsement of a Court nominee from federal employees and judges, but investigating and threatening of government funded lawyers who write letters opposing the nominee.

Attempts to ease non-conformist employees out of the civil service by applying political tests and by reinvestigating their backgrounds for past participation in protest activities.

Inspection of incoming foreign mail by federal authorities.

A concerted effort to interfere with the freedom of the press, led by the Number Two man in the Administration.

Harassing calls to the networks by the Chairman of the Federal Communications Commisson, and to local media by a member of the Subversive Activities Control Board and by our nation's first information czar.

Harassment of the national educational TV network by the Internal Revenue Service.

A constant effort to blame the nation's ills on scapegoats such as the previous Attorney General.

Each of you can probably add to that list, from your own knowledge, items which the public is not yet aware of, and there are others I have omitted.

Nevertheless, it is a shocking and terrifying list. It betrays a total lack of respect for our heritage of freedom and constitutes an immediate threat to our system.*

The reality of increasing repression was consistently felt most keenly by black groups who saw utter danger to their survival. Ministerial and other groups normally given to moderation and the counsel of forbearance and patience were increasingly in the forefront, warning of imminent danger. One such group, a coalition of civil rights organizations in New York, began 1970 with a plain warning of genocide. Reported the New York *Times:*

* Senator Kennedy was addressing the JFK Lodge of B'nai B'rith upon presentation of the sixth Profiles in Courage Award to Former Chief Justice Warren, April 28, 1970. See *Congressional Record,* May 13, 1970, pp. S-7110–S-7112.

A series of programs and rallies yesterday marked the beginning of "Black Liberation Week," a campaign sponsored by the Black Solidarity Day Committee.

The committee is a coalition of civil rights groups led by Dr. Eugene S. Callendar, director of the New York Urban Coalition.

The campaign is designed to protest the "genocide" against black people in this country, according to Reginald Butts, a member of the committee. Mr. Butts and two of his colleagues opened the week yesterday with a 15-minute broadcast at 10 A.M. over radio station WWRL, urging black people to stop work and listen to the program.

Each day of the week has a different theme, Mr. Butts said later in an interview. The first of these themes, "We Charge Genocide," was the subject last night of a rally at I.S. 201 in Harlem.*

Those who look for tangible evidence that concentration camps are myths find, instead, the existence of camps and legal sanctions as well. Those who wish to prove that the government has a policy of genocide can realistically point to the fact that Russia, China, and 73 other countries have signed the 1949 United Nations agreement outlawing genocide—but not the United States.

New rhetoric on the antigenocide pact was stirred, however, in the aftermath of the Song My and My Lai massacres. Reported the New York *Times:*

President Nixon urged the Senate today to ratify the 1949 United Nations agreement out-lawing genocide.

Sources on the Senate Foreign Relations Committee where the genocide agreement has languished about 21 years expressed concern that a Senate vote could lead either to an embarrassing defeat or to only a narrow victory "unless the President is willing and able to twist arms."

In a message to the Senate, the President said, "We should delay no longer in taking the final convincing step which would reaffirm that the United States remains as strongly opposed to the crime of genocide as ever."

. . . Senator J. W. Fulbright, chairman of the Foreign Relations

* New York *Times,* February 17, 1970, p. 28.

Committee, said he had no comment on the genocide agreement. "I haven't thought about it for months," he said.

There were no immediate indications whether Mr. Nixon would actively seek support for ratification of the agreement by states-rights advocates and Southern conservatives, who traditionally have been reluctant to grant their consent.

. . . Officially called the Convention of the Prevention and Punishment of the Crime of Genocide, the agreement bans attempts to wipe out national, ethnic, racial or religious groups by killing their members, or deliberate attempts to cause "serious bodily or mental harm to large numbers of members of such groups."*

The *Times* further reported that the American Bar Association has opposed U.S. ratification of the agreement for 20 years, despite the fact that the pact went into effect in other countries as early as 1951. Opposition to the pact is by no means limited to the ABA; powerful Rice Cup Congressmen also oppose ratification. One of them, Louisiana Congressman John R. Rarick, cloaked his opposition, unsurprisingly, in patriotism:

Our first duty is to safeguard the protection of individual liberties as provided in the Constitution of these United States and the Bill of Rights by preserving the sovereignty of the United States—rights and privileges which would be infringed if the Genocide Treaty is ratified.

The Genocide Treaty was designed to outlaw any mass extermination of any group of humans because of their national, ethnical, racial or religious classification. As Americans there can be no question of our abhorrence of genocide against any peoples or of our desire to prevent such action. But we must stand eternally vigilant so that our emotional reaction to such crimes against humanity does not blind us into surrendering the basic liberties of our heritage as free men.

The wording of the Treaty would grant discretionary powers and is far too vague in its definitions. It includes as an act of genocide "causing mental harm" and makes "complicity" in genocide punishable as a crime.

Further, the Treaty would extend to acts of private citizens—acts,

* New York *Times*, February 20, 1970, pp. 1, 14.

domestic in nature, but which could be brought under the jurisdiction of an international organization and foreign jurists.

I shudder even to consider the stricture of such basic tenets as freedom of speech, religion, press, petition and assembly by nationals of a foreign country whose laws and customs have never permitted the open discussion or individual freedoms which our citizens have historically enjoyed. . . .

We must stand guard against every act which leads to piecemeal over-throw of American sovereignty. Free men, don't, with full understanding, trade in their liberty because of sugar coated appeals to join an organization to prohibit acts they have never committed.

Our responsibility is to perpetuate the liberties of unborn generations under proven American principles. Ratification of the Genocide Treaty will betray to our people the gift of liberty they entrusted to us as their stewards.*

Rarick and many others insist on arguing that committing the nation against killing off a segment of its people somehow undermines constitutional guarantees. However, an editorial in the Washington *Post* in mid-1970 more candidly faced the real issue which Rarick and others will only allude to. Commented the *Post:*

The failure of the United States to ratify the Genocide Convention has left an unsightly stain on the good name and the high pretensions of this nation, a leader in the long quest for international order and justice. It was in very large measure through the effort and leadership of the United States that the General Assembly of the United Nations adopted the Genocide Convention by unanimous vote in 1948. Seventy-five nations speedily ratified it. But, to the perplexity and consternation of the world, the United States Senate, pressured by a cabal of Southern lawyers in the American Bar Association turned from the Convention in anxiety and withheld this country's ratification.

Genocide, as defined in the Convention, consists of the deliberate and systematic extermination of an ethnic or religious group. It was

* John R. Rarick, "Americans Do Not Support the Genocide Treaty," *The American Mercury,* Summer, 1970, p. 10.

obviously inspired by and aimed against the Nazi program of destroying the Jewish people. It is inconceivable that the American people would ever want to engage in genocide. But some Southerners in this country have taken the view that racial discrimination here might be seized upon as a basis for charging the United States with a violation of the Genocide Convention. . . .*

True, President Nixon did make a symbolic call for action by the Senate Foreign Relations Committee, but as the *Times* reported, that political gesture is far from the bold support a President serious about ratification of a pact against genocide would have to give. As the *Times* explained: "If the agreement was approved by the Senate, implementing legislation would have to be adopted to put it into effect. The President said he was not proposing any specific legislation 'at this time,' but said his Administration would be prepared to discuss the subject during Senate consideration of the convention."†

This is the "benign neglect" on which black survival largely depends in the new decade. If it is the choice of the new decade—and it appears to be—then the inevitable second choice belongs to black people in America. That choice is the style in which they—and America—will die.

* Washington *Post,* June 1, 1970, p. A-18.
† New York *Times,* February 20, 1970, pp. 1, 14.

# Index